What Your Colleagues Are Saying . . .

"Shanna Peeples (2015 National Teacher of the Year) speaks a voice that's not heard often enough in the places where critical decisions are made about education—the voice of the experienced, devoted, and passionate teacher. As a nation, we should never make educational policy without asking whether it will support pedagogical practices of the sort this book advocates. If students learned to 'think like Socrates,' it would benefit them, their workplaces and communities, and our democracy in countless ways. May this book find tens of thousands of readers who want to put Peeples's well-tested insights into practice!"

—Parker J. Palmer, Author of *The Courage to Teach*,
Let Your Life Speak, and *On the Brink of Everything*

"Excellent writing and a wealth of inspiring examples from distinguished educators make this possibly the strongest Corwin book I have read in the past ten years."

—Michelle Strom, Middle School Language Arts Teacher
Fort Riley Middle School, KS

"Equal parts affirming and challenging, this book confirms why so much of what feels like good teaching is also messy, emotional, and personal. Peeples is a master teacher and a spectacular writer, and here we have a book that is evidence of both. This is a book that respects the intelligence of teachers. I plan on sharing this book with every teacher I work with."

—Tom Rademacher, Eighth-Grade Language Arts Teacher
St. Anthony Middle School, Minneapolis, MN

"Allowing students to pursue their own questions is upheld as a powerful and driving force in learning. Furthermore, the stories in this book are personal and powerful. They helped get my mind and heart involved and ready to read on. Teachers will be able to recognize their own students in these stories."

—Jane Hunn, Sixth-Grade General Science Teacher
Tippecanoe Valley Middle School, Akron, IN

"Peeples's book is important and relevant. It covers topics that educators are grappling with and provides authentic examples that will connect with them. Both novice and master teachers will be able to put these protocols and lesson plans into practice immediately. This is a resource that both administrators and teachers will revisit over and over again."

—LaQuita Outlaw, Principal, Grades 6–8
Bay Shore Middle School, NY

"Great for staff development, new implementation of Socratic seminar, and enhancing the craft of inquiry. This is a must-have for AVID school sites in particular."

—Valeria C. Ruff, AVID Coordinator and Elective Teacher
Druid Hills Academy, Charlotte, NC

"If you wish your classroom privileged students' questions, and fostered authentic discussion and relationships that support discourse, then *Think Like Socrates* is a must read. Shanna Peeples provides simple but powerful structures to get started but also to make such an environment thrive."

—Kara Vandas, Education Consultant

"Shanna Peeples has dedicated this book to her students and described it as a 'love letter.' It is. It is also a superb and powerful resource for educators committed to designing and developing learning cultures of curiosity and meaning-filled inquiry. Socrates said, 'Wisdom begins in wonder.' As human beings, questions are our North Star; we walk in their direction, so we must ensure they are not too small for our imagination. By grounding learning and teaching in student-generated questions, we invite children to develop agency over their own learning and choose the questions they wish to 'walk' throughout their lives. Adroitly and wisely integrating current research on learning and teaching for deep understanding with her own personal experiences in fostering Socratic thinking within her students, her colleagues, and herself, Peeples has generously gifted us with a new narrative and a new map for inviting curiosity, wonder, and empathy into the classroom, by design. This book is a treasure."

—Stephanie Pace Marshall, PhD
Founding President and President Emerita
Illinois Mathematics and Science Academy
Chancellor, The Lincoln Academy of Illinois
Fellow, The Royal Society of Arts,
Manufactures and Commerce, London

"Teachers and students are parched for authentic and significant conversations in today's schools. Through insightful innovations on an ancient tradition of posing thoughtful questions, Shanna Peeples offers here a practical guide for building wisdom and meaningful learning in today's classrooms. This book will be an asset for deep inquiry among pre-service and in-service educators alike."

—Randy Bomer, PhD, Dean
University of North Texas College of Education
Denton, TX

"If you are looking for a pathway to a remarkable student-centered classroom, Shanna Peeples teaches you how you can use questions to connect with your students, garner deeper engagement, and excavate the deep intellectual thoughts that are within our students, yet seem so difficult to uproot. *Think Like Socrates* is a practical yet soulful book, one that speaks with honesty and compassion to the power of questions and how they can transform your classroom."

—Brian Sztabnik
College Board Advisor for AP Literature and Composition
Miller Place High School, NY

"In this book, master teacher Shanna Peeples takes us inside the world of compelling classrooms, showing us what makes them tick and how they can be made to soar. *Think Like Socrates* is a tour de force that moves effortlessly between theory and practice, advancing an argument about the critical importance of inquiry as a mode for teaching and learning and providing detailed examples and resources which show how this can be accomplished. I learned a lot from this book and think you will too."

—Jal Mehta
Associate Professor
Harvard Graduate School of Education

"Questions are the pulleys of learning. Once that space between question and answer has been created, it's the question, not an answer, that pulls our students to new insight and greater understanding. Shanna Peeples knows this because she lives it and practices it. As soon as you meet her students and see her pedagogy in action, you'll recognize your own students and classroom. You'll see the way Peeples's clear and accessible instructional framework will liberate their thinking and empower their voices. This book has a place on the bookshelf of every teacher I know."

—Sarah Brown Wessling
2010 National Teacher of the Year

For Sister Rita —

THINK
LIKE
SOCRATES

THANK YOU FOR BEING A
WARRIOR OF HOPE FOR
SO MANY! WITH
ADMIRATION,

For my students, a love letter

THINK LIKE SOCRATES

Using Questions to Invite
Wonder & Empathy
Into the Classroom

Grades 4-12

SHANNA PEEPLES

CORWIN
A SAGE Publishing Company

A SAGE Publishing Company

FOR INFORMATION:

Corwin
A SAGE Company
2455 Teller Road
Thousand Oaks, California 91320
(800) 233-9936
www.corwin.com

SAGE Publications Ltd.
1 Oliver's Yard
55 City Road
London EC1Y 1SP
United Kingdom

SAGE Publications India Pvt. Ltd.
B 1/I 1 Mohan Cooperative Industrial Area
Mathura Road, New Delhi 110 044
India

SAGE Publications Asia-Pacific Pte. Ltd.
3 Church Street
#10-04 Samsung Hub
Singapore 049483

Acquisitions Editor: Ariel Curry
Development Editor: Desirée A. Bartlett
Editorial Assistant: Jessica Vidal
Production Editor: Melanie Birdsall
Copy Editor: Megan Markanich
Typesetter: C&M Digitals (P) Ltd.
Proofreader: Barbara Coster
Indexer: Molly Hall
Cover and Interior Designer: Gail Buschman
Marketing Manager: Margaret O'Connor

Printed in the United States of America

Library of Congress Cataloging-in-Publication Data

Names: Peeples, Shanna, author.

Title: Think like Socrates : using questions to invite wonder and empathy into the classroom, grades 4-12 / Shanna Peeples.

Description: First edition. | Thousand Oaks, California : Corwin, 2018. | Includes bibliographical references and index.

Identifiers: LCCN 2018017480 | ISBN 9781506391649 (pbk. : alk. paper)

Subjects: LCSH: Questioning. | Children with social disabilities—Education. | Inquiry-based learning. | Classroom environment.

Classification: LCC LB1027.44 .P43 2018 | DDC 371.3/7—dc23
LC record available at https://lccn.loc.gov/2018017480

This book is printed on acid-free paper.

18 19 20 21 22 10 9 8 7 6 5 4 3 2 1

CONTENTS

ACKNOWLEDGMENTS

No one undertakes a project of this size without considerable help, and I am grateful for my family, friends, colleagues, and students for being the inspiration, advisers, cheerleaders, and taskmasters that pushed me to perform the mental equivalent of lifting a Volkswagen over my head.

Goethe said that "all truly wise thoughts have been thought already thousands of times; but to make them truly ours, we must think them over again honestly, till they take root in our personal experience," and that's what I've attempted to do in this book.

Without the grounding wisdom and influence of Parker Palmer and Margaret Wheatley, both of whom have had a tremendous impact on how I teach, I'm not sure this would've become the book I envisioned, nor would I be as effective as a leader of other teachers.

My deepest gratitude goes to each of the teachers quoted in this book—all of whom are not only colleagues but the kind of brilliant friends who inspire me to reach higher and do better. I'm indebted to my writing partner, Justin Minkel, who gave me untold hours of help, pushed my thinking, and suggested changes with a grace and gentleness that is a gift. Tom Rademacher was an early reader and cheerleader for this project who models powerful teacher voice for me.

Thank you to Arnis Burvikovs, who first approached me from Corwin and connected me to my wonderful editor and patient guide, Ariel Curry.

Finally, and most importantly, I stand in awe of my partner, Diane Farrington-Curtis, and her ability to believe in me and in this book over the years that it has taken to create it; I am nothing without her and the love of our children, Riley, Savannah, and Emma. Anything I create is an empty third carbon copy compared to her love and their support.

Publisher's Acknowledgments

Corwin gratefully acknowledges the contributions of the following contributors:

Jane Hunn, General Science Teacher, Grade 6
Tippecanoe Valley Middle School
Akron, IN

LaQuita Outlaw, Principal, Grades 6–8
Bay Shore Middle School
Bay Shore, NY

Tom Rademacher, Language Arts Teacher, Grade 8
St. Anthony Middle School
Minneapolis, MN

Ernie Rambo, U.S. History, Grade 7
Walter Johnson Academy of International Studies
Las Vegas, NV

Valeria C. Ruff, AVID Coordinator and Elective Teacher
Druid Hills Academy
Charlotte, NC

Michelle Strom, Middle School Language Arts Teacher
Fort Riley Middle School
Fort Riley, KS

ABOUT THE AUTHOR

Shanna Peeples, the 2015 National Teacher of the Year, took the road less traveled on the way to her classroom. She worked as a disc jockey, medical assistant, and journalist before teaching, as she says, chose her.

Shanna taught middle and high school English in low-income schools in Amarillo, Texas, for fourteen years. Because Amarillo is a resettlement area for refugees, students as diverse as the Karen people of Myanmar to the Bantu people of Somalia make up classes in her former assignment at Palo Duro High School.

Currently, Shanna is a doctoral candidate in education leadership at the Harvard Graduate School of Education. She most recently served as the English language arts (ELA) curriculum specialist for her district, where she designed professional development experiences and cocreated curriculum with more than 200 secondary ELA teachers.

A former reporter for the *Amarillo Globe-News*, Shanna won awards for reporting on health issues, schools, and music criticism.

Shanna is a board member of the Longview Foundation, a 2016 National Education Association Global Learning Fellow, and a member of the Global Teacher Prize Academy.

Introduction

> The things that I think about are like what wakes us up, or what if their is lifes on other planets, is their aliens in the planets. I think that that makes us very weird persons or actually very strange thinkers.
>
> **—AMY, AGE 9**

During my second year of teaching, I came to believe that my middle school assigned the meanest twelve-year-olds to my class. They hated me, each other, the school, and seemingly life itself. Though I didn't see how it was possible at the time, this group of children would become my master class in learning how to use questions to spark their desire to learn, to engage with their own futures, and to just become better people.

I wanted them to see the commonalities they had with each other beyond the poverty that blighted their neighborhoods. This was a tall order because of the racial differences within the class and the generational mistrust they had of each other. In the cafeteria, they separated themselves by race and neighborhood, preferring to stay with the people they knew. When I tried to group them in class, it was disastrous: crying, threatening to fight, and hurling insults.

As I struggled to figure out what to do, I began writing, trying to remember what it had been like for me to be in middle school. Sandra Cisneros (1992), in her brilliant short story "Eleven," makes the case that we are all the ages we've ever been "like the rings inside a tree trunk," and when I counted back in my own rings, it helped me see that being twelve is hard.

You're too big to be little and too little to be big. To be twelve, I remembered, is to stand across the gap between childhood and adolescence. Middle school is steeped in insecurities and worries. For many kids, it's the first time they experience love, rejection, or exclusion. This might be what they were feeling, I thought, and it might explain the meanness in my classes.

Perhaps, too, they were feeling that school had become little more than a test preparation factory, and they were the "products" being moved along in a system that didn't seem to value them beyond their scale scores. And when you can't succeed inside such narrow parameters, it's logical to think that school is not for you and even suspect that it might be rigged against you. This is easy to believe if you have physical challenges, untreated health issues, malnutrition, and a home life churning around the relationships that form and fracture among your caregivers.

Several students left my classroom before Christmas, never to return. They had looked at their circumstances, weighed their chances of ever passing tests, and decided to find other avenues to create a sense of accomplishment.

What, I wondered, would happen if I set up an anonymous system for them to share what was going on inside them? If they could just see how much everyone was struggling, I thought, maybe they would develop a bit of empathy for each other. This tiny seed of an idea grew into fourteen years of work in helping children—and adults—voice the questions they carry inside them but rarely ever talk about or discuss. This book owes its creation to those students and is my debt of gratitude to them and that year that began so badly only to become one of the best years of my professional life.

I'm not a philosophy teacher, nor was I ever trained to be one, but I wondered if I could incorporate questions inspired by it—questions, to paraphrase Douglas Adams, about life, the universe, and everything. What philosophy does best is invite inquiry, normalize the uneasy feelings of not knowing something, and encourage thinking and discussion—exactly what I needed my students to practice.

The next day, I handed out index cards to my classes and modeled some of my own deepest, unvoiced questions, thinking aloud about why good things happen to bad people and why people suffer. Then, I invited my students to share their own questions by writing them—anonymously—as fast as they could think of them onto the index cards. I asked them to fold the cards in half so no one could look over them, then hand them in. After school cleared out for the day, I bent over the stack of cards and read:

Why do people ignore the truth? Can peace really exist in this world?

Why do people kill? Why do people have to die?

What happens when we die?

Will animals have rights like us?

How come love never lasts? How come there is always pain in love?

What am I supposed to feel? What am I supposed to do? How am I supposed to act?

As I read these questions, I felt my heart squeeze inside me, cracking the protective shell I'd kept around it. I wanted to find the authors and tell them, "Me too! I wonder these same things." I wanted them to know that they were asking questions that lie at the heart of what it means to be human. How would it change them to know that they were asking the questions that people have been asking since we could talk?

A Book for Curious, Committed, and Caring Teachers

This book is for teachers who want something better for their students and who believe in each child's capacity for deep and creative thinking. It is designed to be a resource for K–12 teachers across all disciplines as well as for those who coach and lead teachers. Those of us who are committed to equity, especially for our students who are in most need of help, will discover support for our work that is practical and concrete as well as deepens our personal understanding of what's possible when we cocreate learning with students.

Our students need to ask questions now more than ever. To shield them from thinking and questioning in a mistaken fear of "pulling them off task" is at best wasted effort and at worst an isolation from what truly makes us human. In a world increasingly uncomfortable with the changes wrought by technology, we seek out authoritarian figures to tell us what to do and how to think. Questioning, therefore is good citizenship. It is the antityranny vaccine.

More than mere strategy or technique, my aim is to make questioning the basis of a classroom culture—where we value learning and listening more than knowing and telling. In work with my own students, we find that we have our most fruitful classes when we sit with questions, continuing to ask them with more and more depth.

In this book, you will find the following:

- Practical strategies for creating a classroom that runs on dialogue, curiosity, inquiry, and respect for the intellectual power of children's minds

- An enhancement to your existing curriculum, regardless of content area or grade level, with examples and advice from award-winning teachers

- Questions of increasing depth paired with sample texts to increase student engagement with your content, from early elementary learners to core content and electives for high school students

- Step-by-step lessons for generating and using children's questions as a way of assessing their thinking and helping them guide that thinking into new learning aligned to national standards in each content area, including fine arts and career and technical education (CTE)

- Lesson extensions for English language learners (ELLs), special education students, and gifted and talented (GT) students

- Writing suggestions, in-class debate questions, and scoring rubrics for each content area

- Recommended multimedia texts (music, video, books) grouped by big questions such as the following:

What can we know?

How do we know what is real?

Why do we suffer?

Who deserves mercy?

How should we use natural resources?

How should we treat each other?

What does it mean to be a man?

What does it mean to be a woman?

Who owns culture?

Who am I?

What is my purpose?

How do we know what to do?

How do we know what and who to trust?

- Detailed protocols for using inquiry with adults as a base for professional learning communities, for guiding staff meetings, and for creating inquiry groups around common areas of practice

Allowing students to use their own questions to form connections to specific content disrupts teaching and learning but not in a way that traumatizes the humans doing the work. It points to a way for students to have a tangible effect on their communities through project-based and problem-based learning without the need for shiny new technology or expensive infrastructure.

Why Students Need Meaning and Purpose Right Now

As it turned out for my first group of middle schoolers, allowing their questions to live at the heart of our classroom changed them in ways I wouldn't have expected. Just opening this small space to think validated them not only as thinkers but as humans with a soul. We accept that the drive for personal meaning and purpose is a fundamental drive for adults, but we don't often extend that to children. And because we don't invite them into the discussion, we create a deep sense of loneliness.

We compound that loneliness by creating meaningless school experiences for many students. There is little to no time given for the time-honored practices of reflection, meaning-making, and understanding ourselves and our place in the world. William Damon, Stanford School of Education professor and psychologist, believes the "biggest problem growing up today is not actually stress; it's meaninglessness" (Lobdell, 2011).

An inability to find personal meaning can feed the alarming numbers of mental health disorders in children. Research estimates that up to one out of every five children from ages three to seventeen suffer from some form of mental illness described as "serious changes in the ways children typically learn, behave, or handle their emotions" (Centers for Disease Control and Prevention, 2013). This data translates into millions of children who experience anxiety, fear, distrust in themselves and others, and depression. It shows up in our classrooms as chronic absences, disengagement with schoolwork, disruptive behavior, and—as I saw for several children I taught—dropping out of school.

Rather than feel overwhelmed by this evidence, I believe we should use it as a catalyst to transform how we teach. That transformation comes, in part, through welcoming all parts of our students' inner lives into the classroom. By inner life, I mean all of those parts of us that make us uniquely human: our emotions, our intellect, our social abilities but also our spiritual lives. This last part of us is the one least welcome in schools and one that I believe our students are most desperate to integrate into their lives.

I've arrived at this conviction after working with children as young as seven and in places as diverse as the Amari refugee camp in Ramallah, Palestine, to a class of middle schoolers in Shanghai, China. Closer to home, I've worked with refugee students from Myanmar and East Africa, students in advanced placement (AP) English classes, and remedial students, as well as teenagers transitioning out of jail or from having a baby who work toward a diploma in night classes.

From these experiences, I've come to believe in my bones that children—especially children in poverty—are desperate for an education to help them discover a sense of meaning and purpose. Yet we have decided to narrow our focus to academic achievement, which creates an unhealthy fixation on grades as a sole indicator of self-worth. We have decided that school is not the place for developing what we would traditionally consider philosophical matters, yet it is the very discipline that allows us to synthesize academics, service learning, and social and emotional principles in support of the whole child. Viewed with a nonjudgmental and nonsectarian lens, students' deepest wonderings can point toward learning experiences that allow them to practice the work of citizenship grounded in empathy.

The Curse of "Teachersplaining"

Edgar H. Schein (2013), in his book *Humble Inquiry*, describes not only teaching but so many other American enterprises as a "telling culture." He argues that in "an increasingly complex, interdependent, and culturally diverse world, we cannot hope to understand and work with people from different occupational, professional, and national cultures if we do not know how to ask questions and build relationships that are based on mutual respect and the recognition that others know things that we may need to know in order to get a job done." He defines humble inquiry as "the fine art of drawing someone out, of asking questions to which you do not already know the answer, of building a relationship based on curiosity and interest in the other person" (Schein, 2013).

We "teachersplain" our kids into distraction. And I'm just as guilty of it as the next person. Fortunately, I had a group of ornery seventh graders to help me break out of this habit. Resisting pressures and temptations to be "teachers as tellers" frees us to see the children in front of us for who they are. When we make a space for students to ask their own questions, we validate them as meaning-makers and honor the hardwired capacity for inquiry that is in each of us.

For those who have grown up in homes filled with violence, poverty, and addiction, being respected by being listened to—truly listened to about their deepest thoughts and feelings—can change how they see themselves and how they view school. When you grow up in a home where dysfunction renders you invisible and silent, it can foster deep rage to come to school where this dysfunction is perpetuated by adult after adult who demands that you sit down, be quiet, and listen to what we have to say.

Eight-year-old Alex, when invited to write about his questions, spoke for so many children when he wrote: "Doe adaults hate kids? Because some adaults say the love ther kids but I don't know if the do or not. Is evrey body hiding something? Becaus some people see staf but they don't tell anybody."

Think Like Socrates

Socrates, one of history's greatest teachers, believed in the power of questions rather than the efficiency of lecturing his students. Long before Latin developed the word we know as *education* from two roots, *educare* (to train) and *educere* (to lead out), Socrates intuitively understood the synthesis of the two ideas (Bass & Good, 2004). He believed that inviting people to question what they think they knew, rather than telling them, would result in deeper understanding.

> [He] pursued this task single-mindedly, questioning people about what matters most, e.g., courage, love, reverence, moderation, and the state of their souls generally. . . . He asked questions of his fellow Athenians in a dialectic method (the Socratic Method) which compelled his audience to think through a problem to a logical conclusion. (Nails, 2014)

Socrates left a lasting imprint on education; his name is formed into an adjective to describe Socratic dialogue and the Socratic seminar, both terms meaning a way to use questions to help students draw from the well of what they know, match it against what they have learned, interrogate it, and build deeper understanding.

If we revere Socrates as one of the greatest teachers, how did we get so far away from his method of inquiry? When did we decide that the answers were all we needed and that questions were almost shameful?

And so, I have continued the practice that I learned with my first group of middle schoolers: asking students and adults to think about and anonymously write down their deepest questions, then reading several aloud. Adults and students alike then use these questions as authentic prompts for writing, reflection, and research. Honoring their questions is a way of honoring not only the cultures of whomever you are working with but also their own sense of humanity.

How This Book Is Organized

Chapter 1 explains the process of generating children's authentic questions.

Chapter 2 presents concrete strategies for using questions to plan academic discussions.

Chapter 3 focuses on building a classroom climate to support inquiry through writing.

Chapter 4 addresses practical processes of helping children become better thinkers through listening.

Chapter 5 shows how to create and sustain trust for deeper learning.

Chapter 6 provides a framework for creating cognitively leveled questions at all levels.

Chapters 7 through 12 use advice from master teachers in core content areas, fine arts, career and technical education (CTE), and those working with special education, English language learners (ELLs), and gifted and talented (GT) students to build and use specific leveled questions around recommended text and resources.

Chapter 13 guides how to use student questions to create powerful project-based and personalized learning.

Chapter 14 shows how teachers can collaborate using their own questions to create professional development around personal problems of practice.

An appendix contains the following:

- A suggested learning schedule
- Blackline masters for handouts
- Recommended books, films, music, and other work to support and extend critical thinking and academic work
- Rubrics for assessment

I believe that we can create vibrant and thoughtful learning spaces where students as young as kindergarten grapple with our deepest and most enduring questions. We can design our teaching for wonder rather than performance, for curiosity rather than testing, and for innovation rather than compliance. All of it starts with welcoming and valuing the inquisitiveness already inside our students.

PART I

BUILDING A QUESTIONING CLASSROOM CULTURE

In this section, you will find the following:

- A protocol to help kids create questions
- Strategies for using the questions as discussion topics
- Plans and processes that use students' questions to help students become better readers and writers
- How to build better thinking through listening skills
- A blueprint for creating and sustaining trust to deepen learning

CHAPTER 1

Kids These Days
Creating Deeper Learning Experiences Framed Around Student Questions

A favorite opening question of mine in designing professional development workshops for teachers is this: What do you struggle with the most as a teacher? And the answers are almost always the same:

1. Students are apathetic, unmotivated, or disengaged.
2. Students don't value education.
3. Parents aren't supportive.
4. Kids don't believe in themselves.
5. Kids are distracted by technology.

During a presentation for K–12 teachers, a man stopped me during the break to ask me when I was going to get to the point in the workshop where I talk about how spoiled kids are. "They need to understand that in the real world no one is going to care about their ideas," he said. "Are you going to show us how to tell them that?"

No, I wasn't.

Instead, I asked him if he felt ignored. "Do you feel like no one cares about your ideas? That you can't make decisions for your classes and your students?" He stopped talking and just stared at me. It made me wonder:

What if we've taken away our own efficacy as teachers by giving in to these assumptions about our students? If we really think this, then why aren't we giving them opportunities to test their ideas in the real world? Why aren't we setting up opportunities for work that requires real and sustained effort?

Maybe one of the reasons students are apathetic is that we've taken all of the choice away from them. Then, we get irritated and annoyed when they can't "think on their own." Too often as a teacher coach, I walk into classrooms where any 19th century student would feel at home: desks in rows, textbooks open on desks, the teacher at the front of the room talking. This classroom design is so familiar that it's almost invisible; we accept it as the default setting for children's learning.

One of our basic human drives is connection. We want and need the company of others. Further, we become smarter by participating in social learning, according to Vygotsky's social development theory. The theory emphasizes the importance of the learning environment in determining how children think and what they think about (Vygotsky, 1962/1986).

This is especially true for adolescents whose developmental needs are centered around a need to discover who they are. If we're not meeting these needs in our classrooms, then how are we any better than a screen on a phone or other device? When we encourage natural social behaviors, we are making ourselves and our learning experiences necessary and ourselves and our teaching difficult to replace with technology or scripts.

What Happens When We Allow Questions Into Our Classrooms

Allowing real curiosity—the kind that fuels philosophers, artists, scientists, historians, explorers, and innovators—is the most fundamental change we can make in our teaching practice. When we step back and allow students to step forward with their own inquiry, it throws a switch in their brains that changes everything. Encouraging students to cocreate their own learning by generating authentic questions grants them an intellectual power and an identity as meaning-makers.

The fastest way to engage anyone's brain is to ask it a question, neuroscience says. Judy Willis, a neurologist and middle school teacher, explains that inquiry is like caffeine for kids' brains. That's because questions kick-start a process inside their heads that works like a kind of prediction machine. Once a question enters this system, the brain begins trying to resolve the uncertainty by formulating answers. The tension that comes from wanting to know if they've guessed correctly is immediately and powerfully engaging:

> Students' curiosity, along with their written or verbal predictions, will tune their brains into the perfect zone for attentive focus. They are like adults placing bets on a horse race. Students may not be interested in the subject matter itself, but their brains need to find out if their predictions are correct, just as the race ticket holder needs to know if he holds a winning ticket. (Willis, 2014)

As teachers, we can use this information as a sort of neurological hack. If we carefully scaffold students' questions in a way that points toward the content we need to teach, we can enlist their natural tendency to find answers into deeper learning experiences. These experiences then, in turn, develop their vocabulary; their speaking and listening skills; their writing skills; their reading; and, most importantly, their critical thinking.

This idea was road tested during my year of service as National Teacher of the Year. In a special partnership with the U.S. Department of State, I visited the Middle East as an ambassador of American teaching. Traveling alone caused the kind of stress that kept my brainpower focused on finding my way around airports and adjusting to the realities of heightened security. This meant that I didn't prepare for one of my first presentations like I normally would have. During times of uncertainty, familiar practices are strength, so I leaned on those that are bedrock for me: inviting students to share their questions.

Even though I'd never met them, the senior class at the American Jerusalem High School in Jerusalem was willing to play along. We gathered in an auditorium, and as I looked at the 200 assembled students, I felt a wave of insecurity wash over me. Seeing their interested faces was all the encouragement I needed to open the lesson the same way I did at my high school: sharing a personally meaningful question.

"Before I was a teacher, I was a reporter and I covered some really sad and scary things," I told them. "And some of them, I don't think I'll ever forget—especially when they happen to children. I accept that bad things happen to good people. That's just the way of the world. What I can't seem to accept is when *good* things happen to *bad* people. Why do some people 'get away with it'? Why are some people never made to answer for what they do to others? I don't know that I'll ever get a good answer, but it's a question that haunts me. What about you? What are the questions that stay with you? What haunts you? Or makes you sad? Or makes you angry? Or just confuses you no matter how much you try to think about it?"

By this point, they were silent. I could see that they were considering whether or not to trust this strange woman from the United States.

"I've asked your teachers to give everyone a piece of paper. I'd love to know what your questions are," I said. "What are the things you've kept inside you that you've been afraid to ask? Would you mind sharing them with me? If you want to, please write them on the paper."

An engaged quiet settled over the room as they began writing. I exhaled. They were repeating the behavior I'd seen in my own classes.

What I've written here is version of my traditional opening for this lesson. Part of the reason the room gets quiet, I think, is because of a willingness to be authentic and vulnerable with my own questions. What I share with them are my own frustrations with the difficult nature of justice, which is also an engaging topic for teenagers.

After a few minutes, I stopped the students and asked who wanted to share. So many hands went up that the administrators were startled.

> "Why is there so much intolerance in the world?"

> "Is it ever okay to tell a lie?"

> "Why do we equate money with success? Are there other ways to be successful?"

Their teachers were as surprised as I was. "We will definitely be talking about these in class today," one of them told me. As I was leaving the school, an older teenage girl stopped me and said, "I just want to give you a hug and say thank you for listening to us."

When we worry that students want more technology or games or for our lessons to be more fun, maybe what they really need is just for us to *listen* to them and trust the intellectual power inside them.

Starting With Your Own Questions

The authenticity of your own questions are all you really need to get started in the process of inviting more authentic inquiry into your classroom. Everything you need is already there inside you. When I ask teachers to share their authentic questions with me—anonymously—I see that they have long-standing struggles that could connect to their students' concerns:

From Montana:

> *"Why is it so hard to forgive and move on?"*
>
> *"Why is it so hard to listen to other people?"*
>
> *"Why do people/corporations treat the planet in such a crappy way?"*

From Ohio:

> *"If I died tomorrow, would I regret how much work has ruled my life?"*
>
> *"Am I being a good person?"*
>
> *"I have deeply loved and valued many beautiful places of the world—will they survive?"*
>
> *"Why do random shootings of innocent people happen? Who is next?"*
>
> *"Why is there so much intolerance in the world?"*

From Texas:

> *"Why can't we value people for who they are and not devalue them because of how they look or what they believe?"*

"What will the future be like?"

"How will the present trauma of so many students affect the brains of future generations?"

Reading these, I see the grounds of our common humanity. What's more amazing than the fact that we share these ideas around the world is that young children wonder the same things. If we step back and make a space for students to speak and really listen to them, they will show us what is in their hearts and minds.

Justin Minkel, a second-grade teacher at a high-poverty school in Fayetteville, Arkansas, gave an opening to his students, during the first weeks of school, to share what they would ask the smartest person in the world (see Figure 1.1).

Figure 1.1 Sample Questions From Second Graders

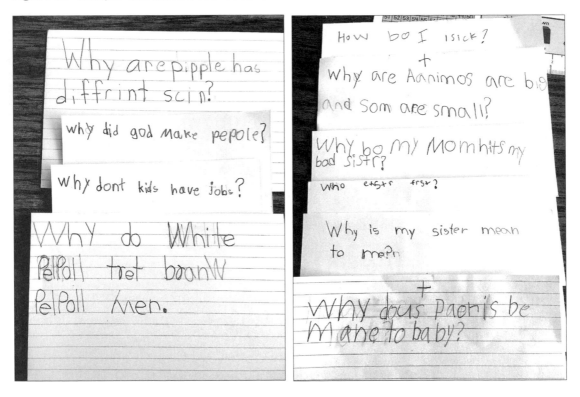

This reminded me of the cards my seventh-grade class turned in that first year (see Figure 1.2).

Figure 1.2 Sample Questions From Seventh Graders

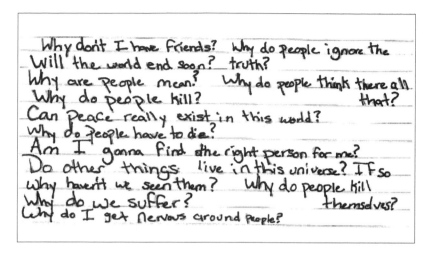

Finally, all of the questions seem connected to this writing from Joseph, a young man I worked with in the night program who was transitioning out of jail where he served time for his involvement in a drive-by shooting. Not sure of how to assess his writing skills, I asked him if he would write down the thoughts and questions that haunt him, sadden him, and nag at him. In one furious burst, he wrote the text in Figure 1.3 on the next page.

Your students are no different than these. If you give them time, space, and respect, they will stun you with their depth.

Figure 1.3 Sample Questions From High School

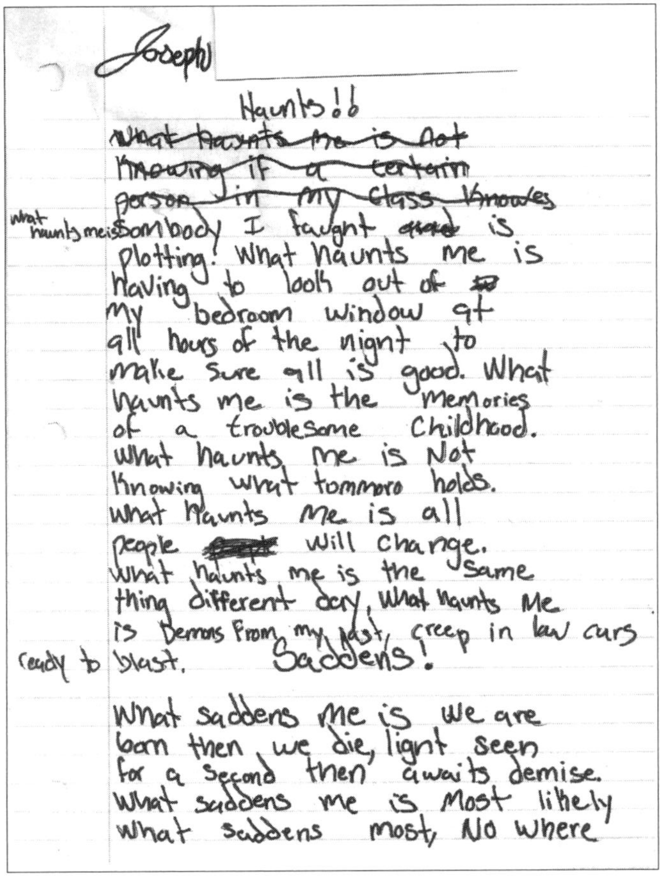

Joseph

Haunts?!!

What haunts me is not knowing if a certain person in my class knows

what haunts me is somebody I taught me is plotting. What haunts me is having to look out of my bedroom window at all hrs of the night to make sure all is good. What haunts me is the memories of a troublesome childhood. What haunts me is Not knowing what tomorro holds. What haunts me is all people will change. What haunts me is the same thing different day. What haunts Me is demons from my past creep in new cars ready to blast. Saddens.

What saddens me is we are born then we die, light seen for a second then awaits demise. What saddens me is most likely what saddens most. No where

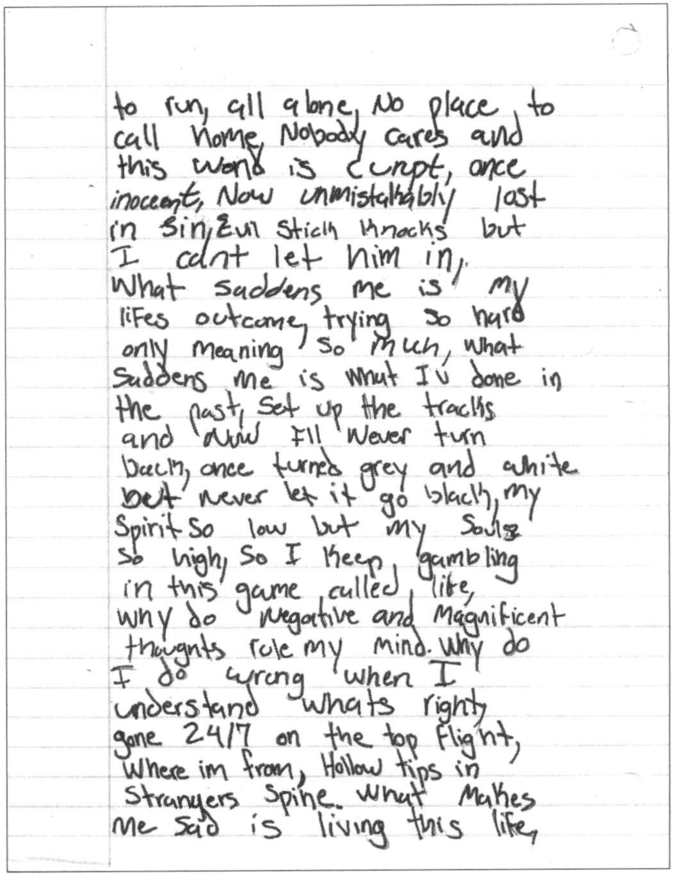

to run, all alone, no place to call home. Nobody cares and this world is corrupt, are innocent, now unmistakably lost in Sin/Zin which knocks but I can't let him in, my life's outcome trying so hard only meaning so much, what saddens me is what I've done in the past, set up the tracks and now I'll never turn back, once turned grey and white but never let it go 'bach, my Spirit so low but my song so high. So I keep gambling in this game called life, why do negative and magnificent thoughts rule my mind. Why do I go wrong when I understand whats right, gone 24/7 on the top flight, where im from, Hollow tips in Strangers Spine, what makes me sad is living this life.

Starting the Process

The conditions you need are the following:

- A sacred space for writing and thinking
- A culture of respect, kindness, and openness to new ideas
- A comfort with discussion and basic facilitation skills
- A willingness to listen down deep to children

PROTOCOL 1.1   Generating Students' Authentic Questions

MATERIALS

- A reading to open the session (your own or my suggestions; see the appendix)
- Some reflective writing from yourself with the questions that haunt you highlighted
- Examples of student questions as idea starters that are provided here
- A timer of some kind
- Quiet
- Index cards (enough so that each student gets one)
- Chart paper (younger, struggling, or language-learning students may share questions verbally as you scribe them.)

TIME

Ten minutes—This time is to allow for a mini-lesson format that will fit into any secondary schedule. You may extend the time, if needed, for double-blocked classes or for younger students. However, keeping time short will produce better quality work.

(Continued)

(Continued)

INTRODUCTION

There are many problems in our world right now—problems with how we treat each other, problems with how we share the earth, problems with technology, problems with money, problems with families, and many others. These problems, if we think about them, make us ask questions like the following:

- How should we live?
- Who am I?
- Why was I born?
- What can we know?

And so many other questions. People have wondered about these questions for a long time, so if you think about these things, you are not alone. In school, we don't often take the time to think about deep and serious questions, but what if we did? If you could ask the smartest person in the world questions, what would you ask?

PURPOSE

The purpose is to help students think about the questions that really matter to them, to draw out those questions and make them explicit, and then use those questions as a base for the work of your classroom. With this base, you can help students link what they are deeply curious about to what you need to teach. This link makes the work of learning explicit and engaging for students of all ages and across all content areas.

DIRECTIONS

Don't write your name on the cards; these are anonymous, so you can write honestly. Write down the questions that you would like to ask the smartest person in the world. Write as many questions as you can. Don't stop to talk about them, worry about them, or try to answer them. Just write the questions as fast as you can. [For younger students, students who struggle, or who are language learners, you may scribe questions.]

- **One minute**—Read the introduction and directions.
- **Five minutes**—Students write (or scribe questions as appropriate). Encourage them to keep asking questions. Model the process by writing with students and/or providing them with one of your own deep questions. (One of mine is this: I accept that bad things happen to good people—that's life. But what really bugs me is this: Why do *good* things happen to *bad* people?)

- **Three minutes**—Debrief by sharing one of your questions. Ask students to answer questions about the process of writing questions: What was hard? What was easy? What surprised them?

- **One minute**—Ask students to fold cards in half for privacy and then collect them. Tell students you will be working with these questions during another class.

MODIFICATIONS FOR YOUNGER STUDENTS AND ENGLISH LANGUAGE LEARNERS

- Allow students to draw as a way of helping them form thoughts, and then ask them about the drawing, listening for a topic that you can help them turn into a question.

- Allow students to share their questions orally as a rehearsal for writing. You might scribe some of the questions on the board or an anchor chart for them to use as they attempt to write questions. ●

CHAPTER 2

Designing for Engagement

Strategies for Using Student Questions to Plan Academic Discussions

True life is lived when tiny changes occur.

—LEO TOLSTOY

School reform that feels much more natural and respectful of those who are in classrooms every day can begin in shifts toward student-centered curriculum as well as in our readiness to make small physical changes in the learning environment. When we are brave enough to question all the ways we take how we "do school" for granted, we begin to find answers that work for the unique needs of those whom we teach.

While it's tempting to try out questioning as a lesson for a couple of days and then go "back to normal," I believe the true power happens when we adopt a culture of inquiry. This starts when we apply it to the climate and construction of our learning spaces.

What happens when we change desks into tables and group kids in pods of three, or try flexible seating where the room has some tables, some desks, some groups, and individual chairs? How does this change the dynamic of the room?

For me, changing the physical arrangement of the room helped me to begin changing how I thought of lesson delivery and even learning. Suddenly, it wasn't "the Ms. Peeples's Show" and the room wasn't designed for all eyes to be on me. The new design meant some students had their backs to me. Grouping students meant that they were turned toward each other rather than all facing me. Practically, this meant that getting the attention of kids at tables was harder and required creating signals that would allow us to equitably share communication. These groupings also meant I would need to move from the front of the class and join conversations already in progress.

Changing up the seating and allowing students to decide where they wanted to sit and who they wanted to listen to was a way for me to put my beliefs about student learning into actual practice rather than just paying them lip service.

Rearranging the room was a way to rearrange my practice. It wasn't exactly painless to take myself "off the stage." The old way was familiar and gave me the illusion of control. But so much more was gained by the willingness to change. Initially, this meant I had to work harder to create the norms and agreements we would use to work together, but it was worth it to cultivate engagement. To arrange a room into tables, desk groups, and individual seating immediately invited choice, and these choices increased both my own and my students' energy and enthusiasm.

It's difficult for me to be patient when I hear comments that boil down to head shaking over "kids these days." But I also lose patience with the guilting of teachers on social media through Twitter memes that ask, "Would you want to be a student in your own class?" That feels like it carries an undercurrent of guilt and shame, which never inspires anyone to do their best work. It's also the wrong question if we want to make things better. Teachers aren't the "end user" of our learning experiences—kids are. A better move is to turn toward your students and ask them this: What is it like to be a student in this class?

Our students don't necessarily want what we want or even what we would like for them to want. However, we can begin to affect our user experiences the same way that Apple or Walgreens or even Domino's Pizza does: by inviting input from those we're trying to "sell" on our content. It invites us to analyze our processes and commit to continually improving the experiences we give our students every day. If we cling to the argument that disengagement is all the students' fault and has nothing to do with how we've set up our schools, then we will miss the chance to transform learning.

A Design Problem

Within computer science there's a way of thinking we would be smart to adopt in education. It's called user experience and considers how easy and personally useful something like an app or an operating system is for the person using it. The international standard definition of user experience considers how a system, process, or product affects "all the users' emotions, beliefs, preferences, perceptions, physical and psychological responses, behaviors and accomplishments that occur before, during and after use" (International Organization for Standardization [ISO], 2015).

The idea of designing for what we want to see in our classrooms is a shift toward what Rolf Faste (2001), a professor of industrial design and mechanical engineering, terms "design thinking as a method of creative action." His way of thinking about engineering is centered on a core principle: Design isn't just about making products but is a way of designing behaviors and experiences of the user. He makes a strong case for viewing everything from a user's perspective in an effort to not only be sensitive to people and cultures but to create meaning for them in the design.

To transfer and modify this discipline to school settings, we can begin with reflecting on the following questions and answering them for our individual classes, as a teacher team, or even schoolwide staff:

1. **How is the design of our class (or school) creating apathy in our students? Disengagement? Lack of motivation?**

   For example, the truism "the person doing the work is the person doing the learning" applies here. If the teacher is the one doing most of the talking in the class, not only are students more likely to be disengaged but they are also shut out of practicing discussion, inquiry, and critical thinking.

2. **How is our design failing to communicate the value of our content?**

   If we are presenting our content as "preparation for the test" or "something you will need in the next grade," we are likely communicating that students will find little worth in what we're teaching. Making deliberate choices to find the relevance in our content for our students' lives as they live them right now communicates a much more compelling reason to learn what we are teaching.

3. **How is our design keeping parents from participating?**

   Many parents are overwhelmed in ways we don't often think about. Many have a patchwork of part-time jobs and often are the primary caregivers for elderly parents, according to research (Pew Social Trends, 2015). Meeting parents where they are by engaging them through social media, texts, discussion boards, or even home visits help them to be involved. Other, more direct forms of parental involvement have been created in Houston through "parent super centers" (Fleming, 2018) or through the use of laundry services in exchange for school attendance, like a program in California (CBS SF Bay Area, 2016).

4. **How is our design undermining kids' belief in their abilities?**

   Behavior charts in elementary school, for example, demean and shame students into compliance rather than help them build self-control. It's worth the extended time to connect with students and discuss behaviors and alternatives rather than rely on a chart that is probably not reflected in any other part of the students' lives outside the classroom. Secondary schools also erode self-efficacy with an overemphasis on grades or, worse, rewarding behaviors that we want students to develop intrinsically. One particularly bad example is giving external rewards like free pizza for filling out a reading log. The better goal is to develop students' love of reading. We want students to embrace effort, welcome challenges, and learn how to recover from setbacks because that is what they will truly learn apart from charts and rewards.

5. **How is our design creating distraction?**

   Consider the amount of work you are asking students to complete using digital classroom tools, both in and outside of schools. Learning spaces centered on building concentration and focus help students become less distracted. Discussion about their need for devices is one way to create awareness of why they are turning to them and away from each other. Some schools are using mindfulness exercises or engaging with the outdoors as a way of shifting students into a calmer, more receptive state.

In my experience with teenagers, they wanted me to teach them techniques like the "20/20," a modification of the Pomodoro Technique (Cirillo, 2011), where they use a timer to complete twenty minutes of focused, effortful work and then give themselves twenty minutes of unfocused "free time" to do whatever they want, also on a timer. If they can complete two rounds of the 20/20, they will have completed almost an hour and a half of work. The more we can help students with concrete methods of managing their attention, the better able they will be to transfer this skill to their other classes and their lives outside school.

At its simplest, design thinking calls on us as teachers and administrators to "understand, improve, and apply" solutions to our educational problems. These are the seeds of *innovation*, that newest buzzword in education. Innovation isn't a one-time thing that we do with the help of an expensive consultant, or by wheeling in carts of the latest hardware, or uploads of the newest software or turnkey programs. And we can't order, threaten, or guilt people to innovate. However, we can be systematic in creating the conditions and systems for innovation to regularly happen inside the walls of our schools.

Using Divergent Thinking

What if many of the problems we see in our classrooms are design problems? What if it's possible to design for behaviors and experiences? At its heart, design thinking is a continual action always in search of newer and better ways to solve problems. It uses analysis to separate a problem into pieces as in, for example, the problem of disengagement.

To think like both Socrates and a designer, we can use *divergent thinking*. This way of thinking creates multiple perspectives and generates many kinds of solutions. An easy way of beginning this process is to alter a prewriting strategy called cubing (because

> Students have lost their curiosity because what we are teaching them is discrete. Our school structure is to blame for this. We need a structure because otherwise it is difficult to manage, but in theory, the more unstructured a classroom is, in terms of freedom of how to learn and what materials to use, students learn better.
>
> **—REVATHI BALAKRISHNAN, TALENTED AND GIFTED SPECIALIST, ROUND ROCK ISD, 2016 TEXAS TEACHER OF THE YEAR**

Table 2.1 Cubing Design Strategy

Describe it	**Think about:** The learning environment Use your senses: What does it look like? Sound like? Smell like? Feel like?	**Try it:** Sit in your student desks at different places in your room. Pay attention to how you feel, and imagine what it is like to be one of your students.
Compare it **Contrast it**	**Think about:** What the space reminds you of, both positively and negatively	**Try it:** Make one deliberate comparison to home by adding one or two "soft elements" like rugs, beanbags, or floor pillows.
Associate it	**Think about:** What does the activity remind you of or make you think about?	**Try it:** Find a video clip, song, or other piece of pop culture to tie your main idea into what students already know.
Analyze it	**Think about:** Who your students are, where they come from and what their goals are	**Try it:** Create a simple survey for your students that asks them about their families, favorite things, and goals. Use what you find out to craft more personally meaningful lessons for them.
Apply it	**Think about:** The relevance of what you are asking students to do	**Try it:** Find a correlation between what you are teaching and what they can use that day in their lives. How does your lesson help them think, create, communicate, or collaborate better?
Argue for or against it	**Think about:** What needs to happen in your classroom—your answer is your claim or argument	**Try it:** Imagine how students or parents would answer your claim. Make one change in your lesson or classroom that comes from this different perspective.

there are six questions or prompts that can be written on a cube). We can modify the prompts and use them to think about our classrooms and other learning spaces or places in our buildings as we answer probing questions (see Table 2.1).

Once you've worked through a set of questions on the cube, you can begin to create a bank of ideas and possible solutions for your classroom. The final shift is to use *convergent thinking*, or thinking that brings together all of the information gleaned from cubing or other brainstorming exercises, to focus on the most promising ideas. From the narrowed focus, you can synthesize ideas and insights into a plan for implementing the change you want to see. Ultimately, all of your mental work will pay off in better learning experiences for students.

The following chapters will give you in-depth guidance in redesigning your spaces, thinking, and practice. Award-winning teachers in different content areas and grade levels will demonstrate how changing the way you think changes how students think about themselves.

Make One Change

In my experience, one of the most enriching changes in our school happened when the eleventh-grade English team of teachers began to turn over a day each week to Socratic circle questioning. My colleagues, students, and I worked on the design problem of discussion in our classrooms. We asked ourselves how we could make classroom discussions more interesting for everyone and began researching, experimenting, and trying out new ways of talking and listening.

High School Juniors Engage in a Socratic Circle Discussion

By the end of one year's investigation, we had a structure that was completely student run. By design, my only tasks were to film the discussions (and I actually could've turned that over to another student) and keep time (which I began turning over to other students). This structure was built out of redesigning all of the elements: airtime, seating, and texts. And though it required quite a bit of planning, the end result was some of the most meaningful learning I've ever witnessed. Students agreed in anonymous surveys at the end of the year, naming these Socratic discussions as the most helpful experience.

If we want kids to connect with the heart of learning, we have to risk the messiness of it. But in the risk is the reward.

Together, students and teachers decided how to construct the text for the discussion. As teachers, we worked together to find various sources to support each discussion and grouped them into mixes of nonfiction, fiction, poetry, and multimedia connected to our standards and content. Students chose what they wanted to read to support the discussion, and we practiced annotating, reading critically, and thinking critically—all in service to a question chosen for discussion or examination.

PROTOCOL 2.1   Socratic Circle

ROLES/DESCRIPTION

- **Speakers**—You will discuss the question or topic and demonstrate the use of academic language, use of text evidence, and good discussion behaviors.

- **Speaker coaches** (each speaker will have a coach)—You will watch or listen to your assigned speaker and take notes on what they do well in discussion and what they need to work on.

- **Comment counter**—You will keep a chart of speakers and tally a mark beside the name of the person who speaks every time they contribute to the conversation.

- **Evidence coach**—You will listen for use of evidence and take notes on who is using it and what kind it is. (You can assign a "logic or reason" coach if you are working on argument skills and/or fallacies.)

- **Academic language coach**—You will listen for use of vocabulary that is used in the discussion and evaluate it for its appropriateness and correct usage. Then you will report on what you find.

- **Big board**—You will listen for "tweetables"—short, interesting takeaways from the discussion that you will then write on the board or chart for everyone to study later.

- **Devil's advocate**—You will listen for the perspectives being used and encourage the discussion toward multiple and possible new and unpopular perspectives.

- **Hot seat**—You will listen for an appropriate place to join the conversation if you feel it is going off course or no one is speaking. You will encourage those who haven't spoken to speak and those who aren't listening to listen. You may leave the conversation whenever you decide you've done your work.

- **Videographer**—You will make sure you are documenting the discussion so that everyone can judge their performance later as well as creating a record for those who missed class to watch later.

MATERIALS

- Question or topic to discuss (see sample questions in content chapters for each grade level or use student-generated questions)

- Roles assigned before the discussion based on student preference

- Texts that support discussion (enough for each person to have one, preferably annotated) [In our classes, we gave students the choice of three texts to choose from: a current news source; fiction or poetry; or philosophical reading, analysis, or expository essay. The texts provided perspective on whatever question or topic was under discussion.]

- Timer

- Video camera (optional; used for students to evaluate their performance)

- Board or chart paper

- Paper for students to take notes

TIME

Forty minutes—Broken into two fifteen-minute "halves," with a five-minute halftime and five-minute debrief

(Continued)

(Continued)

PURPOSE

To help students think about a question, topic, or text more deeply and critically while also supporting their use of and growth in academic language and academic discussion skills

DIRECTIONS

Students should get their support texts and move into position for the role they signed up for previous to this class period. Students who are playing the role of Speaker move into the center of the room. Students playing speaker coaches sit directly behind their "player." Other roles create an outside ring so they can hear, except for the person playing big board, who will stand at the board or chart to scribe. As soon as possible, begin the discussion and have a designated timekeeper (usually the teacher) who will put fifteen minutes on the clock. The timer times halftime at five minutes; debrief at five minutes. The second half starts with another fifteen minutes on the clock. Student speakers begin the discussion, and the videographer begins recording as soon as time starts.

- **Fifteen minutes**—The timer starts time and signals speakers. The speakers begin discussion, and all others begin taking notes as their roles describe.
- **Five minutes**—It's halftime. The timer starts time. Speakers and coaches confer. Other coaches may confer, and the teacher checks in with each of the outer-ring coaches.
- **Five minutes**—The timer restarts five minutes. Debrief the first half. The teacher calls on different coaches or roles to report.
- **Fifteen minutes**—The timer puts fifteen more minutes on the clock and signals to speakers to begin the second half.

CONCLUSION

Time permitting, the teacher may want to lead another short debrief.

You may extend the activity with a reflective writing. I have taken photos of the big board notes, converted them to PDFs, and posted them on my classroom website so students can access ideas as they complete a reflective writing. Students who missed class may also view the video. I conclude the discussion during a dedicated speaking and listening workshop where students evaluate their discussion based on a rubric we've cocreated. They set speaking, listening, and thinking goals for next time and note their strengths and weaknesses.

You may also wish to extend the assignment by using it as a way to develop background knowledge and thinking before a timed writing on the same question or topic.

Source: Cocreated by English teachers and students at Palo Duro High School. ●

What Engaged Discussion Looks and Sounds Like

As I held the video camera to record my students during a Socratic circle discussion, a mix of feelings washed over me. Pride was first. Pride in them for choosing to explore this question: How can we know what is real? Pride in them for coming prepared for the discussion by annotating texts that they'd chosen to read from my suggestions as well as song lyrics and readings they found on their own. Pride in them for choosing to take on the responsibility of thinking seriously about a difficult question. But I also felt a small sting of grief because they didn't seem to need me to tell them what to do.

I watched them lean in as Adam argued, "You know reality is just something that a group of people say it is. Like, they agree to believe something even if it may not be true, like the way people are prejudiced against Mexicans for being lazy. They don't see how hard my dad works. They don't see that reality. They choose to believe that their bias is the reality." Kimber furiously wrote this on the interactive whiteboard, while Karen and Pamela took coaching notes as they sat behind the speakers. Enrique kept count of who was speaking on a small dry-erase board; Alex nodded as Jazmin spoke, "You're making me think about this in a way I never did before, Adam. So, you're saying that reality is something we create by what we believe?"

It was difficult to frame the action like I wanted and hard to hear sometimes, but the discussion was becoming much deeper than I had anticipated, and I was amazed. They didn't need me to tell them what to do, but they did need me to create the space for them and to facilitate the conversation. Sometimes, I moved into the hot seat to challenge one of them. "What about the paranormal?" I asked. "Do ghosts exist? Is there such a thing as a soul that we can prove?" I moved out of the hot seat to make room for Natalie. I knew my question would provoke her into more challenges and I smiled, knowing that we would approach Nathaniel Hawthorne's "Young Goodman Brown" in a much deeper way when we read it together later in the week.

CHAPTER 3

Teaching Like Socrates

Composing a Classroom Climate to Encourage Inquiry

The content of your character is your choice.
Day by day, what you choose, what you think
and what you do is who you become.

—HERACLITUS

Some readers may find it odd to begin a book about questioning with chapters about design followed by ones on listening and trust. However, it's absolutely critical to support intellectual risk for ourselves and our students by deliberately focusing on the physical and emotional aspects of our classrooms. Without being willing to make these changes first, I argue that it's much more difficult—if not impossible—to create better teaching and learning.

For years, I made the mistake of viewing my classroom as a "fixer-upper," and like the remodelers on many do-it-yourself television shows, I believed that if I just made a few cosmetic changes, I could reap major teaching rewards. What I found instead—to continue the real estate metaphor—was that it was necessary for me to "take it to the slab," as builders say when they deconstruct a building down to its foundation, and be willing to reconfigure, reimagine, and reconstruct everything.

But it's so difficult to do this in practice. We are in love with "tips and tricks" in education, reducing our challenging cognitive, emotional, and spiritual labor to a few bland, quick fixes that can be simplified for use by an entire department, particularly during test prep season. As a teacher, there's almost nothing more flattering than when another teacher says, "I really like your lesson. Tell me how you do that because I'd like to try it." When one of my colleagues said this to me about using questions with kids, I reverted to fixer-upper problem solving, barging right into telling her all about the nuts and bolts of the lesson. But what I forgot to tell her—or even reflect on myself—was how long it had taken me to establish the trust, community, and respect that make this kind of inquiry possible.

The lesson, when reduced to just its mechanics, was disastrous for her in a way that all these years later I wish I could take back. My colleague had taken me at my word: Use your own questions as a model for your students, and then share a deeply personal story with your students. She came to me the next day, in tears.

"I did what you said, and it was awful," she said. "Most of them didn't even pay attention when I talked to them about my cancer, and even worse, some of them were laughing."

Right then, I felt like the biggest jerk in the world. Here I'd gone and exposed this kind person to suffering I never would've wished on anyone because I didn't think about how much classroom climate matters.

"I'll never do anything like that again," she cried. "They don't deserve it. They're getting worksheets and the textbook from now on. I should've known I couldn't trust them with anything."

What I knew about her students was that they were competently taught by her in what for most of us is a familiar high school English class. She had a poster of rules for the class on the wall at the front of the room and had high behavioral expectations for her students. She told them what to write—in the form of essays, concentrating on grammar and mechanics. They were told what to read—in the form of the traditional canon of classics. They were told what to talk about—in the form of preset questions from the teacher's edition of the text. So when she abruptly shifted the nature of her class by becoming uncharacteristically vulnerable, it was too much for her students to process.

There's nothing wrong with the way she usually taught her class—it's exactly how all of my teachers, including my English professors in college, taught me. I'm not arguing that it is wrong to teach grammar or mechanics or classic literature, but I am arguing that our teaching should be about something more than mere lessons in search of a right answer or predictable performance. Technique, as Parker Palmer (1998) so eloquently said, is what we use until the real teacher arrives.

Teaching is the most difficult work I've ever tried, and I certainly need every model of successful outcomes I can find. However, the best part of my teaching—the parts that I believe helped me to grow and, more importantly, helped my students to grow as thinkers and creators—were those times when I became "the real teacher." The real teacher in me teaches out of my own humanity, when I am vulnerable enough to model my own learning, my own questioning, my own lack of certainty. This stance—teaching from who we are and connecting to those who are in front of us—is what raises teaching from a set of discrete skills into the realm of something only humans can do. It calls on us to be unguarded, empathetic, authentic, and brave.

Our teaching should come from the deepest part of who we are and engage the deepest part of who our students are. This can't happen without the groundwork of building respect for everyone in your classroom. It begins with something as simple as a smile.

Research also seems to suggest that we can build better relationships by focusing on what makes us alike rather than focusing on our differences. When Harvard researchers tested an intervention for ninth-grade students and their teachers based on finding five similarities between them, the relationship between teachers and students not only improved but "[appeared] to close the achievement gap at this school by over 60%" (Gelbach et al., 2016).

Respectability was synonymous with what Socrates's contemporaries called virtue. In his lectures, he wove knowledge and virtue together and believed that as you can teach knowledge, you can also teach virtue. He also believed that knowledge was a means to ethical behavior and positive action. This positive action has the outflow, Socrates says, in the sense of happiness that comes from promoting right action. For teachers, that translates into concrete strategies that help everyone practice rituals of respect that I will explain in this chapter.

Privileges as a Form of Respect

The most basic form of respect is attending to the bottom of Maslow's hierarchy of needs. This is also pedagogically smart. My colleague James Ford (2017) says that "Maslow eats Bloom's for lunch," so taking the time to create safety and a sense of belonging is key, and "when students enter a classroom with so many different base-level needs, a certain foundation has to be laid before true learning can take place."

Maslow's theory is well-known in education, but we often forget that it rests on a base of physical needs. Students need rest, water, movement, safety, and security for their mental health, and when we provide for these needs, it communicates a profound sense of being seen and respected. For me, this was borne out in doorway conversations before class. Students were able to privately tell me if they needed to see the nurse or counselor.

It's troubling, for example, how many girls in poverty don't have access to feminine hygiene products. This became clear to me from students' regular requests to visit either the school nurse or the athletic trainer—both places where they could privately secure these products. No girl will feel comfortable telling you this, but it can cause deep anxiety to worry about starting your period at school or running out of supplies. Because of this, I began making my hall pass available to students. It hung on a hook near my door, and I pointed it out during the first day of school along with these basic guidelines:

1. It may be used anytime in class by one student at a time.
2. Quietly and with as little disruption as possible, exit the class.
3. Return the pass quickly, quietly, and with as little disruption as possible.

This practice evolved into similar instructions for seeing a counselor, getting a drink of water, or going to the restroom. Later, with the advent of cell phones, it became a way for students to access their phones outside of class as they used it to make phone calls or text while in the hall or in the bathroom.

More than anything I've ever done as a teacher, this practice was viewed most favorably by students and most unfavorably by colleagues and administrators. However, in fifteen years of teaching, not one of the thousands of students I taught ever abused this privilege. And this was true of the middle schoolers I taught. Many of my students were responsible for getting their siblings ready for school or taking care of them after school when their parents were at work. Older students were regularly relied upon to make decisions in their jobs, drive cars, and exercise leadership decisions in their extracurricular activities like athletics, ROTC, band, and theater. But for some reason, the school day was designed to relegate them to passivity and dependence.

In classes, I didn't lose learning time from disruptions caused by students raising their hand to ask if they could go to the bathroom or the nurse or the counselor. Students were more attentive because their needs were taken care of. Most importantly, students practiced responsibility. What good does it do to bemoan the "lack of responsibility" in students if we never give them chances to build it? This practice of privileges allows students to practice self-regulation, responsibility, and trust.

Privileges of Choice

Once these basic needs are met, the next step is to begin meeting student needs for acceptance, group membership, independence, status, and mastery. Fortunately, it is easy to both provide for these needs as well as put them in service to creating a climate that grows trust and goodwill.

The choices we allow our students—to opt out, to take a break, to laugh, and to move—are just as important to their development as whatever content or skills we want to teach them. The success that came from allowing students to take responsibility for their physical needs helped me to trust them to take more responsibility for their emotional needs. This came about in the form of the choice to opt out of participating, especially if they were feeling angry, heartbroken, or anxious.

Those feelings are particularly stormy for students, and their effects can last long after the initial trigger. Even pleasant distractions can upend students' ability to focus. A study on focus found that it can take an average of twenty-three minutes and fifteen seconds for adults to reset their attention, so how much more might it take for students to reset their emotions (Pattison, 2008)?

Students who conferred with me at the door before class and asked for opt outs were the ones I knew were serious. To some, I offered an opt out because it was obvious that they needed one from their tears, anger, or other signs of distress. Most kids reset themselves within fifteen minutes and acclimated to class. Often, a suggestion to write about whatever was going on with them sped up this process. Middle schoolers needed the technique to manage their emotions before doing something impulsive like starting a fight.

An invitation to write about what's going on with them is all that most kids needed. Students wrote privately, unless they chose to share them with me—and for good reason. My first year of teaching, I naively responded to a parent's request to see her son's journal during "meet the parents night" at our middle school. In it, he had written something private—the page was folded over to prevent casual viewing. As I watched the boy's face twitch with panic, his mother unfolded it and began reading it aloud. Too late, I understood what was going on and asked her to please hand it to me because I needed to grade it. Tears began in his eyes as she ignored me and kept reading. Other parents in the room shifted uncomfortably.

"Please," I begged. "Give me his journal."

Her expression was savage.

"Oh, you want me to give you this?" she said, tearing the page out of the notebook. "What other shit have you written?"

By this time, I had my hands on the notebook, but it didn't matter. The damage was done. He was devastated. She was triumphant. I felt nauseous with guilt.

Student trust is partially built on these kinds of moments, and I realized that I'd clumsily caused it to be broken for this child. He didn't write much of anything for me the rest of the year. And I began cocreating privacy policies with my students around their personal writing:

1. If you write in the journal, I won't grade it, but I will read it.

2. Please know it is subject to being read by others, such as a parent or administrator.

3. If you write that you are being harmed, that you have harmed someone, or that you want to harm yourself, I'm legally required to report it.

4. If you need to write things that are too private to risk being read, please keep a separate journal.

This policy worked to grant privacy to my students, create trust in our classroom, boost writing practice, and alert me to some serious issues with students. Each year, at least one person confessed that they were being sexually abused or felt suicidal.

Privileges of Thought and Purpose

Choices in what we read, what we listened to, and what to write about were a way to achieve two goals: (1) Build their identities as thinkers and critical consumers of the media surrounding them, and (2) stay current in finding relevant connections to what they deemed interesting or important. On writing workshop days, students presented the opening mini-lesson, chosen from any kind of text that connected to a writing question. The only limits were that the text had to be able to be read, watched, or listened to in two to three minutes and needed to be something thought-provoking to help all of us learn and think more deeply about the world.

From my students, I learned about the philosophical inspiration for and literary allusions in video games like the *Fallout* series and *BioShock*, studied translated lyrics to songs from all over the world, and even learned how professional wrestling video clips can be used as writing prompts. On Fridays, we shared music playlists. Students brought in CDs early on, then shifted, as technology changed, to plugging a set of speakers into their phones to share specially created music for class.

Another way students helped to create our physical environment each year was through the use of their own artwork. About four years into my teaching, I stopped buying the "inspirational" posters at the teacher store and started asking students to create the inspiration for the room. This custom spread throughout the building. A colleague covered an entire chalkboard with black paper each year so teenage artists could use different colors of chalk to create murals. These pieces were museum-grade and featured work like a large scene of Martin Luther King interlaced with his quotes.

Part of the summer reading assignment asked students to craft a personal mission statement based on their reading. They brought these in during the first week of school, and the classroom's bare walls began to fill with collages, drawings, and paintings to illustrate quotes, lyrics, and sayings.

The best student choice, however, was the choice of whether to revise work for a higher grade or choose an independent learning for extra credit points. Researchers into mindset and grit make a great case for its importance (Duckworth, 2016), but I needed practical ways to apply it for my students to show them that the more you read and write, the better you get. But I didn't want it to be a dry exercise in "point grubbing," so the choices were somewhat constrained. If a student was willing to keep revising a piece of writing and completing a short reflection about what he or she learned about writing from it, I was willing to keep looking at it and raising the grade accordingly. The catch was that it had to be handed in before the last week of the marking period.

PROTOCOL 3.1 Practice Critical Thinking With Big Questions

Those who wanted or needed to replace a failing grade with a 70 or higher may choose from among several tasks:

- Watch a TED Talk or video from Big Think of your choice, write a two-page response explaining why you chose the one you chose, what you learned from it or how it deepened your understanding of the subject, how you connect it to other learning, and what questions it made you think of.

- Or do the same reflection after listening to a *This American Life*, *Radiolab*, or *Hidden Brain* podcast.

- Read any Text to Text lesson from the New York Times Learning Network, and answer five of the provided questions.

- Present a PechaKucha based on any of these (many great examples and instructions on how to make them online are at www.pechakucha .org), or choose an Oscar-nominated documentary short film that you can find online at the Oscars official site.

- Take a selfie of yourself completing this assignment.

A required conference, scheduled by the student with me, followed the activity and took place before or after school.

CONFERENCE EXPECTATIONS

- There are no set questions. I will ask you to discuss your chosen text based upon questions that occur to me during the conversation.

- I will ask you for your written response.

- I will ask to see the photo of you working on the assignment.

- I will ask to see a copy of your chosen text.

- We will have an informal conversation for about ten minutes during which I will become convinced that you engaged with the text or are simply pretending to have done the work.

If you complete the extra credit assignment and conference, you will be given a 70 or higher to stand in place of your lowest grade (except for timed writings). Points will be awarded based on your effort. If you attempt to bluff your way through the conference, no points will be awarded. Extra credit also will override a test grade (except for semester tests).

You may apply for extra credit up to three times a semester.

MODIFICATIONS

Modifications for elementary may include accessing sites specifically designed for younger students like NeoK12, MIT+K12 (Massachusetts Institute of Technology, MIT), and *Schoolhouse Rock!* videos on YouTube. ●

Privileges of Collaboration and Independence

As serious a thinker as Plato was, he also believed that play is an important part of living. Play in service of real academic learning is something we rarely structure in our classrooms, yet it can naturally support the kinds of questions that drive problem-based learning. Not only does it help students practice divergent and convergent thinking (the kind that fuels creativity and innovation) but it can change how students feel about whatever topic or content you're studying while boosting their confidence as learners.

An easy way to incorporate this is to have students tackle an open-ended challenge with a group that previews whatever skill or content you will be teaching. In ten minutes, students working in groups bond with each other, collaborate, and try out "what if?" solutions in a low-stakes situation. For example, when

I wanted to give students an introduction to expository writing without using that heavy term, I gave them a problem to solve in teams. After they finished the challenge, they wrote about their experience in an authentic practice of explanatory, illustration, or descriptive genres. This is the lesson I used as a demonstration lesson for teachers in Shanghai, China, who asked me to help them design lessons to spark creative thinking. The bonus, they said, was seeing how well it helped students practice expository writing.

The problem is easy to set up but not so easy to solve creatively: Propel a table tennis ball as far as you can with only a paper clip, a rubber band, or a rolled-up magazine. Chris, who'd struggled as not only the new kid in class but also with serious health issues, generated one of the most creative solutions I've ever seen to this problem. He convinced his group to choose the paper clip, bent it into the rough shape of the egg dippers inside Easter egg coloring kits, and used it to pick up and hold the table tennis ball as he walked it to the end of the hall and back. This solved for distance in a way no one previously considered.

Kris Bordessa (2006) calls these kinds of dilemmas "tiny tasks," and she inspired me to modify and alter these for my classes.

PROTOCOL 3.2   Tiny Tasks for Bonding Small Groups

SUGGESTIONS

- Start with the easiest and most low-risk activities you can imagine.
- Have an objective for the activity. For example: reflecting on their behavior as a team or what they can do next time to work together better. Later, you can tie the activity to actual content you need to teach or as background for a text or discussion.
- Pretest the particular activity with some colleagues to make sure it works.

CONDITIONS

- Opportunities for movement and interaction with peers
- No "right" answers

- Encouragement of discovery, creativity, and teamwork
- Groups of four or five members each (groupings can be as easy as counting off to four or five and putting all the same numbers together, to premade groups of high-, medium-, and low-achieving students)

VARIATIONS OF TASKS

1. Choose one of three objects to do the following:

   - Create the longest bridge.
   - Propel a table tennis ball the farthest down the hall.
   - Build the tallest structure.

2. Make a hot chocolate river, traffic jam, Blind Line, or do some other physical team challenge. (Videos of how to play these are available on YouTube.)

3. Produce creative solutions to problems like survival scenario games (instructions are online).

4. Have teams work toward a common objective (e.g., build something useful or workable) but use different materials.

5. Solve a mystery or play the Detective Game by working together.

6. Develop new perspectives or ideas by asking questions like those used for conversation starters. You can find hundreds of these by searching for "table topics" or "better conversations questions."

   - More ideas here on my Pinterest site, www.pinterest.com/shannapeeples
   - Demonstrations of similar activities in my YouTube playlist titled "Tiny Tasks"

MATERIALS

- Any office supplies or other objects that have piled up in the storage areas of your classroom or campus: paper clips, rubber bands, boxes of transparency film, index cards, magazines—I've used all of these

- Or unused or extra things you or a colleague have at your home: marshmallows, toothpicks, uncooked spaghetti noodles, cardboard tubes, inexpensive toy balls or table tennis balls from discount stores

- A pair of scissors for each group that can also be used as part of the solution

(Continued)

(Continued)

- Timer
- Optional: small prizes for winners like those collected from fast-food children's meals or dollar store tchotchkes

INTRODUCTION

All problems have a solution, but finding that solution by yourself is sometimes really hard. That's why we need help from each other. More brains are always better at thinking up new ideas than just one brain. We're going to practice putting our brains together to solve some silly problems, but this practice will help you develop several skills: how to communicate, how to work together, and how to think in different ways. You can take these skills into your other classes and outside the school to help you whenever you need to solve a problem. Plus, it's fun and will help you get to know and trust each other.

DIRECTIONS

I'm going to give you a problem that you will solve using one of three items. You'll get in groups. You will be timed. You will have think time and planning time. The timer will be set for actively solving the problem so no one has an unfair advantage. Your job is to work together quickly to figure out the problem.

- **Five minutes**—Set the timer: groups choose materials, think, plan, and discuss options.

- **Five minutes**—Reset the timer: groups have five minutes to begin building solutions or engaging in puzzle or mystery.

- **Five minutes**—Choose a winner, award prize, and debrief activity.

- **Two minutes**—Tie it into the lesson, text, or discussion.

EXTENSIONS

Have students practice the following:

- **Informational or expository writing**—Describing how they solved it or explaining why the winner won

- **Reflective writing**—Writing what they noticed about what worked and didn't work and what they could have done

- **Persuasive writing**—Making an argument for why students should or shouldn't do team-building exercises

- **Narrative writing**—Creating a story inspired by the activity ●

Writing Groups or Circles

Writing circles grew out of a need for me to create a larger audience for my students' writing than just me. It started in "coffee house" author celebrations where students read a piece of their writing they particularly loved for an audience of peers, teachers, and family. It was a way for students to experience the instant gratification of "open mic" with the additional boost to their speaking and listening skills. It also bonded them because everyone was in it together. We publicly celebrated at the end of the semester, both fall and spring, by inviting family members and other significant people in the students' lives to attend the coffee house performance in a donated space—like the church across from our school. I provided coffee and hot chocolate; our city's chain of donut shops gave us donuts, but then it grew to include students bringing food, which I'm sure violated some sort of rule, but we somehow never got sick or in trouble for it. When we couldn't get the church space, it became a practice in my room over two days. Because students responded so well to this, I knew that it needed to be more than a twice-a-year thing, even though it was a fun party. And so, writing groups became a natural outgrowth of that, along with a need for me to multiply myself as a responder and editor, based on my own experiences of being involved with writers' groups.

During my time teaching middle school, I was able to find some dirt cheap rugs and get hand-me-down beanbags and floor pillows from another teacher. We moved the desks back and put the rugs and pillows down; then, the students met in their groups. Something became immediately clear to me with this—students stopped fidgeting when they were freed from the desks. The novelty of sitting on the floor in a circle helped them focus. I kept this up through my first years of teaching remedial classes in high school. I first tried grouping students randomly, which was a mistake because it was often like putting Betta fighting fish together in a small bowl. From my mentor, Elaine Loughlin, I learned to have students fill out cards stating who they preferred to work with and who they knew they would have trouble working with. This initially took a little time up front, but it saved so much more time down the road.

As the circles were tweaked from student feedback, they became weekly meetings, both in and out of school. Students began using collaborative apps to "meet virtually" because so many of them were in athletics or other extracurriculars that kept them from meeting together during class.

It was helpful to teach them in gradual release as I scaffolded them toward the hardest writing task: expository essays. This looked like Figure 3.1.

Figure 3.1 Gradual Release of the Writing Process

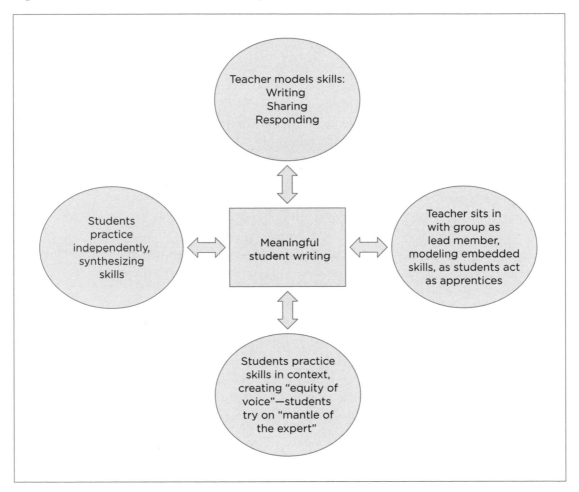

My friend and fellow writing teacher, Steve Peha (personal communication, April 5, 2017), believes that "if you have to choose between having time for reading and time for writing, favor writing. Writing requires all the skills of reading plus the logical thinking of math."

The conditions that you need are as follows:

A dedicated time for writing workshop that functions in three sections:

- Teacher modeling of a specific skill
- Time for students to write
- Time for students to get feedback—either in a one-on-one conference with the teacher or in their groups

Modeling of how to read and respond in a group—a fishbowl demonstration of each part such as how to read your work aloud where others can hear it or how to be a good listener of others' writing (see Figure 3.2 and Protocol 3.3).

> Learning how to think really means learning how to exercise some control over how and what to think. It means being conscious and aware enough to choose what you pay attention to and to choose how you construct meaning from experience.
>
> **—DAVID FOSTER WALLACE**

Figure 3.2 Writing Workshop as Minutes of Class

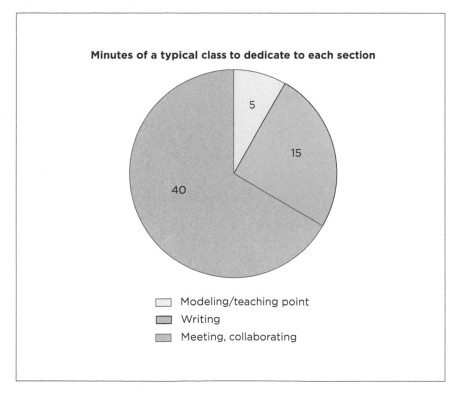

PROTOCOL 3.3   How to Create and Meet in Writing Groups

MATERIALS

- Cards with questions you have copied from student responses to Protocol 1.1: Generating Students' Authentic Questions in Chapter 1 (at least three per small writing group)

- A writer's notebook of some kind, composition or spiral (can store or make students responsible for)—to experiment with writing techniques, recorded thoughts, feelings, seed ideas, etc.

- A working portfolio stored in the classroom

- Your own writer's notebook that you commit to using, if only for ten minutes a day

- Groups of four or five students formed beforehand from student input. You can make the groups bigger, but smaller groups are able to process the writing easier within class time. Ask students to list three people they know could work well with them. If they know they absolutely can't work with someone, have them note the name of that student so you can be sure not to group them together.

TIME

About thirty minutes

INTRODUCTION

Writing groups are a good way to get better at writing, and they will help you by giving you a real audience for your work: each other. All writers need others to give them help in knowing what is working in their writing and also what needs work because it's confusing. This group is your chance to be both a writer and a good audience for other writers. Because it can be scary to share your writing, it's important that you feel comfortable with each other. That's why you will stay with this group for at least six weeks. With your group members, you will learn how to work together as readers and responders to make your writing better. I will give you some cards with questions on them that have been generated from other students. As a group, you will decide which question you most want to write about.

PURPOSE

We are meeting in writing groups for several reasons:

1. Reading our writing out loud helps us get better at fixing it and finding mistakes. It also lets us know if the funny parts are funny.

2. Working with a group helps us learn to trust each other enough to be honest about each other's writing. This helps us get better as writers and as friends.

3. Listening to others' writing helps us develop empathy for each other and realize that the old saying is true: Everyone you meet is dealing with problems you probably would never guess they're dealing with.

4. Bonding with a group of other writers helps you to develop confidence as a writer and as a communicator.

DIRECTIONS

You will move with your group to different spots in the room. Bring your notebooks and a pen or pencil with you. Choose who will lead the discussion (the easiest way is to pick whoever's birthday is closest to today). Choose a monitor to make sure everyone stays on time in the group and finishes the task. The leader will read the cards, and the group will vote on which one seems the most interesting to write about.

- **Ninety seconds**—Read the introduction and directions.

- **Three minutes**—Students gather in groups and choose a leader and monitor.

- **Three minutes**—The leader reads cards and makes sure everyone understands the questions. The monitor makes sure everyone stays on task and finishes within three minutes. The leader then counts the votes for each question and will cast the tie-breaking vote if necessary.

- **Five minutes**—The leader will get everyone's ideas on how to write about the topic (e.g., different ways to connect the question to what you are learning or thinking about, or something that happened to you).

- **Ten minutes**—After discussion, you will write silently. You may choose to stay with the group or move to another spot if that helps you concentrate.

Students are able to practice any of the writing skills, genres, or rhetorical modes you are teaching within this group. This frees you as a teacher to sit with struggling groups or to check in with everyone during the class period.

(Continued)

(Continued)

EXTENSIONS

- These groups may stay together and work as inquiry circles or book clubs. Inquiry circles may choose to investigate a particular question and create a product from it. Book clubs similarly choose a book or work with another text that the group reads and processes collaboratively to create meaning. Students identified as needing special education thrive in these groups because everyone is focused on making meaning rather than getting a right answer.

- Students may use these groups as a support for goal-setting, reflection, recognition, and concerns. Those identified as gifted and talented (GT) often need this extra support to help them plan for new learning as well as begin to identify strategies that have worked to help them learn the material.

- Groups may meet as "study buddies" who use reciprocal teaching to help each other process material for a test, understand a particularly difficult concept within your content, or practice language skills with their peers. Speaking and listening in authentic contexts is critical for English language learners (ELLs), and these groups help them to both process content and practice language. ●

CHAPTER 4

Learning to Listen

Processes to Support Better Thinking Through Focused Attention

We learn an art by doing that which we wish to do when we have learned of it; we become builders by building, and harpers by harping. And so by doing just acts we become just, and by doing acts of temperance and courage we become temperate and courageous.

—ARISTOTLE

When we listen to others without prejudice, advice, a connected story of our own, or to score rhetorical points, we are making the first moves in growing a community. Learning to listen, as Aristotle knew, is a skill we get better at the more we practice. Giving our full attention to someone is one of the easiest ways to begin building the trusting climate that an inquiry-based classroom demands. If I'm too busy filling your head with my words, then it becomes harder for you to connect to your thoughts and questions.

This realization didn't come to me through classical reading but from working as a newspaper features reporter. Listening, as much as writing, became a critical tool for my work. The ability to create interesting reporting about an event rested on the information I could gain from asking questions and then shutting up to listen to the answer. Features reporters are frequently called in as "color commentary" on news that's often traumatic: crime, death, reversals of fortune, medical mysteries, and so on. Meeting people on what was often their worst day taught me that listening is a deeply human gift that helps those we listen to feel as though they matter. But this is true for all of us, regardless of the context. We only share what's real and true when we believe someone is genuinely listening.

Switching to the classroom from the newsroom, I seemed to lose these skills as well as the motivation to listen. To my memory, there wasn't even one day of learning listening skills during all of my teacher preparation. Part of the reason for that, I believe, is decades of conditioning to the lecture mode of many of our teachers, who were themselves taught by lecture. As students, we expected teachers to tell us what we needed to know, repeat the important point over and over, and make it easy for us to tune out. This commonality among my teachers allowed me to always be somewhere else with my attention. Good students, it seemed, were those who could listen for what the teachers found important and then repeat it on tests. There was little to no opportunity or encouragement to listen to each other. Certainly, we didn't have the encouragement to learn to listen to ourselves in moments of mindfulness or quiet reflection.

However, there is power in learning to slow the traffic inside our heads—as students and as teachers. In this mental quiet, we can connect to the deepest parts of ourselves, which, in turn, allows for teaching and learning to make the mysteries of our own minds explicit as we bend toward our own unvoiced thoughts and questions.

Listening on Paper

Teaching is by its very nature emotionally, spiritually, and cognitively demanding. Scheduling reflective writing into my days helped me cope with these demands as well as giving me a way to remain present and productive. Those minutes added up into teaching days in a way that proved the truth of Annie Dillard's (1989) observation that how we spend our days is how we spend our lives, so regular writing becomes "a net for catching days" (p. 32). Teaching can become so chaotic that it's hard to find your way back to yourself and your motivation for doing this work.

A week of study with writing teacher Natalie Goldberg (personal communication, January 15, 2005) taught me the potential of ten-minute writings to, as she said, "[p]enetrate your life and make you sane." Carving out those minutes within my classes became a way to put pauses in my chaotic day and create a space where I could, as Thich Nhat Hanh advises, validate my own strong feelings without spilling them over onto my students or colleagues.

The process of writing in short bursts is easy, but committing to it as a daily practice is more difficult. Because this structure worked for me, I wondered if it would work for students, with some alteration. I began to look for ways to build the habit of these tiny writings into our days, finding places where it could help them, as Goldberg taught me, to "meditate on paper." Writing is a way to be present with your own experience. This is a life skill for our children in the age of smartphones and their siren calls to always be responsive to others and forever insecure about missing out on something.

Enough former students told me how practicing this one habit helped them that I decided to keep it as an ironclad structure over all of the years of my teaching. Finding these splinters of time in a school day is easier when you start to think about the occasions where students might need to slow their scattered thoughts and think more deeply. For example, when my students showed up on the in-school suspension rolls, I often had no idea why they were there or who sent them. An assignment that served the dual purpose of allowing me to find out what was going on, as well as give them an authentic writing activity, was to send a set of sentence stems along with their makeup work:

- What I'm feeling right now is . . .
- I hate/I love . . .
- What I wish people understood is . . .
- What I'm wondering about is . . .

Each stem is answered on a separate sheet of paper because I expected the writer to use at least one page to explain their thinking or emotions. Students who came to class visibly upset often opted to do a ten-minute writing to downshift their brains out of high alert. Sometimes they shared these with me, but most times they found that it comforted them just to have time to feel listened to on paper. Once they did this, it was much easier for them to rejoin class. Some students need to draw until they can find the words, and we often forget that drawing is a form of prewriting.

Paradoxically, for me and many of my students, the more you learn to listen to yourself on paper, the more you learn to listen to others in your daily life. This is even more true when listening feels threatening as in those times when you are faced with anger or imagine that you will face anger, like listening to parents.

Listening in Difficult Conversations

Speaking to parents, especially parents with whom I had to have difficult conversations, was nearly impossible for me for many years. Because most of my students' parents were a different race and culture from me, I was afraid that I would unintentionally offend them or make them angry. My own discomfort with conflict of any kind made this worse. Calling home, at first, was excruciating for me, provoking my anxiety to the point that I would find any excuse to avoid the call. A colleague suggested that I write out a script, much like a telemarketer, before I called (see the appendix for the script I used until it became a habit).

It was hard for me to extend the validation or adopt an active listening stance with parents in the way that I did for students. Compounding this difficulty was the lack of support on discipline issues that teachers received from administrators, who it seemed were overloaded with so many other tasks that they often weren't available. Some of the teachers told me that it didn't matter if you called a conference with a parent because administrators would agree to any request from a parent and defer to them over a teacher, no matter the issue. This was doubly true if the student was an athlete, they said. This seemed to ring true for me because early on in the school year, I'd already had run-ins with coaches who wanted me to change failing grades so a student could play.

We don't do a good job of making parents feel welcome in schools. Too often, we don't feel supported and so become defensive, which makes parents defensive. What breaks through this cycle, in my experience, is the acceptance that comes from being listened to in an open and present manner. I had a sticky note inside the folder I carried to parent conferences that said this:

Talk less; ask more questions.

Being present helps me notice the facial expressions and body language of another, which helps me to affirm the emotion that seems the strongest.

Validation Is Magic

Active or reflective listening is a way to help students and parents feel heard, seen, and respected. In the heat of conflict or when we're afraid of consequences, listening is the first skill we seem to lose. In school, we buy into the illusion of efficiency that seems to come from the hierarchies and authoritarian nature of many interactions. Asserting our titles and positions may make us feel more confident, but it often cuts off discussions and escalates tensions. This drives a cycle of defensiveness that causes everyone to feel attacked.

A magic phrase for beginning difficult conversations that avoids a tense scenario is this: What's going on that I need to know? With administrators or parents, I made it more formal: What do you need me to understand? The key is to keep people talking by asking them this: Can you say more about that?

As you get more information, the other key move is to reflect back, as accurately as you can, what you're hearing, without arguing or interpreting or getting defensive. This is really hard in the school day with the pressure of the bell and shifting classes. But it's actually more efficient in helping to manage tension, conflict, and other strong emotions.

Often, a student hearing you use their words makes them feel heard, and that's enough to make strong feelings dissipate: I'm hearing you say . . . is that right?

For those who dismiss this as a "touchy-feely" exercise that wastes time and distracts from learning, I'd argue that Socrates's main power was his ability to listen closely to whoever was speaking. This allowed him to ask such good questions that the speaker would convince himself or herself of the better argument. This ability to listen and respond appropriately made him beloved by his students and influential among those he sought to engage in discussion.

Key Phrases for Reflective Listening

- You sound really _____ (fill in the blank with the emotion you're seeing).

- I can understand why you feel . . . (repeat what you've heard them say).

- Let me make sure I heard you correctly (repeat what you heard).

- That must be really _____ (find a word that validates their experience, such as hard, sad, upsetting, exciting, challenging, etc.).

Active listening also includes body language that demonstrates your engagement, such as eye contact and head nods. Just being quiet and looking at the person may cause you to zone out. Leaning forward helps to slow down the person you're listening to, while leaning back gives the signal that you need them to open up more.

Listening well—whether it's student to student or teacher to student, teacher to teacher, or administrators to teachers—dissolves fear. Fear, in my experience, is one of the biggest barriers to creativity and innovative solutions. Being heard is deeply validating. It communicates respect in a way that no classroom rules can because it's the active practice of relationship.

Philosopher Erich Fromm (1994) says that good listening is a practice of empathy "strong enough to feel the experience of the other as if it were [our] own" and that it opens our hearts to understanding another as a "crucial facet of the capacity for love. To understand another means to love him—not in the erotic sense, but in the sense of reaching out to him and of overcoming the fear of losing oneself."

Common Problems

Students are no different from the rest of our culture when it comes to listening skills. They've been rewarded for having quick answers, certainty, and confidence. This causes them to adopt the stance that listening is really just a way of waiting for someone to stop talking so you can make your own points without having listened to what others say or attempting to relate to their ideas.

As a teacher, I found myself either holding my students hostage to what was often something I'd describe as bad performance art, where I talked from bell to bell about whatever I felt was the most important or interesting parts of the "lesson," or rambling off on tangents involving personal anecdotes. Or worse, I was stringing together lots of disjointed advice like Polonius's obtuse lectures in *Hamlet*. Once I became aware of my worst tendencies of "teacher as teller," I overcorrected by handing over all conversation to students, encouraging them to talk regardless of the connection to whatever we were learning.

We can only change what we become aware of in ourselves, so the way forward is to bring these issues into class and create solutions for them together.

Table 4.1 is adapted from several sources in addition to my own observations as an instructional coach. It summarizes the roadblocks to effective listening and cripples the learning we might gain.

Table 4.1 Common Obstacles to Effective Listening in the Classroom

STUDENT PROBLEMS	TEACHER PROBLEMS
1. Only prepared a single point and waits to use it 2. Waits for any pause to jump in with their own idea 3. Doesn't answer original question, uses it to jump to another topic they'd rather discuss 4. Stuck on their own issue that they repeat in every discussion 5. Tune out because they don't think whatever is being discussed is important 6. Tune out because they think they already know whatever is being discussed	1. So focused on lesson plan that student input isn't noticeable—and when it is, it's not listened to very well 2. Discussion is set up as "guess what answer I want you to have" and ends whenever a student manages to give the teacher the "right" answer 3. Everyone is encouraged to say whatever they're thinking and it's treated as equally insightful, so no one really has to think about what to say or listen to anyone

Source: Adapted from Leonard (1991).

Lyon Terry (personal communication, April 2, 2017), a fourth-grade teacher in Seattle, Washington, shares his ongoing practice in learning listening skills with his students. "Teachers are bad about repeating what is said. That shows kids that they don't have to listen to what each other says because the teacher will just repeat it for them and repeat the important stuff," he said. "And I have kids watch me for that and keep me accountable."

He presents listening skills as life skills and something that everyone needs to practice. Students in his class practice greetings and goodbyes every day, with an emphasis on paying attention to each other and looking at each other when they speak. His introverted students struggle with this and need these daily interactions, he said.

"I'm really intentional about saying, yes, we're learning about science, but what you're really learning is how to talk to somebody and be able to work on a project together," Terry said. "I have kids who don't like to go to recess. They want to stay inside and read. I tell them, 'Your job is to go find other kids to interact with and talk to on the playground. This is something you need to work on. Other kids need to work on the skill you already have, which is reading. You need to work on your getting along with others skill. Those are equal skills.'"

To listen to each other is practice in being human and one that can't easily be taken over by technology. Through listening, we learn how to see others and to feel seen and understood by them. Everyone is able to contribute to the community we build from space and time to listen to each other, no matter their age or ability level or language skills. This is a shift into what Margaret Wheatley (2009) believes is conversation as trust building:

Listening Agreements

- Acknowledge one another as equals.
- Stay curious about each other.
- Understand that we need each other's help to become better listeners.
- Slow down so we have time to think and reflect.
- Remember that conversation is the natural way humans think together.
- Expect it to be messy.

A pragmatic reason to teach explicit listening skills, agreements, and the tools to resolve conflict is because it will save you time in not having to "police" your classroom. This saved time can then be redirected into academic tasks.

The more important reason to teach these skills and create routines around them is that they give students experience with peaceful and productive collaboration. "Teaching kids intentionally how to speak to one another isn't fluffy," Ann Marie Corgill (personal communication, March 21, 2017), a first-grade teacher in Birmingham, Alabama, says. She believes that deliberately teaching communication skills builds the kind of agency she needs students to have so they can authentically participate in writing workshop learning with each other. "They've been controlled, and ticketed, and stoplighted to death. That creates a controlling environment, and I want them to feel empowered that this is our classroom," she said.

That empowerment comes from the concrete ways she teaches them to listen to each other. "I'll ask them, What does it look like when someone's listening to you? Even down to the place where I'll take photographs and we'll look at them. We'll look at eye contact and body language," she said.

The one practice that changed Corgill's work is the listening she does during writing conferences with her students. "I'm stepping back and letting them do the talking. At first, they don't know what to say or what a conference is. But I start by talking to them about what they're working on and asking how I can help them," she said. "Conferring is where they realize that I'm really listening to them."

During her time teaching at the Manhattan New School in New York, Corgill once had a class of thirty-two second graders that seemed too large for her to effectively confer with them. Her solution was to create a classroom of peer teachers who used "share time" to synthesize the concepts they learned in conferences and explain that to their classmates. For example, Miles shared that as he showed Ms. Corgill his drawings, she didn't understand how they fit with his writing, so he learned that he needed to put words underneath the pictures. Students then turned to talk with a partner to solidify the learning that writers add words to their pictures so the reader can understand.

"It's that daily, repetitive, 'I'm going to hear you, and then you're going to teach your classmates how to listen as well' that creates the listening skill," she said.

Justin Minkel (personal communication, September 9, 2016), a second-grade teacher in Springdale, Arkansas, developed a process called Peace Talks that help younger students process conflict and learn listening skills at the same time. He has an anchor chart on the wall of the conversation stems for students to use and models the procedure in fishbowl demonstrations. In the demonstrations, students use a made-up or actual conflict to model these stems:

Peace Talks Routine

1. The first student says, "When you_____, I felt _____. Next time I want you to_____."
2. The second student repeats the stem, adding their input.
3. The kids work out a solution.
4. They shake hands.

Source: Justin Minkel (personal communication, 2016).

He supports the Peace Talks with synonyms for emotion words so students can identify what they're feeling and from read-alouds like *When Sophie Gets Angry—Really, Really Angry* (Bang, 2004) or *The Butter Battle Book* (Dr. Seuss, 1984).

"I was amazed at how little the process required from me. All I had to do was ask Marina, 'Do you want to have a Peace Talk with Michael?' Then the two of them would work it out," he said. "I don't listen in, hover, or coach. The kids didn't even report back to me. They just went to the back of the room, out of earshot of the other students, worked out their problem, and returned to their seats. Every year since, one of the first things I teach my new class is how to do a Peace Talk."

Learning to listen well is difficult. That's partly because it's much easier to set the parameters of discussion in classes around encouraging everyone to speak and for everyone to think of an answer. True listening requires a different kind of mental energy. It requires us to stop performing as teachers and to stop requiring our students to perform.

> One of the easiest human acts is also the most healing. Listening to someone. Simply listening. Not advising or coaching, but silently and fully listening. (Wheatley, 2009)

The following listening protocol is one I've used with students as well as teachers in professional development workshops as a way of beginning serious practice in learning to listen to each other.

PROTOCOL 4.1
Practicing Listening Skills

SUGGESTIONS

- Use the protocol before, during, or after any discussion as a way for everyone in class to practice speaking and listening. If you have an uneven number of students, be a listening partner with a student.

- Explain the reason for a protocol: It helps us feel safe with each other. You can use the idea of training wheels on a bike that help us until we can ride on our own, or explain that it's like the bumpers on a bowling alley lane that help the ball stay on the lane and head toward the pins.

- Explain that listening is one of the best gifts we can give each other because it helps us feel like someone cares.

- It is also one of the best skills to have for your life because it will help you have better friendships, better marriages, and even be a better parent. Have an objective for the activity.

- Becoming a good listener also helps you in whatever work you want to do. The scientist and teacher Bill Nye wants us to remember that everyone we will ever meet knows something we don't. Listening is the way we learn from each other so we can get smarter every day.

- Partnerships of two people are a good way to practice listening.

PROMPTS

- My preference is to use student-generated questions. You may choose to use any of the questions that students have generated or ones that you have saved from other classes or groups.

- What do you like to do when you are not at school?

- What is the best thing about a friend?

- What are you really good at?

- What are five ways you are strong?

CONDITIONS

- Students are able to sit with each other for a short time, in places of their choosing—rug or moving chairs or desks to a spot in the room

(Continued)

(Continued)

where they can hear each other. The physical space begins to help create the mental space.

- Students have watched or seen a model of good listening and speaking.

- Students are encouraged to take turns listening and speaking.

- Students should be in groups of two to start, then can extend it to four.

MATERIALS

- Timer

- You may want to use some variation of a "talking stick"—some object that helps to concretely remind students who is supposed to be talking. I have used inflatable microphones I found at a dollar store, or the kinds of squeezable objects people give away as "de-stressors." Anything you have will work as a concrete reminder, even paper towel tubes.

- Determine who will go first as the speaker. You may use variations of ideas such as whose birthday is closest to today's date, who has more pets, who has more brothers and sisters, and so on. This helps the students know something about each other right away.

TIME

Eight minutes is a good beginning time. As students become more comfortable with it, extend the time to fifteen minutes.

INTRODUCTION

Everyone deserves to be listened to, and everyone deserves the right to speak about whatever is in their hearts or their heads that they need to say. Listening and speaking are like two puzzle pieces. When we do a good job, it's a good fit. But it takes practice. We need to make sure that we help each other feel safe, so let's agree that what we tell each other is private until we have permission to share it.

DIRECTIONS

We are going to take turns practicing listening and practicing speaking for two minutes each. I will set a timer to make sure everyone gets the same time to practice. Listeners will only listen. There is no interrupting or asking questions.

- **Two minutes**—Set the timer: The first speaker answers the prompt; the listener remembers to listen only. The speaker speaks for the entire time.

- **Two minutes**—Reset the timer: The second speaker answers the prompt; the listener remembers to listen only. The speaker speaks for the entire time.

- **One to two minutes**—Debrief by having volunteers describe how it felt to have someone listen without interrupting. What was easy? What was hard? What did you like? How could this help you in your life?

- **Two minutes**—Optional: tie it into the lesson, text, or discussion.

EXTENSIONS

- Use it to begin class or to help students begin thinking about the topic or question under discussion. Pairs can become discussion groups of four as students get more comfortable with the process.

- Use it to teach students to pay attention to environmental distractors—like phones. You can have kids stack their phones in the middle of the table, and the first person to check it loses their discussion points.

- Use it as a "time-out" whenever a discussion breaks down to help students process the strong feelings that may have arisen or think about why a discussion broke down.

- Use it after an activity or discussion to help students reflect on what they learned, and synthesize it with new learning.

- Use it as a silent "conversation" with nature by taking kids outdoors to listen to environmental sounds. They then write about what they learned from listening to the space around them.

- A deeper extension is to use this with colleagues and/or administrators—see Part IV of this book for adapted protocols for adult work.

Source: Adapted from Marjorie Larner (2007), Parker Palmer, Victor Cary, and National Coalition for Equity in Education. ●

Listening well is also another practice in responsibility—in trusting students to manage and practice speaking responsibly in a way that doesn't provoke or offend but that contributes to the intellectual culture of the class.

As students become more adept in discussion, you may choose to teach them specific conversational moves that support mental models of responding to text. Academic writing, at its simplest, is a form of conversation with a source where the writer clarifies, adds, questions, agrees, or disagrees with the source.

National standards for college and career readiness emphasize speaking and listening, as do many state standards like those in Texas. Students are expected to develop and demonstrate independence in their speaking and listening skills. Table 4.2 highlights discussion skills that serve as concrete practice in the movement of academic discourse that Graff and Birkenstein (2009) so brilliantly summarize as "they say, I say."

Table 4.2 Discussion Skills and Corresponding Standards

SKILLS	STEMS TO SUPPORT	NATIONAL AND STATE STANDARDS ADDRESSED
1. Effectively challenge or respectfully disagree. 2. Build on others' ideas or work toward "equity of voice." 3. Reflect or paraphrase. 4. Use examples. 5. Manage conflicts of opinions. 6. Clarify. 7. Summarize.	1. Another way to look at this is . . . /When you say . . . , it makes me think . . . /I want to challenge that point a bit . . . 2. I want to expand on your point about . . . 3. What I'm hearing you say is . . . /It sounds like what you're saying is . . . 4. The author/text/problem said . . . /It's like when . . . 5. Let me make sure I understand you . . . /I'm hearing you say . . . , is that right?/Tell me more about why you think that . . . 6. What I mean by that is . . . 7. So we're saying that . . . /Our main points seem to be . . .	• Listen actively in informal and formal situations. • Use strategies to enhance listening comprehension. • Understand important information. • Ask for clarification when they don't understand. • Ask questions connected to the topic under discussion. • Add to others' ideas, and clearly explain their own. • Have a clear purpose for speaking and listening related to the current task. • Understand how the nuances of tone and inflection in the speaker's voice affect the meaning of a message. • Analyze and evaluate the effectiveness of a presentation. • Respectfully question assumptions and arguments while assessing their accuracy. • Value evidence.

Sources: Fisher, Frey, and Rothenberg (2008); National Governors Association Center for Best Practices and Council of Chief State School Officers (2010); Texas Higher Education Coordinating Board and Texas Education Agency Division of Curriculum (2009); Zwiers and Crawford (2010).

These moves are also practice in notetaking, one of the nine learning strategies with a significant probability of boosting student achievement across all subject areas and at all grade levels discovered in Marzano, Pickering, and

Pollock's (2001) meta-analysis. Students taking notes using these stems are trying on a social rehearsal of the basic moves of critical thinking. A strategy to help students blend these skills plus practice questioning, get to know another person in class, and create a product for publication is my alteration of Proust's questionnaire shown in Protocol 4.2.

PROTOCOL 4.2
Famous for Fifteen Minutes

SUGGESTIONS

- Generate questions that don't have a one-word answer before the activity by having students think about what they'd like to know about someone. Post them on an anchor chart, or have students write the ones they like in their notebooks.

- Alternatively, you can have students section off a piece of notebook paper into four squares and use these as starters for questions:

Questions About Facts	Questions About Opinions
Sample: Are you oldest, middle, or youngest in your family, and what is good about that?	**Sample:** What is the best food, and why is it the best?
Questions About the Past	**Questions About the Future**
Sample: What is something that used to scare you but doesn't anymore?	**Sample:** When you imagine what the world will be like when you graduate from high school, what do you imagine?

- Show examples of magazine interviews. Good examples are the "Talk" Q&A feature in the *New York Times Magazine* or "The Q&A" in the *Guardian* newspaper. My students used these to help them visualize a final product. We deliberately designed our features to look like the layouts from magazines.

OTHER SAMPLE QUESTIONS (A VERSION OF THE VICTORIAN WRITER MARCEL PROUST'S FAMOUS QUESTIONNAIRE)

What is your main characteristic?

What do you appreciate the most in your friends?

(Continued)

(Continued)

What is your main flaw?

What is your best personal trait?

What is your idea of happiness?

What is your idea of misery?

If you could be anyone, who would you be?

Who is your hero?

What's the funniest thing that's ever happened to you?

If you could learn about anything, what would it be and why?

Who can you talk to about anything and why do you trust that person?

How would your best friend describe you?

CONDITIONS

Students need to be able to take notes from listening and then be able to use them to write a profile. However, you can adapt the lesson to short videos or audio files for younger or struggling students. Check with your digital learning leaders for help in creating, housing, and showing these as well as permissions guidelines for recording students.

MATERIALS

- Timer
- A place to take notes, preferably in their notebooks so the notes don't get lost
- Each student should have a partner. An easy way to do this is to "break the line" by having students line up single file. Then, tell everyone to follow the line leader. The line leader guides the line until he or she has doubled it. Each student should be across from another one. That's their partner. If the class is uneven, partner with a student.

TIME

Forty-five minutes

INTRODUCTION

We are going to make each other famous for fifteen minutes today. We are also going to be reporters who will create a one-page feature of each other that will be posted for others to read. This is also going to help us get to know each other.

DIRECTIONS

- **Five minutes**—Generate interesting questions.

- **Three minutes**—Partner up, and find a place to interview each other where you can hear.

- **Ten minutes**—Set the timer. The first partner asks questions to the second partner and takes notes.

- **Ten minutes**—Reset the timer. The second partner asks questions to the first partner and then takes notes.

- **Five minutes**—Debrief with the students [sample questions].

EXTENSIONS

Students create a page to display that's designed as a magazine layout. Struggling students and English language learners (ELLs) can just bold the questions they asked and write the answers. Gifted and talented (GT) students can write features about the person. Get permission to take photos and post finished products outside your classroom to introduce your class. You can extend this exercise with multimedia applications with students using the format to ask questions of family members, faculty, or people they'd like to interview in the community, either on video or for a podcast.

Source: Adapted from Linda Rief, Joyce Armstrong Carroll (Carroll & Wilson, 1993), and the New Jersey Writing Project in Texas. ●

Making It Work for You

- What listening experiences have been particularly rich for you personally? What made them so helpful? What could you pull from those experiences to help students?

- How are your students listening in class? Why do you think that is?

(Continued)

(Continued)

- What have you modified from this chapter for use in your own classroom? How did it go?

- What would you like to try next?

- What would an ideal classroom look like, sound like, and feel like if everyone was skilled in listening?

- What would change with colleagues if you tried out some of the listening ideas with each other?

- What would change for administrators if listening was a priority?

See the appendix for lesson ideas and texts for all ages.

CHAPTER 5

Constructing Trust

Foundational Practices to Build Empathy, Belonging, and a Culture of Thinking

There is a deep—and usually frustrated—desire in the heart of everyone to act with benevolence rather than selfishness, and one fine instance of generosity can inspire dozens more. Thus I established a stately court where all my friends showed respect to each other and cultivated courtesy until it bloomed into perfect harmony.

—XENOPHON

Everyone who arrives at your classroom door asks themselves a form of this question: Can I trust you? This is true even if they are an administrator, a parent, a colleague, or a student. How we answer that question is important because an essential part of trust is understanding that it carries the possibility of loss whether of tangible things or intangibles like respect, according to philosophy professor Carolyn McLeod (2015). She writes that the act of trust involves four separate actions:

1. Allowing yourself to be vulnerable to others
2. Thinking well of others

3. Believing that the other is competent to do what you ask

4. Adopting a generous mindset about the motives of others

McLeod explains that trustworthiness can be viewed through Aristotle's conception of virtue. A trustworthy person, in this view, is someone who can be counted on to take care of the things we entrust to them and "whose ways of caring are neither excessive nor deficient" (McLeod, 2015).

Further, the research of Lewicki and Wiethoff (2000) found that trust is built when we do the following:

1. Act consistently and reliably.

2. Meet deadlines and commitments.

3. Repeatedly do so over time. (p. 111)

Taken together, these actions create a willingness to care which, in turn, creates the conditions for us to be open-hearted to whoever enters our classrooms.

ANGEL, BULL SNAKES, AND BIRTHDAY CAKE

Ironically named teenagers often filled the tables in the night class at my high school: Dulce is the name of the girl repeatedly suspended for fighting. Christian is the boy who draws anarchy symbols on his forearms. Angel, the stereotypical "student from hell," is the one who glares at me and who rolls his eyes at me. It's Angel who tempts me to make it personal between me and him.

Angel would die if he knew this, but I consider him one of my best teachers of trust. Court-ordered to attend my class, he glared at me when I registered him. Many teachers know that look. However, what I've learned from kids like Angel is that expression, the "mean mug" as they call it, is a front.

Growing up in Texas, I've seen my share of bull snakes. They look just like rattlesnakes, but they're not dangerous. When you scare them, they puff up to make themselves look as big as possible, hissing like crazy while simultaneously striking and moving backward. Angel behaved just like a bull snake.

For years, I've fallen for this act. Gradually, with the help and model of the excellent teachers with whom I worked, I've learned to calm down and lean on a standby: food.

The fastest way around an attitude is also one of the oldest: Offer food, particularly something sweet. For Angel, like many children in poverty, celebrations are rare, and those that involve big, colored confections even more so.

One night, my coteacher brought in a sheet cake from a party she'd attended. Angel eyed the waves of piped white frosting, the beads of colored sugar sprinkled among plump mounds of fondant flowers. A tiny spark of longing flashed across his face so quickly that if you blinked, you'd miss it.

I asked him if he wanted a piece. He stared, irritation simmering inside his brown eyes. He needed to get the cake without me seeing him do it. It's a small but important part of trust to grant these small entitlements.

"Well, it's there if you want it," I said, walking away. When I came back, he'd gotten himself a corner piece and eaten it.

"Oh, good," I said. "I'm glad you got some. But now you owe me. One page of writing for one piece of cake."

"I ain't writing nothing," he said, smirking.

To maintain my temper and teach myself to see and connect to the invisible child inside the big, often rude bodies of my teenagers, I use another kind of sugar: verbal honey. I call these irritated students "sweet baby," another Texas custom. Using this endearment softens me and helps me remember that learning something from someone you don't really know is a vulnerable experience. It also really puts the listener off guard, something Texas women have known for a long time.

"Sweet baby, don't write, then. Tell me why the judge ordered you here."

He puffed up, telling me what a "bad kid" he was. As he talked, I noticed that the frosting had stained his teeth blue.

"Angel, if you can tell me all that, why don't you write it? I want to show it to a guy in my class who says everything I give him to read is stupid and not real. He'd love your story. Would you like a laptop, or paper and a pencil?"

The question startled him. "A laptop, I guess," he said, his face registering a kind of shock at his own answer. As the computer booted up, I drew a few boxes on a piece of paper to give him a structure to begin writing from and walked away.

To see a struggling student actually begin to attempt real work is like watching a butterfly land. You have to see it sideways, so you won't frighten it away.

When I came back around toward the end of class, I saw that he had written nearly an entire page.

"You are a writer, Angel. I knew it." I could see the beginnings of a smile on his face.

"It was pretty easy," he said, tilting the screen toward me.

What I read was rife with misspellings and barely intelligible sentences. But what I've learned about the first steps of trust in a classroom is that you have to meet each student where they are, celebrate what they can do, and show them a small success.

"You have all kinds of stories inside you," I told him. He smiled.

That smile meant that, for a small moment, he believed that he could. That smile meant that he felt actual pride in himself. That he believed he mattered. That his words have meaning and he has value.

Source: Peeples (2015); previously published in "The Blog," HuffPost, on May 25, 2015.

◇◇◇

Trust Begins With Safety

Parker Palmer (personal communication, March 23, 2017) is a major influence on my thinking around the necessity of vulnerability in education. He shared advice with me on how to begin the process of creating the kind of trusting climate necessary for real transformation in education. He suggested starting with this question: What makes education unsafe?

"If you think about what makes education unsafe, you start to get a lot of clues of course," he said. "One of the things that makes it unsafe is that it's very oriented toward getting the right answer. So, if we're to make safe spaces for self examination, we have to put out problems and issues and questions that don't have right answers. That would be huge in education if we could create even a little space for things that aren't connected to the right answer."

> To believe that one can teach respect through coercion is to confuse respect with obedience.
>
> **—LARRY BRENDTRO AND NICHOLAS LONG, *RECLAIMING CHILDREN AND YOUTH***

Another way we unintentionally create unsafe spaces in schools is to allow the kind of judgment that makes students feel embarrassed. This, Palmer said, leads to students learning to be quiet and only give "right" answers rather than take the kinds of risks necessary for learning. The end result is a marginalization of their voices and ideas.

For me, this is the ground of the work. If we don't create trust, safety, and respect in our classrooms, then why bother with any of the other bits of school? Because students are struggling with so many more issues than they have in the past, it's essential that when they walk into our classrooms, they know they will be safe physically, emotionally, and intellectually. This means that it starts with real conversations about these very topics.

Safety requires deliberate cultivation, yet it's one of the hardest things for those of us in a school to do. We don't trust each other. We view each other transactionally: What do I have to give you to get what I want? We lack the deep well of confidence that comes from owning what we're doing because we're so fearful of the judgment or punishment that we fear will come. This fear keeps so many of us—teachers, administrators, students, and parents—siloed from each other and prevented from the shared understanding that creates and sustains trust.

Vulnerability, however, is not to be confused with a failure to set boundaries. Indeed, it is not until a teacher develops boundaries that he or she can be truly approachable.

You can start conversations about trust inside your classroom with an invitation to consider questions of community: Have you been part of a group—inside or outside of school—that felt like a community to you? What does community feel like or mean to you?

Asking students to cocreate the space with me by deciding what will go on the walls in the form of inspirational quotes or lyrics, anchor charts, and images is a successful ongoing practice. The walls are blank when students arrive on the first day because I want each piece we post on it to be intentional. One of the first posters to go up is the result of our discussion and agreement on creating a safe space, like this one:

Ground Rules About Safe Space

Emotional safety—No one will use offensive or insulting terms when speaking to or about anyone in this room.

Physical safety—Respect the bodies around you, and keep yours from invading theirs. Respect your own needs by quietly attending to them with the hall pass by the door.

Intellectual safety—Respect perspectives—everyone knows something you don't. You're free to read, write, and speak about your confusions, questions, and new learning.

Spiritual safety—Respect the beliefs or lack of belief of those around you. All world religions agree on one rule: Treat others as you want to be treated. Everyone is entitled to the integrity of their heart and soul.

Students don't make all the decisions, but the more time I spend in creating the conditions for trust along with a positive environment, the fewer problems I encounter during the rest of the year. Holding their hearts frees their minds for discovery.

"Plato went so far as to say that philosophy is about falling in love. I think he's actually right about that. You have to fall in love a little with your students and you have to let them fall in love a little with you," Sharon Kaye (personal communication, March 8, 2017), a professor of philosophy at John Carroll University, who helps children and teens access philosophy through innovative lessons, said in a discussion.

"That can't happen if you are holding back, presenting a professional facade," she said. "It takes a lot of trust to be yourself in the classroom. And sometimes you get burned by rejection. But when they do, it is magic, because, in the end, you're not really in love with each other, you're in love with the beautiful ideas that you've brought to life together."

How Do You Turn These Principles Into Concrete Action?

The first steps toward cultivating trust are to practice what Rachel Kessler (2001) defines as "the teaching presence." This is a teacher's deliberate openness to whatever is happening right now: the choice to be responsive to the needs of this moment, rather than stressing over what has happened or worrying about what will happen.

Many readers will recognize this as the basics of mindfulness, a discipline whose rewards will serve you in the difficult work of teaching. Being present gives you more flexibility and creativity as you "monitor and adjust" when things go wrong. Presence allows us to problem-solve around things like the typically difficult after-lunch class, sleepiness of first period, or disengagement of last class. Teachable moments happen more often when we call on honesty and humility, admitting when things are going wrong and questioning if the lesson's goal is more important than what's going on right now.

As simplistic as it may sound, trust begins with a willingness to smile. Hattie and Yates (2013) devote a whole chapter of their book to research on smiling, finding that your smile "[invites] your students to share your view of the world and in so doing you are providing a strong model for implicit emulation. . . ." (p. 268). They explain that when we smile at our students, they smile back almost all of the time. Our faces create reactions from those we interact with, according to their cited research, and this "indicates that teachers' liking for their students is linked to whether or not students exhibit responsive smiling" (p. 269).

For my part, smiling helps me feel more positive about any situation and makes me more inclined to offer goodwill to whoever comes into my classroom. I'm also more open to the idea of seeing what's right with my students instead of what's wrong. Searching for my students' strengths so that we could build on them together was the mindset that helps me work with children in poverty more than any other strategy. This search is helped by finding out as much as I can about them as soon as I can.

On the first day of school, I give students a questionnaire to work on as they arrive. I also give it to new students who join my classes throughout the year.

First-Day Assignment

What name do you want me to use for you?

_____

Who would you like me to call when I have good news about you to share? Please write their names:

_____

What are you good at (inside of school)?

_____

What are you good at (outside of school)?

_____

What was the last movie you saw that you really liked, and why did you like it?

_____

_____

If you could study anything, what would you want to know more about?

_____

What's easiest about school for you?

_____

(Continued)

(Continued)

What's hardest about school for you?

_____

What would your friends say about you?

_____

What would you like me to know about you?

_____

_____

How do you feel about working in groups?

_____

When we work in groups, who would you like to work with?

_____

_____

When we work in groups, who do you know you'll have trouble with or will cause you to get in trouble?

_____

What questions do you have for me? I will write my answers back to you on another piece of paper.

FOR OLDER STUDENTS

Please share your schedule with me so I will know what your day is like:

Wake up:

Responsibilities before school:

Time you usually arrive at school:

Responsibilities after school:

Time you go to sleep:

What do you usually do after school?

What do you usually do on weekends?

Tech note: Have students answer these in a Google Form; the answers will be compiled into a report you can use to help you keep track of individual student preferences.

How to Process These Answers

Make a folder for each student, and keep this information in it, along with samples of work, conference notes, and correspondence concerning the student from themselves, parents, or school personnel.

During the first weeks, try to make contact with the person the student identified as someone with whom to share something good so you can make sure the first things they hear from you are positive.

Depending on your content area, you may decide on different ways to use the information. Some teachers report trends in the answers as statistics of the class or classes or ask more in-depth questions about a student's experience with different subjects. My inventories, since I needed to know about their attitudes toward reading, included questions about how many books they had at home, whether they thought books were a good gift, and so on.

In middle school, I used the student self-report of strengths to make a "directory of experts" for my classes, listing who they might go to if they needed help or wanted to learn more about a topic. Laminated, they become a usable reference.

The answers helped me to suggest books or other texts and writing topics, and it also gave me topics for conferences. Although it takes more time up front, grouping students by putting them with people they prefer to work with decreases issues and increases collaboration. Later in the year, it's easier to change up groups because students feel more comfortable with each other. Being willing to take their preferences seriously goes a long way toward establishing trust and good relationships.

In high school, the student self-report of difficulties guided me in forming study groups or matching study buddies. Additionally, the student schedule helped me find trouble spots with time, which helped me bolster their executive functioning skills.

Every year, I have a few students who take me up on the questions and write to me. Many ask a form of this question: Are you nice? That question is one I often have when I meet someone new too. We always want to know what we're getting into when we start a new relationship, especially one where the person has authority over us. I write back to the student personally and privately but use short stories about me to illustrate the answers. For example, they find out what kind of disciplinarian I am in the story about a student who climbed on my filing cabinets and wouldn't come down my first year of teaching. I encourage them to share similar school stories with each other and then, if they want to, with the class. Stories bond students faster than almost any other activity.

Five Suggestions for Building Healthy Relationships

Finding qualities and actions I can genuinely praise helps students feel validated in their efforts, which in turn makes them want to keep getting that validation. Sincere and specific recognition of what you appreciate is key—the transformative potential of this practice lies in its authenticity, not in phony gushing. We underestimate the power of unconditional and relentless positive regard. Our evolutionary bias toward negative events often keeps us from remembering all those instances where influential mentors did the same for us.

This is echoed in an unlikely place to find guidance for creating trusting relationships: a divorce researcher. John Gottman became famous for creating a scientifically based model of predicting divorce with more than 90 percent accuracy. Decades of watching couples revealed patterns of behavior that literally make or break relationships. Good relationships, he found, are based on a deliberate nurturing of fondness, of attention to knowing the goals, worries, hopes, and dreams of the other person. His suggestions, when adapted for classroom use, look like Table 5.1.

These actions lower stress and fear in students and ourselves, which, in turn, helps the brain learn faster and more efficiently, according to a raft of neurological research. All of us do better within a climate of positivity—we're more creative and resilient. Students in poverty are especially in need of affirmational language because they tend to experience double the amount of discouraging or prohibitive words as do children in working-class or professional families. Hart and Risley (2003) found that "by the age of 4, the average child in a welfare family might have had 144,000 fewer encouragements and 84,000 more discouragements of his or her behavior than the average child in a working-class family" (p. 6).

Table 5.1 Five Practices to Build Trust, Safety, and Empathy

FINDINGS FROM RESEARCH	CLASSROOM ADAPTATION
Turn toward each other—respond to bids for attention	Meet others at the door, allow students to opt out of activities, allow students to go to the restroom without having to interrupt class.
Let your partner influence you	Allow students to be classroom DJs and choose the music in class, or share playlists; allow them to choose video clips or other examples as the texts to support your content or essential questions.
Solve your solvable problems	Know when to get help. Some students have trusting relationships with another teacher or coach—seek their advice and try to meet together as a group.
Overcome gridlock	Be willing to have amnesia about previous behaviors. Move on by finding an admirable quality that you can sincerely compliment.
Create shared meaning	Remember your own feelings and experiences when you were this age. Bridge your age gap by allowing your "inner child" of this age to guide your interactions.

Source: Adapted from Gottman (2014).

Many of my students, by the time they got to my classroom in high school, had a kind of music of disapproval in their heads that was difficult to drown out, much less change.

A "neuroscience of trust" exists and research shows that it's correlated with the levels of the brain chemical oxytocin (Zak, 2017). The more oxytocin in your brain, the greater your ability to trust others as well as increase your empathy. Over a decade, Zak looked at what boosts this chemical and what suppresses it to determine why trust varies in people and environments. Chronic stress inhibits oxytocin, which is also corrosive to collaboration among students as well as for colleagues working together, or in conferences with parents. Oxytocin is enhanced with specific activities.

Zak identified management behaviors correlated with higher levels of trust and uses this matrix to gauge trust in companies. Some of those behaviors track with suggestions already mentioned in earlier chapters like introducing

> The brain is like Velcro for negative experiences and like Teflon for positive ones.
>
> **—RICK HANSON**

"challenge stress" where a difficult but achievable goal, like those of the tiny tasks and writing groups, promote bonding and collaboration. Likewise, choice—of how, when, and where students learn—combined with encouraging student solutions to existing problems creates a dynamic class.

PART II

CURATING QUESTIONS FOR USE IN THE CONTENT AREAS

I do nothing but go about persuading you all,
old and young alike, not to take thought for your
persons or your properties, but to care about the
greatest improvement of the soul. . . . This is my
teaching, and if this is the doctrine which corrupts
the youth, I am a mischievous person.

—SOCRATES

If we choose to see our students as possessors of skills we haven't traditionally labeled as *literacy,* like the ability to read people, situations, and visuals, then we can connect these innate competencies to our content literacy. Working with refugee and remedial students taught me this as I noticed how easily they used context clues; connected background knowledge; and made inferences in viewing images, videos, and experiences.

For example, even beginning language learners laughed at the wordless short video *For the Birds* (Eggleston, 2000), easily grasping the humor of the characters and plot. Likewise, athletes who struggled with text could predict behavior and explain sophisticated inferences about their opponents based on subtle body movements and facial expressions. This is true of even young children who, when I've asked them to tell me how they know who they want as a friend, can interpret behavioral details and dialogue to draw conclusions about someone else. In class, we created anchor charts to capture this expertise and use it as a bridge to reading text (see Table II.1).

Showing them the explicit connection between their rhetorical analysis of visuals and written texts created academic confidence for many of them because they'd only ever seen themselves as one kind of reader: struggling or failing. Viewing themselves as accomplished readers of the world around them instilled pride and motivation to add to their literacy skills.

Table II.1 Students' Visual and Interpersonal Literacies to Connect Them to Textual Literacy

READING VIDEO	READING IMAGES	READING PEOPLE AND SITUATIONS
• Pay attention to the title. • Notice where the story is happening. • What are the characters doing? • What does this remind me of that I've already seen? • How does one scene connect to another—what's the same?	• Look at all four corners of the image. • Notice details: What do you see when you look closely? • What are the main colors? • How is the photo put together: What's in front? What's in the background?	• What actions do you notice in this person? • How is he or she standing or sitting? • What is his or her face doing? • What do you notice about what he or she says? • What do you notice about his or her eyes and tone of voice?

For many students, reading is a pseudo-concept: They know they are supposed to "get something out of the text," but until we make explicit connections between what they already know and are able to do with what we need them to do, they pretend to read. Worse, they will believe that reading, or learning for that matter, is a game to see how many wild inferences they can generate, hoping that one of these will be the "right" answer. They've seen their peers and teachers perform what looks like a magic trick, effortlessly pulling meaning from a text with seemingly little or no effort.

This is not only a "struggling reader" problem. This behavior happens in advanced placement (AP) classes too because these students have always been rewarded for playing the game of school so well. They are adept at persuading their teachers to answer their own questions, which they then regurgitate in their writing. When asked to create meaning, they often freeze because of an intolerance for mistakes and the discomfort of being wrong. Visual literacy works just as well in persuading them to attempt difficulty and tolerate ambiguity.

When we give students thinking tools, like leveled questions, they're more willing to engage in academic literacy tasks. Leveled questions aren't new, but applying them as a specific scaffold with developmentally specific texts and tasks allows students to build their critical thinking muscles for other work (see Figure II.1).

Figure II.1 Leveled Questions

LEVEL 1

"Right There" Questions

- Finger put on or pointed to the answer
- Who, what, where, when, and how questions
- Important details
- Bloom's remembering and understanding levels; Depth of Knowledge (DOK) recall and reproduction level

LEVEL 2

Detective Questions

- What you know and what's in the text
- Make inferences, analyze, create meaning
- Why questions
- More than one answer
- Bloom's applying and analyzing levels; DOK skills and concepts/strategic thinking levels

LEVEL 3

Big Questions

- Start with text; go beyond it to connect to other thinking
- Philosophical questions that humans have been asking since ancient times
- Answer not in text; good practice for high-stakes testing to bring a universal perspective to written responses
- Bloom's evaluating and creating levels; DOK extended thinking level

Source: Bloom, Anderson, and Krathwohl (2001).

Three representative grade-level texts illustrate how leveled questions work: *Lilly's Purple Plastic Purse* by Kevin Henkes (1996) for elementary, *The Giver* by Lois Lowry (1993) for middle school, and *Romeo and Juliet* by William Shakespeare for high school:

Examples of Level 1 questions:

1. What is inside Lilly's purple plastic purse?
2. Who is Jonas's best friend?
3. What is Romeo's last name?

Examples of Level 2 questions:

1. Think about what you know about Mr. Slinger as a person. Why do you think he sent a note back to Lilly instead of sending her to the principal's office or calling her parents?
2. Based on what you know from everything that happens in *The Giver*, do you think Jonas and Gabriel live or die at the end of the book? Why?
3. Based on what you know about people and what you know about his character, why is Mercutio so sarcastic?

Examples of Level 3 questions:

1. What makes a good teacher?
2. Is a "perfect society" possible? Why?
3. How do you know when you've met "the one"—the person for you?

LESSON II.1   Make a Leveled Questions Foldable for Student Reference

MATERIALS

- A copy of "Cinderella" for younger children or English language learners (ELLs); older children will be familiar with the tale

(Continued)

(Continued)

- Enough sheets of 9 x 12 construction paper (any color) so that each student has one piece
- Scissors
- Markers
- Chart paper (three pieces) or easel pad

TIME

About forty minutes or one class period

DIRECTIONS

- Begin teaching leveled questioning by choosing a well-known story like "Cinderella" or "The Three Little Pigs," even for secondary students. They're simple and help students understand the levels of thinking quickly.

- Students may create a foldable by halving a sheet of 9 x 12 construction paper in a "hot dog" fold (long side to long side) and section off three flaps on one side. Cut these flaps to make doors that will open. Label one door Level 1, the next Level 2, and the final flap Level 3.

- Have students write a description of each level on the flap under each descriptor.

- Next, have a student volunteer to retell the story of "Cinderella," and then ask students to group brainstorm questions for each level. In elementary, they will need some help in Levels 2 and 3, but they will eventually be able to generate these on their own. For younger children, you may want to have another child volunteer to retell the story a third time as you group brainstorm.

- Get three big pieces of chart paper to collect the questions from brainstorming, placing them under the corresponding categories of Level 1, Level 2, and Level 3.

- Next, have students choose an example from the chart to write under the flaps of their foldables, making sure they are copying them under the correct flap.

- Talk about why they go with each level. The key is to generate lots of questions to demonstrate that reading is rereading (and thinking and wondering and asking questions). ●

LESSON II.2 Visual Literacy Practice With Leveled Questions

MATERIALS

- Images like those collected in annual "best of" photography awards (see my Pinterest board: "Images for Use as Writing Prompts and Visual Thinking Lessons" or my "Social Media, Social Justice" or "Visual Thinking Prompts" collections at Unsplash)

- Short videos like the Pixar short films or see my YouTube collection: "Using Video for Critical Thinking" (https://bit.ly/2GZNNoz)

DIRECTIONS

- Once students are comfortable with the levels of questions, have them try it out with images or a video.

- Make another foldable, and have them label the flaps, helping them rewrite the descriptors for each level in their own words. This activity in itself is heavy lifting for some kids as they've never attempted metacognition before and often have trouble paraphrasing ideas. Gently insist and model profusely. Paraphrasing is a key strategy for comprehension, so the more practice, the better.

- Pixar short films are an excellent resource for this, but you may use it for a longer film such as *Wall-E* (used with high school ELLs), or *The Incredibles* (used with middle schoolers), or *Finding Nemo* (used with elementary learners). In beginning this strategy, I used Pixar shorts because we could watch them three times in one class, noting new details and questions each time. We collected all of our thinking on anchor charts. ●

Students now have some confidence with familiar texts (and some practice using literary analysis by "reading" the video or photographs) and are able to begin tackling written text. Students may work with partners to either create shared notes or another foldable for use in practicing with a short text, poem, or song lyrics (see the appendix for an annotated critical thinking music playlist, flash fiction and children's book suggestions, and suitable poems).

The best leveled questions work as student-made essay prompts—whether you use them as formal timed writing, or free writing prompts, or warm-ups/do-nows. Students can use their own questions to begin self-generated inquiry, the highest use of leveled questions that I've found in my teaching career. Answers to students' questions can then become formal presentations, whether as research papers and projects or multimedia products.

These questions also connect students who are often labeled as "struggling" or otherwise in need of more "basic skills" to content in a way that doesn't perpetuate a cycle of low expectations. Harvard professor Jal Mehta (2018), an expert on the conditions for creating deeper learning, believes that giving students opportunities to determine the why of content also helps create equity:

> There is also the fact that the "basics first" approach also tends to reproduce inequalities in schools. This line of thinking tends to foreground students' deficits over their assets; for disadvantaged and lower-track students, it serves to justify teaching as transmission and what Freire called the "banking model" of education. Writ large, this line of thinking is a powerful force for social reproduction—no matter how well-intentioned it is, the result in practice is that, yet again, the most privileged students are being taught how to think, whereas less advantaged students, who are often students of color, are being taught how to follow the directions of authorities. Research suggests this divide starts as early as kindergarten, and continues through high school.

Possibilities for Using Questions Across Content Areas

Content areas can be seen as lenses that allow us to see different aspects of the problems embedded within philosophical questions. For example, the question "What can we know?" drove not only Socrates but the greatest thinkers in each course and specialty. Putting on our "scientist glasses," we can examine what we know through physical, measurable phenomena; our "math glasses" will allow us to see how equations, statistics, functions, and numerical probabilities give us more answers to consider.

Likewise, "historian glasses" provide answers with documented events and records. "Artist glasses" offer us the perspective of human imagination, with words, music, paint, clay, ink, costumes, and performance giving us a deeper perspective still, through examining character, theme, and even transcendence.

The beauty of these responses, varied as they are, is that the curriculum begins to insert itself into lives. When curriculum is seen in a broader, multifocal attempt to answer humanity's questions, it "ensures access and opportunity for all children by creating lessons that are student-centered, culturally relevant, and deeply meaningful" (Kirk, 2006).

The following chapters use the advice of some of the best teachers in the country to look at how inquiry functions in different content areas and across different grade levels. They invite you to ground your teaching in questions as a gateway into the thinking of your particular discipline or curriculum.

CHAPTER 6

Using Questions in Multiple Disciplines and Grade Levels

Connections between courses create the kind of deep understanding that points to solutions for some of our greatest challenges. The ability to view a question from multiple perspectives is critical, yet we don't design our curricula this way. However, giving our students opportunities to see how a question about our place in the universe can be answered from multiple classes makes them innovative.

Researchers have found this to be true, particularly with students who aren't identified as gifted and talented (GT), nor in honors or other advanced classes:

> Nontraditional students appear to be more at home and successful as learners in classrooms where teachers connect them to subjects in new ways. The students we interviewed recognized and appreciated teachers' efforts to get to know them and to create classroom settings that encouraged academic engagement and expression of ideas. Yet nontraditional students describe most of their classes as highly structured, teacher-controlled and regimented. (McLaughlin & Talbert, 2001)

This is increasingly the view outside of education in companies like Google, where intellectual curiosity is prized above merely being smart. Judy Gilbert, Google's director of talent, is responsible for generating innovative thinkers and believes that we as teachers "need to eliminate the bright lines between subjects. A more interdisciplinary approach to learning will better prepare people for the kind of problems they'll be confronting" (Wagner, 2012).

In-Class Debate as Interdisciplinary Connector

Thinking is social, as Vygotsky reminds us. Beyond its social benefits, discussion and debate help to clarify and deepen our own reasoning skills. Productive classroom talk is a powerful way to make the invisible mechanisms of thought explicit. In speaking and listening, students build their understanding, purposefully tie into others' ideas, and strengthen their abilities to participate in academic discourse. In short, talking about something helps us to make sense of it for ourselves. An aphorism applies here, which is that the person doing the work is the person doing the learning.

Moreover, building background knowledge, academic vocabulary, and rich connections among and across various content areas happens efficiently and memorably when students are given multiple opportunities for constructed academic discourse. Supporting it takes patience and practice, but it's worth the gains in confidence that will transfer to college and career settings.

Managing Controversial Issues

Because my students often choose to discuss political, spiritual, race, and gender topics, discussions sometimes become strained. You may need to call a time-out to diffuse attention and have everyone take a few deep breaths in silence, or allow agitated students to leave the room and get a drink of water. The point is to help students stay in conversation with each other. To facilitate useful dialogue, have students recall their listening stems and commitments (see Chapter 4) and consider adding in these ground rules:

Planning Questions for Teachers and Facilitators

1. How can you help students articulate their first thoughts about controversial issues, paying special attention to those related to their personal values?

2. Is my classroom a safe place to have unpopular, unusual, or opinions that disagree with my own?

3. Am I choosing to water down or avoid a topic because it is socially controversial even though it is an important part of my content? This can exacerbate educational inequities, especially for children who are not often allowed to engage in intellectual exchanges.

4. How am I putting a human face on the controversy? Am I including diverse perspectives from the community?

5. Am I welcoming the viewpoints of students from nondominant cultures and communities?

6. How is what I'm teaching with this lesson empowering students to see themselves as thinkers, creators, questioners, and contributors?

Students in My Eleventh-Grade English Class Engage in an In-Class Debate

PROTOCOL 6.1   In-Class Debate

TIME

Two forty-five-minute class periods

PREPARATION

Use one class period to vote on and choose a debate topic; use one to engage in debate. You may have students vote on how to use points

(Continued)

(Continued)

awarded for teams—each member of winning teams in my classes were able to substitute a 100 for a failing or missing grade. Make sure students understand vocabulary (e.g., rebuttal, counterargument).

Day 1: Have a coin flip to decide pro and con (for advanced learners—have them prepare for both sides, and the coin flip happens immediately before debate). Begin researching questions and complete argument planner as a team (see handout in the appendix). Choose speakers, researchers, and coaches.

Day 2: The debate begins as soon as class bell rings with room setup to reflect debate (e.g., a podium for speaker, desks to either side of podium for seating other speakers, desks arranged into tables for other team members at the back of room to give privacy during team huddles).

ROLES

(**Note:** Everyone is expected to listen to the opposing team to find mistakes in thinking, logic, or evidence.)

- **Speakers**—Use best public speaking skills to argue their team's side using note cards, if needed. Speakers may break up speaking responsibilities according to their strengths, but every speaker must speak at least once during the debate.

- **Researchers**—Listen to the opposite team to understand counterargument, and make sure speakers have the best information and points by quickly finding evidence to support or challenge.

- **Coaches**—Consult the rubric, and make sure the team is doing what's necessary to gain the most points.

MATERIALS

- Teacher (or judging panel, if desired) needs two copies of debate scoring sheets (see handout in the appendix) to keep score.

- Laptops (preferable for each team, at least two), but smartphones may be substituted if laptops are not available.

- Internet access to www.ProCon.org or other debate prep site like SIRS Issues Researcher (many school libraries have access to this site). Elementary learners may access https://idebate.org and search for "junior" topics like banning animal testing.

- Copies of the scoring rubric are needed for each team.

- Two teams are divided into pro and con.
- Three members on each team will argue; all other members of the team will be researchers and coaches for their respective teams.

FORMAT

Six minutes—Position presentation—Pro

Six minutes—Position presentation—Con

Five minutes—Research or revision of argument period

Four minutes—Rebuttal—Pro

Four minutes—Rebuttal—Con

Three minutes—Research or revision of argument period

Two minutes—Response—Pro

Two minutes—Response—Con

One minute—Huddle with team

Two minutes—Position summary—Pro or con

Two minutes—Position summary—Pro or con

Five minutes—Tallying of scoring sheets, announcement of winner, and awarding of points

EXTENSIONS

- Have teams switch sides and summarize the others' position; then, create a consensus position based on arguments and evidence from both sides.

- Student teams section a piece of chart paper into quadrants and think collaboratively to identify four stakeholder positions and the concerns and values of each group. For example, what do businesses believe and care about the issue? What do health care professionals believe and care about the issue? (Teachers will need to assist this process, but it is a valuable exercise in democratic thinking.)

- Each student writes a reflection about their individual and team performance. This can be used as a quiz grade, an in-class essay, prewrite for a timed writing, or other writing task (see the rubric in the appendix). ●

Eleventh Graders Work as a Team to Plan
Debate Strategy During the Revision Huddle

Questions from students, I realized as I began using them as instructional hooks, meet the criteria of what McTighe and Wiggins (2013) define as an "essential question" because they are as follows:

- Open-ended and typically will not have a single, final, and correct answer

- Thought-provoking and intellectually engaging, often sparking discussion and debate

- Pointing toward important, transferable ideas within (and sometimes across) disciplines

- Able to raise additional questions and spark further inquiry

- Able to be revisited again and again

They warn that the rich questions posed by students can be blunted and rendered into a way for the teacher to retake control of the thinking: "Instructors display intellectual dishonesty when they ask for students' opinions on controversial issues but actually seek or highlight responses that they deem politically or morally correct" (McTighe & Wiggins, 2013, p. 8).

This is another way to think about "flipped learning," but instead of having students work on content first, it uses their own questions as an entry into content. Starting with a student's own question flips the work back to the student, engages them in authentic inquiry, and personalizes the learning. Teachers don't have to generate essential questions themselves or create something extra. Student understanding then becomes the end goal rather than "the test." Assessments don't change, but the engagement and motivation for learning what's assessed changes.

Figure 6.1   Flowchart to Connect Classroom Content With Student Learning Outcomes

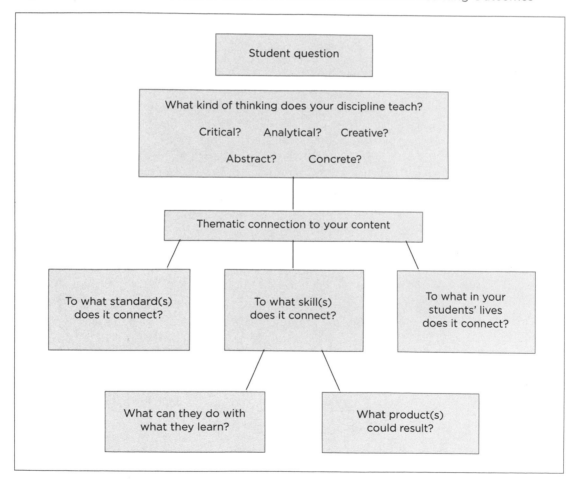

What might it look like to put a spin on flipped learning and begin with a question generated by students? The flowchart in Figure 6.1 visually describes the process.

For example, consider the following questions:

Why are white people mean to brown people? (elementary student)

Why do people kill? (middle school student)

Will peace ever exist in this world? (high school student)

When I'm trying to connect the student question to my content, it's helpful to find the theme or idea embedded in the question. Notice what repeats in the question, or use a thesaurus to find synonyms for words in the question. Alternatively, pull the main idea out of the student question, and compare it to something familiar: What is this like? How is it different?

In the student sample questions, themes of relationships and prejudice and how we relate to each other in destructive ways emerge. The commonality across all of them is a discomfort with people who are different from us.

Next, ask how what you teach tries to answer these questions. Because I teach English, I know that my discipline seeks creative answers in literature through the use of plot and character. Thinking through my content this way helps me discover transferable understandings that students can use outside of class as a way to think about their own experiences. Flipping the learning this way also helps me understand why I'm teaching a particular lesson or skill. If I as an English teacher look at the theme of how we relate to each other in destructive ways, one of the main ways is through the various "isms" of our society: racism, sexism, etc. Prejudice is the commonality. Prejudice can be viewed as a difficulty with handling differences.

I examine my content through literature as my "big box" to work with. Inside the big boxes are smaller boxes of skills (reading and writing) and standards (what I have to teach) (see Figure 6.2). For example, fiction may answer the question in books such as the following:

- *The Butter Battle Book* (Dr. Seuss, 1984)—Because it shows how discomfort with differences is the root of conflict (elementary)

- *The Giver* (Lowry, 1993)—Because it shows how trying to erase differences has unintended consequences (middle school)
- *To Kill a Mockingbird* (Lee, 1960/2002) and *Huckleberry Finn* (Twain, 1884/2003)—Because they show how social rules about difference create violence (high school)

Figure 6.2 Connecting Students' Questions to Themes and Standards

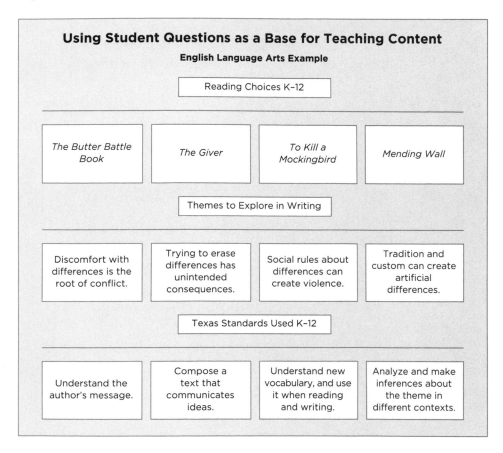

The reading and writing standards in Texas, for example, ask students to use reading skills to understand an author's message and then to compose a text that communicates ideas to an audience. The student's question becomes a guide into the content, providing a purpose for reading and writing. Part of my lesson might be to show students how reading the particular text is the author's way of answering the question. The writing task could become an expository analysis of how the author answers the question or a creative writing where the student writes about dealing with differences.

However, great teachers who are featured in later chapters show how they use the same process in their content areas. If, for example, my content is math, I might show, like Jose Luis Vilson, the probability of violent encounters with authorities by race and what those numbers might tell us about how we process difference as a society. If my content is science, I might use, like Jeff Charbonneau, a discrepant event to engage students, but then debrief it to examine how well they worked together to formulate an answer for it. If my content is social studies, I might show, like Nate Bowling, the power of government over people who look and live like them. If my content is fine arts, I might show, like Mairi Cooper, how deliberately building a culture of empathy for our differences helps performance (see Figure 6.3).

Figure 6.3 Using a Student Question to Show Cross-Content Connections

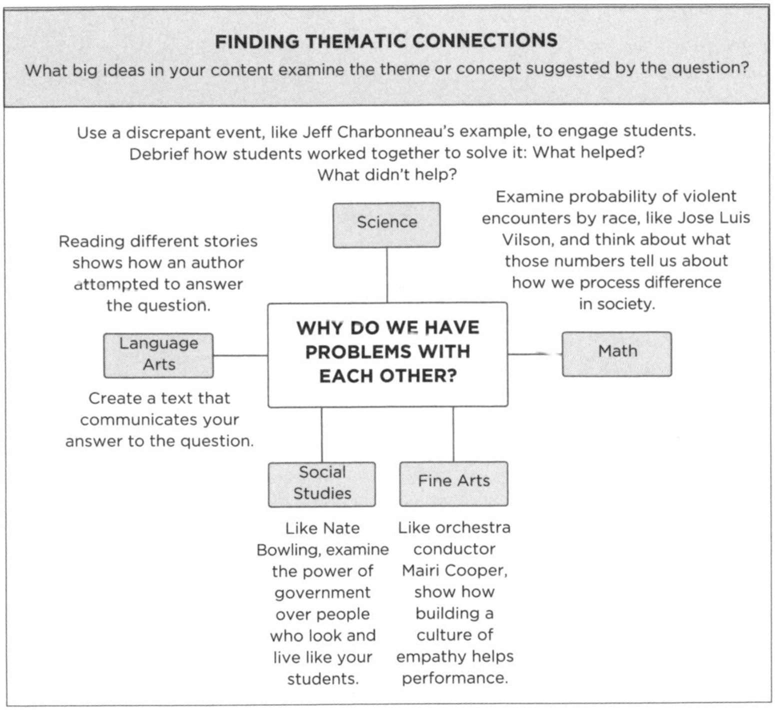

We can extend learning for students by showing them how their questions connect to classical questions from philosophy, as Figure 6.4 shows.

Complexity, connections, and developing the ability to reason abstractly are dominant themes of the Common Core State Standards for English language arts (ELA) and math (the standards for math mention a

Figure 6.4 Connecting Student Questions to Larger Philosophical Questions

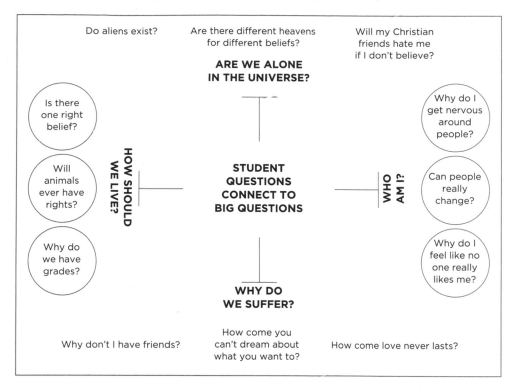

"productive disposition" that sees math as "sensible, useful, and worthwhile"), and anything that helps us help our student approach higher-order thinking prepares them for tests.

Each of the content chapters in Part II highlights the practice of award-winning teachers and situates their practice within the larger framework of national standards and practices for each discipline, which illustrates how inquiry is a foundational skill across all content areas plus career and technical education (CTE), and, of course, the fine arts. Additionally, each chapter features grade- and content-specific examples of leveled questions; links to extension activities and resources like in-class debate questions; and where to find material supporting inclusion, diversity, and equity in lessons.

> Don't be afraid of philosophy—it has been spreading love and advancing human ideals for centuries. Be afraid of a world without philosophy. Be afraid of what you will become if you turn your back on the beautiful possibilities it has to offer.
>
> **—SHARON KAYE**

Teachers who need to modify or introduce content to ELLs or those who need special education services may want to try the texts and questions identified for younger students.

Even if you don't teach in these content areas, I encourage you to look at the ideas from these master teachers as ways to connect what you teach to other content students will be studying. An insight I gained from interviewing so many teachers is that we are essentially the same person. The people who choose to teach are like brothers and sisters in the same family—all of us sharing a belief in the hope provided by education, a passion for the social justice underlying the act of teaching, and a deep and fierce loyalty to the students we love and serve.

CHAPTER 7

Science

The important thing is not to stop questioning.
Curiosity has its own reason for existence. One
cannot help but be in awe when he contemplates
the mysteries of eternity, of life, of the marvelous
structure of reality. It is enough if one tries merely
to comprehend a little of this mystery each day.

—ALBERT EINSTEIN

When Timmy, age eight, wanted to know "What do ants think about us? I wonder if they know we are persons and they are not?," he was asking a question that entomologists wonder about. Or when Magaly, age six, wanted to know "Why are some animals big and some are small?," she was thinking like a zoologist. Wade, age twelve, in asking, "Do other things live in this universe?," was asking the same question that Neil DeGrasse Tyson and other astrophysicists ask. And eighteen-year-old Jasmine's question—"Will we be able to order babies like we order stuff on Amazon?"—puts her in the same curious territory as a bioethicist. These four questions fall into the areas of life science, space science, and engineering and technology, which make them perfect for engaging students with the inquiry that drives science.

"Every invention, advancement, nugget of knowledge, equation, exploration, discovery started with authentic questions—how, what, why, when, etcetera," my colleague Craig Beals, a chemistry teacher, told me. "Questioning, in itself, is the foundation of everything in science."

Another colleague of mine, Rich Ognibene, teaches physics, and far from being utterly cerebral, he has the heart of a poet. When we talked together at a conference in 2017, he said he thinks that it takes courage to teach with questions: "Given that there's this infinite knowledge and we only have about seventy years on this planet, the defining question of teaching right now is 'What is worth knowing?' If a lot of the stuff I teach could be looked up, then how do I add value?" he said. "I think we hide behind our content

Table 7.1 Science Guides

Craig Beals

2015 Montana Teacher of the Year

2016 NEA Teaching Excellence Award

Billings Senior High School

Billings, MT

Chemistry; formerly taught Earth Sciences and Biology

Follow him on his YouTube channel, *Beals Science*: www.youtube.com/user/bealsscience

Jeff Charbonneau

2013 National Teacher of the Year

Global Teacher Prize, Top 40 Finalist

Zillah High School

Zillah, WA

Chemistry, Physics, and Engineering

Follow Jeff on Twitter @JeffCharbonneau

Richard Ognibene

2008 New York Teacher of the Year

2015 Inductee, National Teachers Hall of Fame

Fairport High School

Rochester, NY

Physics and Chemistry

Keri Randolph

2005 Chatham County Teacher of the Year

Director of Innovation, Hamilton County Department of Education, Chattanooga, TN

Former Vice President of Learning at PEF/Southeast Tennessee STEM Innovation Hub

Science Master Teacher at University of Tennessee at Chattanooga

Science Master Teacher, Pittsboro, NC

at the secondary level to avoid questions of the heart. If you have this knowledge, should you be using it to make a lot of money or to help humanity? Our value added is actually in these philosophical questions."

Keri Randolph left microbial ecology research to teach high school biology, chemistry, and earth science. She helped me to frame my thinking about how science is taught and why we should be wary of just teaching content. She stressed the need to take the longer view and focus on what she calls "those beautiful questions" in each of the scientific disciplines.

"Over the course of my career, I've really shifted my perspective on science education from teaching science *to* students to teaching students as scientists," she said. "I think it is an important distinction. Teaching science implies content and subject matters (biology, chemistry physics)—and these are important—but teaching kids to think like scientists not only nurtures beautiful questions and curiosity but it hones skills like critical thinking, problem solving, arguments from evidence. I don't expect every student to become a scientist, but teaching them to think like scientists supports their development as critical consumers of information, great questioners and better decision makers."

This chapter is a small guidebook of suggestions for creating a culture of curiosity while also motivating and engaging students to love science.

> Some of children's early intuitions about the world can be used as a foundation to build remarkable understanding, even in the earliest grades. Indeed, both building on and refining prior conceptions (which can include misconceptions) are important in teaching science at any grade level.
>
> **—NATIONAL RESEARCH COUNCIL**

Four Takeaway Ideas That You Can Put to Work in Your Classroom

1. Invite Big Questions to Begin the Year

Beals: I continually engage my students in the scientific process where we always start with two things: first with observations, second with questioning. For example, I have my students brainstorm five "I wonder" questions. They can be about anything. Then, they turn those questions into "testable questions," or questions wherein they could collect data, or build a contraption, or engineer a solution so they can attempt to answer their question.

Next, they "chase" their favorite question with research and experimentation and analysis to come up with a conclusion to answer their question. This is a requirement in my class, and I call it the "Independent Study Project," and the main goal is for them to change the world. It is one of the most powerful science experiences for my students because they are answering their own questions using science.

Randolph: Science really is a way of knowing and understanding the world—not a list of facts, which is how we have so often taught it. That list is now way too big to teach, so we've got to think about teaching science differently.

This also gets at the depth vs. breadth conversation. I would start the semester with something that I knew kids could relate to—like ecology in biology. We'd find some questions we were interested in to go after as a class. It was messy, but it hooked them. They'd present their findings in poster sessions. Some of them were ridiculous, like what Coca-Cola does to plants (it kills them), but I was interested in process and experimental design and curiosity toward content as well as argumentation and data-driven discussion. Once they got this, we could do a lot together—but I always sacrificed depth for breadth—and it didn't impact my test results. Did they know every standard? Nope—but what they did know, they really knew and hopefully still do—and they gained a healthy respect for the field of science and how it works. That's much more important than learning the steps of the water cycle.

2. Use Analogies Tied to What Kids Are Interested In

Charbonneau: Analogies are so important because they tie into something that you know already and allow you to make some level of inference. You do have to be careful of analogies because sometimes that can lead to wide misconceptions about the topic you're trying to convey.

And the only way to have a good analogy is to have a good knowledge of students' backgrounds. If I give you an analogy of baseball and you've never played the game, then that analogy just simply isn't going to work and it's not doing you any good. I very often have foreign exchange students in my classroom or students from very different cultural backgrounds than my own, and I've got to be very careful if I make a pop culture reference because not everybody has the same pop culture.

Randolph: I think the most value for a teacher in an analogy is having students find where they break down. For example, we often use the analogy of a factory when discussing cell structure and function. This works—and yet it doesn't—but it really works when kids analyze the analogy to find discrepancies. That's real learning—like the mitochondria is the power-house of the cell, but it isn't like a battery. It doesn't store energy; it just takes glucose and converts it into ATP, which is the currency of energy in the cell, etc.

3. Artfully Deploy Discrepant Events

Charbonneau: Scientists, science teachers, we love the discrepant event. You show them a discrepant event and they're like, "Why does that happen?" This is where magic becomes science. The difference between magic and science is that in magic they don't explain the science behind it. They're doing a scientific phenomenon in some way, shape, or form; they're just not explaining how it's done. Because I put so much emphasis on student inquiry, I'm able to frame that really well.

You say to kids, "Okay, let's deconstruct this. How did this happen?" And then you introduce the concept and allow the students to experiment: Allow them that inquiry time to discover how things are reacting. Allow them to notice trends. Ask them to come up with a rule to explain what they've found. Then ask them to justify it: "What evidence can you come up with to support that?" Or, I can say, "Guess what, here's one that's going to throw you a curveball," and introduce this other chemical, but it doesn't do what you thought it would, so you'll have to readjust your rules. This is the same thing that scientists have to go through when they're trying to make scientific discoveries.

It's a continuation of question after question after question. You put a problem in front of them and ask them to come up with the rules rather than say, here's the rules for these chemicals and here's how they work.

4. Accept That This Kind of Teaching Takes Time

Ognibene: The mistake we make as educators is to believe that we're filling heads with our knowledge rather than constructing something together. In a classroom, you've got finite time; it's like a pizza—you've only got so many slices you can make. So just the act of asking questions shows a willingness to value you as a human being.

If the work is engaging to a student, they can actually work very quickly and make some very quick connections to prior learning when the work is

> I'm firmly of the mind that education is about developing the best humans.
>
> **—RICHARD OGNIBENE**

relevant and engaging. I claim that I can get through virtually the same amount of material in the same amount of time because I'm not having to go back and reteach it over and over and over again because they get it right the first time. Where some teachers may take three days to get through a unit, because they're going to introduce it, then they're going to reinforce it and reinforce it and reinforce it and then review it. I can introduce it one time; they got it because they developed the rule for it, and we can move forward.

LESSON 7.1   Applying Leveled and Big Questions in Science

Early childhood text: *My Five Senses* by Aliki (2015)

Summary: Young readers are encouraged to use their five senses to explore the environment around them.

> **Level 1:** What are the five senses?
>
> **Level 2:** How do your eyes help you to learn new things?
>
> **Level 3** (for debate or discussion): What does it mean when people tell you to pay attention? How do you know what to pay attention to? How do you decide what is important?

Elementary text: *Because of an Acorn* by Lola M. Schaefer and Adam Schaefer (2016)

Summary: Engaging illustrations accompany this story of a forest's interconnected ecosystem.

> **Level 1:** What happens to most acorns in the forest?
>
> **Level 2:** How is our school like the forest? How are we connected?
>
> **Level 3** (for debate or discussion): Why is nature important? Should we make laws about the environment? What are the most important parts of nature to protect and why?

Middle school text: *Bubonic Panic: When Plague Invaded America* by Gail Jarrow (2016)

Summary: This high-interest historical account of a medical mystery is illustrated with grim photographs and vivid detail.

> **Level 1:** How do people get infected with bubonic plague?
>
> **Level 2:** What is the connection between people's living conditions and their chances of getting infected?
>
> **Level 3** (for debate or discussion): In a pandemic, what actions are justifiable? Should we worry about people's rights or their safety? Why does misinformation spread so easily?

High school text: *A Global Warming Primer: Answering Your Questions About the Science, the Consequences, and the Solutions* by Jeffrey Bennett (2016)

Summary: This easy read, using a Q&A format, explores the facts about the human impact on Earth's climate.

> **Level 1:** What is a greenhouse gas?
>
> **Level 2:** What local consequences are possible from storms and extreme weather, and why do they matter?
>
> **Level 3** (for debate or discussion): Are human activities causing climate change, or is it a natural occurrence? How can we determine the validity of evidence? What do we owe future generations? Is it more important to think about the future or the present?

EXTENSIONS FOR SPEAKING AND LISTENING (IN-CLASS DEBATE HANDOUT IN THE APPENDIX)

Debate or discuss Level 3 questions.

Sample science-related debate questions:

- **Animal testing**—Should animals be used for biomedical research? Should animals be kept in zoos and aquariums? Are conditions for cage-free or crate-free farm animals better?

- **Cell phones**—Are they safe? Is social media contributing to mental illness?

- **Alternative energy**—Should renewable energy sources replace fossil fuels? Should the United States open federally protected lands and waters to oil well drilling? Is nuclear energy safe?

(Continued)

(Continued)

- **Stem cells**—Is stem cell research ethical?
- **Climate change**—Is climate change causing more natural disasters?

EXTENSIONS FOR ACADEMIC WRITING PRACTICE

Students complete a debate reflection (handout in the appendix). ●

"We can't ignore the social dimensions in science, but we can work to make sure our students are scientifically literate and think like scientists. The climate change debate has most scientists scratching our heads as to why we are debating whether climate is changing," Randolph said. "It is—the evidence is clear the Earth is warming. Politics and the media confuse the issue and dispute the what, why and how. As science teachers, it is important that we help our students understand the scientific basis for something like climate change—and think like a scientist as they read and examine evidence. We can't do this by teaching science as a bunch of facts. We have to teach them how to ask good questions and think like a scientist."

A *Framework for K–12 Science Education* (National Research Council, 2012), in its guiding assumptions and organization, argues for the inclusion of children's questions at all levels, especially those from younger learners:

"As a strategy for building on prior interest, the disciplinary core ideas identified here are described not only with an eye toward the knowledge that students bring with them to school but also toward the kinds of questions they are likely to pose themselves at different ages. Such questions as "Where do we come from?" "Why is the sky blue?" and "What is the smallest piece of matter?" are fundamental hooks that engage young people. Framing a curriculum around such sets of questions helps to communicate relevance and salience to this audience" (National Research Council, 2012, p. 28).

Asking questions, defining problems, and engaging in argument from evidence are core practices in the Next Generation Science Standards. Far from taking kids "off task," using class time to cultivate curiosity, collect and discuss questions, and debate them in class will help solidify scientific concepts for students. Further, giving students these experiences helps to connect their thinking and learning to their other coursework, which deepens their academic competencies.

Standards Met by Activities, Strategies, and Practice in This Chapter

National Science Education Standards

When engaging in inquiry, students describe objects and events, ask questions, construct explanations, test those explanations against current scientific knowledge, and communicate their ideas to others. They identify their assumptions, use critical and logical thinking, and consider alternative explanations. In this way, students actively develop their understanding of science by combining scientific knowledge with reasoning and thinking skills.

Next Generation Science Standards

Disciplinary core ideas have the power to focus K–12 science curriculum, instruction, and assessments on the most important aspects of science. To be considered core, the ideas should meet at least two of the following criteria and ideally all four:

- Have broad importance across multiple sciences or engineering disciplines or be a key organizing concept of a single discipline.

- Provide a key tool for understanding or investigating more complex ideas and solving problems.

- Relate to the interests and life experiences of students or be connected to societal or personal concerns that require scientific or technological knowledge.

- Be teachable and learnable over multiple grades at increasing levels of depth and sophistication.

Disciplinary ideas are grouped in four domains: the physical sciences; the life sciences; the earth and space sciences; and engineering, technology, and applications of science. (National Research Council, 2012)

Resources for Further Exploration and Enrichment

Massachusetts Institute of Technology (MIT) science videos designed for use in K–12: www.k12videos.mit.edu/videos

MIT Moral Machine—Designing and playing an updated version of philosophy's classic "trolley problem" using driverless cars: http://moralmachine.mit.edu

Discrepant events for use with all ages: http://sciencing.com/list-discrepant-event-science-activities-8018044.html

Social Justice Toolkit of questions to probe the implications of various science topics from the Southern Poverty Law Center's *Teaching Tolerance* archive: www.tolerance.org/toolkit/toolkit-just-science

Using analogies with Grades 5 to 8 from the National Science Teachers Association: www.nsta.org/publications/news/story.aspx?id=53640

Videos of science concepts and questions for all ages at TEDEd: https://ed.ted.com/lessons?category=science-technology

CHAPTER 8

Math

In my opinion, all things in nature
occur mathematically.

—RENÉ DESCARTES

You have thirty minutes to decide: Who gets the donor heart that's packed in ice and on its way to your hospital? Will it be Susan, a single mother of four children between the ages of one and eight who uses public assistance to meet her family's needs? Will it be Amal, a young, single man who is an expert in military strategy? Will it be Ben, a junior high student with a congenital heart defect? Or will it be Toni, an older woman who won the Nobel Prize in literature? There are three others on the list from which you and your small team of medical ethicists must choose a candidate to be prepped for surgery. All of them suffer from a heart condition that will kill them unless they get a transplant.

This is a question in Shelby Aaberg's Pre-Calculus and Trigonometry class. Aaberg, who is the 2015 Nebraska Teacher of the Year and recipient of a prestigious Presidential Award for Excellence in Mathematics and Science Teaching, wants students to use math as a lens to understand the world around them in a way that goes beyond simple computation. He writes the organ transplant dilemma on the board early in the year to communicate his expectation that students will bring more than just an ability to crunch numbers into the class—and that they will leave with an ability to apply what they do to any place outside the class. Students work in small teams under time pressure to come up with the best forced choice of who should get the organ transplant. He's looking for struggle, for the messiness of real life, and the transplant dilemma forces both while resisting easy answers.

"It's okay to walk into a room and not know—that's what this says," Aaberg told me. "Too often in schools, we give a lot of priority to exercises, which are things we already know how to do. We repeatedly assess what kids already know. A problem is something you don't know how to do."

Aaberg believes that dilemmas are an even more intellectually intriguing puzzle and students need more practice with them in the classroom. "Doing life and being in the workforce is finding dilemmas to be optimized. There's lots of times in your life that you can't solve the problems, you just have to find the Goldilocks amount of everything and move on. How can we effectively prepare students for a world in which you have to make difficult moral decisions? Like the organ trade market, like being able to grow living tissue. Does the billionaire get infinite livers just because he can afford them? What will we find when we're forced to abandon this planet?

This chapter is a small guidebook of suggestions for creating a culture of productive struggle with real-world problems that also points toward a new way for students to authentically connect with math. The teachers featured here have unofficially adopted a math curriculum that seeks to be what David Perkins deems "lifeworthy."

> The uncomfortable fact is that almost everyone studies quadratic equations, relatively few people use them, and hardly anyone uses them outside of teaching them. The topic of quadratic equations lives on in schools largely to equip the next generation of teachers to impart quadratic equations. (Perkins, 2014, p. 13)

See Figure 8.1.

Figure 8.1 Sample Questions From Early Elementary and Middle School

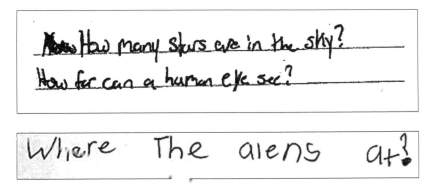

Table 8.1 Math Guides

Shelby Aaberg

2015 Nebraska Teacher of the Year

2013 Presidential Award for Excellence in Mathematics and Science Teaching

Scottsbluff High School

Scottsbluff, NE

AP Statistics, Precalculus/Trigonometry, Geometry, STEM

Follow Shelby on Twitter @ShelbyAaberg

Shawn Sheehan

2016 National Teacher of the Year Finalist

2016 Oklahoma Teacher of the Year

Lewisville High School Harmon

Lewisville, TX

Algebra 1

Follow Shawn Sheehan's *Teach Like Me* channel on YouTube:
www.youtube.com/user/TeachLikeMeCampaign

And on Twitter @SPSheehan

Jose Luis Vilson

Founder, EduColor

Author, *This Is Not a Test*

Inwood/Washington Heights Middle School

New York, NY

Math

Follow Jose Luis Vilson on Twitter @TheJLV
and his website: https://thejosevilson.com

Mariel Novas

Teach For America Teacher Leadership Development Manager

Former English as a Second Language (ESL) Math Teacher—Grades 6, 7, and 8

Lilla G. Frederick Pilot Middle School

Dorcester, MA

Four Takeaway Ideas That You Can Put to Work in Your Classroom

1. Math Helps Us Understand Political Forces

Sheehan: Statistics—I'm always striving to talk about the lesser-known statistics or the ones that I know my students and their families, the community at large, glaze over. If we're just accepting the fact that 40 percent of the population in Syria is under age twenty-three, we don't really process it or what it means. We think long and hard about what it's going to take for Kevin Durant to average three-pointers with Golden State. But what does it mean that the life span in Japan is double what it is in Syria? This is the area where decisions are being made. Statistics are what tell us if something is really a problem.

Aaberg: Look at the "Parable of the Polygons"—it's a simulator that I use in class that shows how segregation works using some simple rules about the placement of different shapes. I put it up and just let it run. They see pretty fast how something that looks so easy and innocent starts to take on a life of its own. They see that decisions about where a shape goes affects the rest of the game, which is what I want them to understand and apply to what they see in our state. Decisions about who lives where follow the same rules of the game.

2. Just Doing Exercises Is Not Enough

Novas: The questions I started to use in my second year were more conceptual. We very much frame a problem in terms of finding a single solution, but that is not the purpose of math. The purpose of math is to explore and discover. Ask, How can you prove that? What other ways can you solve that? It's less about 56 divided by 7 is 8 and more about how many ways can you represent that? It deemphasizes the answer and emphasizes the process. I had many students who didn't have all of their math facts, but they could still participate and show their genius. It gets to their ability to think.

Rote facts do nothing for your brain. Math is practice in a way of thinking that can be applied to solve any problem—it teaches you to think of alternatives. I tried to teach math in a way that was contrary to how I was taught. I did not operate with testing as the North Star. I identified the standards that cut across all three levels versus the ones that just show up in one level. Because we only had two sections and I had three grade levels, I wanted to maximize my instruction. I wanted to make sure we created our schedule, that we could teach those cross-level standards to everyone and then pull smaller groups for the grade-specific standards. It created an awesome culture in the classroom where I could help them with what they needed but that didn't push them beyond their capacity yet allowed those who wanted to go deeper to do that.

Depth of understanding was my goal, not the test. I wanted them to understand ratios, rates, and proportions at a deep level. I was intentional about spiraling the curriculum as well. It was the first time in the school's history that newcomer ESL students scored advanced on the [Massachusetts test], but everyone grew. The second year, we saw the exact same pattern. Because I focused on open response and how to approach an open-ended question, I think that helped them grow faster.

3. Math Is Both a Form of and a Lens for Social Justice

Vilson: There are some folks who believe that the test is perhaps the most important thing in terms of equity, because in their eyes, they don't see a test as a reflection of a culture or of what society says because it's supposed to be very normal; it's supposed to be unbiased and it will tell you exactly what the student knows and what the student doesn't, which as we know full well is pretty far from the truth. That's been one of the biggest pushbacks against what I'm trying to tell them in terms of students and their learning. My response is fairly simple: so, are you trying to teach to the test, and if you are, then does that test accurately reflect everything you've taught, and if it hasn't, then what are you teaching to? Who are you teaching?

I don't think our society is ready for a whole set of question askers, which is why so many of our most vulnerable students aren't taught to ask questions when they're very young versus the most privileged who do.

Robert Moses said recently that even just teaching mathematics well is a form of social justice in the sense that our systems were not meant to teach certain students well. There's that form of social justice where you try to make an equitable attempt at teaching students deeper, harder math instead of just a shallow level of math.

[Learning scientific notation] piqued a lot of students' interest in how science actually works and how numbers connect to astronomy or engineering even. These ideas are often inaccessible to our students because some say, "Oh, that's too complex. They'll never understand it." But all the while, my students are trying to find ways to crunch those numbers to determine the difference and then use that to actually create a scale model. They created class projects that a lot of my colleagues said could not be done with my kids because it's too deep, it's too intense, and it takes too long.

I am curious about the implications of learning how to develop questions and what it would look like if a student was able to use question developing in the outside world outside of the math concepts—instead of just asking what the daily basics of my life consist of, like being able to ask why it is constructed as such or looking at the deeper issues around the neighborhood using that math. That seems to be a social justice issue, if anything. This idea [then is] that we can actually construct good questions in the classroom and then use the same sort of formulations to construct those questions out of classrooms.

4. Teach Concepts Rather Than Hammering Facts

Novas: Every month, I had a philosophical question on the board, sometimes connected to math, sometimes not. I thought it was important to have their voices front and center and the first thing you'd see. I'd see a really great question, and it would surface some great thinking, so we started having a weekly Community Hour on Fridays that was pretty flexible and where we could respond to what was on students' minds. I really believed in their genius—and I talked about them that way. And I tried to get to think about math and think about it outside of class. Most were Caribbean or Dominican, from Puerto Rico or the Dominican Republic, and there's a significant custom of oral tradition in our cultures—tall tales and stories and sayings. I did essential questions with a twist. I would start any new unit with a story—typically on Monday—and I would make up wild stories and make it start where they thought it was real life, but it became crazier and had an embedded mathematical dilemma that we would preview. I made up this story—a mangu story—mangu is like mashed plantains, and you have it with salami and eggs and onions and cheese and it's just like heaven. And I started a story—we were doing a lesson on grouping/divisibility—and I said we were going to have a mangu party, and I'm going to get so many of each ingredient and enough to make a plate for everyone in class. How much am I going to have to buy to make that happen? What do you think I'm going to have to do? What's my strategy? What's the approach? How are you thinking about the problem? That's metacognitive, and it transfers to other areas.

LESSON 8.1 Applying Leveled and Big Questions in Math

Early childhood text: *The Right Number of Elephants* by Jeff Sheppard (1993)

Summary: By answering the repeating question—What is the right number of elephants? (for various silly tasks)—children practice the concept of counting.

> **Level 1:** What is the right number of elephants for a quick circus?
>
> **Level 2:** The author says two elephants can make a swing for a little kid, but what other games could two elephants help someone play?
>
> **Level 3** (for debate or discussion): What is the right number of friends to have, and why do you think that?

Elementary text: *It's Probably Penny* by Loreen Leedy (2007)

Summary: This introduction to probability uses the story of Lisa and her homework to think of an event that will happen, one that might happen, and one that can't happen.

> **Level 1:** What group of jelly beans makes it impossible for Mr. Jayson to pick a green one?
>
> **Level 2:** Lisa says there's a tiny chance that Penny might dig up a treasure chest on the beach, but what is something that Penny will find if she goes to the beach?
>
> **Level 3** (for debate or discussion): What is something you know for sure will happen? Something that might happen? Something that can't happen? Why do you know that?

Middle school text: *The Way Things Work Now: From Levers to Lasers, Windmills to Wi-Fi, A Visual Guide to the World of Machines* by David Macauley (2016)

Summary: This well-illustrated, humorous explainer of physics helps students understand how math and science work together to create so much of our technology.

(Continued)

(Continued)

Level 1: What is a binary number ?

Level 2: Which two of the book's inventions do you think are the most important to our lives and why?

Level 3 (for debate or discussion): Will there ever be a machine that can think and act like a human—and if so, would it deserve the same treatment as humans?

High school text: *Information Is Beautiful* by David McCandless (2012)

(If you can't find the book, he has a website of the same name with many examples, some animated.)

Summary: This book is an engaging design of statistics, percentages, ratios, and other numbers that works as a primer for data visualization for students to use as inspiration for designing their own infographics of numerical information.

Level 1: Based on the infographic "Mean Happiness," which country has the highest proportion of happy people?

Level 2: In the "Mountains Out of Molehills" chart, how does the visual representation of the information help you understand the relationship between the content of a story and how likely it is to become viral?

Level 3 (for debate or discussion): How can we be sure something is true—especially if we can't see it (either because it moves too fast for us to see, like the individual flaps of a hummingbird's wings, or too slow, like a flower blooming, or it is invisible like Wi-Fi)?

EXTENSIONS FOR SPEAKING AND LISTENING (IN-CLASS DEBATE HANDOUT IN THE APPENDIX)

- Does lowering the federal corporate income tax rate create jobs?
- Should fantasy sports be considered a form of gambling, or are they just a creative use of statistics?
- Will cryptocurrencies, like Bitcoin, replace traditional currency?
- Is it smarter to buy a car or lease a car?
- Are lotteries ethical?
- Should we try to save energy? Does it really make a difference?

EXTENSIONS FOR ACADEMIC WRITING PRACTICE

Students complete a debate reflection (handout in the appendix). ●

Standards Met by Activities, Strategies, and Practice in This Chapter

National Council of Teachers of Mathematics (2018)

- **Equity.** Excellence in mathematics education requires equity—high expectations and strong support for all students.

- **Curriculum**. A curriculum is more than a collection of activities: it must be coherent, focused on important mathematics, and well-articulated across the grades

- **Learning**. Students must learn mathematics with understanding, actively building new knowledge from experience and prior knowledge.

- **Assessment**. Assessment should support the learning of important mathematics and furnish useful information to both teachers and students.

- Solve problems that arise in mathematics and in other contexts.

- Recognize and use connections among mathematical ideas.

- Recognize and apply mathematics in contexts outside of mathematics.

College and Career Readiness Math Standards

College and Career Readiness Math standards expect students to make connections between the strands of mathematics to the study of other disciplines, to situations and problems, to "**nature**, real world situations, and everyday life."

> There is a societal acceptance of the idea: I'm not good at math, especially for people of color and women who have internalized the idea. It prevents you from doing more complex mathematics that will in turn keep you from certain careers. We should be trying to remove that fear in our kids. Math should be driven by their questions.
>
> **—MARIEL NOVAS**

Resources for Further Exploration and Enrichment

Nicky Case's site for students to explore math through play:
http://explorabl.es/math

MIT Moral Machine—Designing and playing an updated version of philosophy's classic "trolley problem" using driverless cars:
http://moralmachine.mit.edu

Excellent dilemma resources here:

www.friesian.com/valley/dilemmas.htm (classic)

www.goodcharacter.com/dilemma/archive.html (student based)

More about Thomas Schelling's model of desegregation (the basis for the "Parable of the Polygons" game) here:
http://nifty.stanford.edu/2014/mccown-schelling-model-segregation

Teaching math from a social justice perspective: www.radicalmath.org

Videos of math concepts and questions for all ages at TEDEd:
https://ed.ted.com/lessons?category=mathematics

CHAPTER 9

Social Studies, Government, and Humanities

Men have no more ready corrective of conduct than knowledge of the past.

—POLYBIUS

"Why do white pepoll treet brown pepoll meen?" a second grader asked when prompted to share her deepest questions. Within her words are themes of justice, race, rights, and relationships, which mirror current news reports about the shooting deaths of Black people by police officers or the right-wing demands that immigrants leave the country. Academics, like researchers studying racial preferences as part of Harvard's Project Implicit, focus on the implications of the idea at the heart of her question.

Justice is a concept that allows us to think about our connections and disconnections with each other. In a larger sense, the disciplines of history, government, and social studies give us a frame for considering our connections to each other, to the people who came before us, and the people we might become. Thinking about how groups organize in creative or destructive ways, particularly around race and class, is naturally interesting to students. This is especially true for children who already know and live in broken relationships with their government and each other through hostilities in their streets or states.

> Basically, in my class, there are two questions that I ask all the time: What is this telling us, and how does it connect to what we already know? And why does that matter to us as citizens and us as individuals? Those questions drive the conversations in my classroom.
>
> **—NATE BOWLING**

Even very young children begin much of their play by establishing some sort of rule or guide. When they feel mistreated, they appeal to an authority. This inclination assumes that there is a larger power, a right of appeal, and a standard of fairness. The second grader's question is one Nelson Mandela answered by saying that children are taught to hate. If that's true, he says, then they also can be taught to love.

Social studies, cultural studies, and history are often the study of what went wrong in a group of people. The promise of this broad content area, encompassing as it does the subjects of geography, economics, sociology, and even psychology, is that learning about people, how they live, and their places in the world helps us to become better people. Stanford University (n.d.) is succinct in its definition of the humanities as an analysis of "how people process and document the human experience."

Three teachers—Nate Bowling, who teaches advanced placement (AP) government, Jahana Hayes, who teaches history, and Sydney Chaffee, who teaches humanities—bring their content to life through the lens of relationships. They want students to see that history is a continually moving case study in how we treat each other, especially those who are different from us and especially about race. They deliberately lean into the difficult conversations that come from their students' questions.

"I put a lot of things in front of them that don't have right answers, asking them what they make of it and what questions they have," said Chaffee.

"For example, as we're learning about Puerto Rico, about the history of Puerto Rico and the United States, we think about the question: Is the relationship just? What should the relationship be? Giving them time to think and write and read about these huge questions that have no right answers is really important to me as a teacher," she said.

Some of the questions asked by students responding to the protocol include these connections to the topics of social studies (see Figure 9.1).

Figure 9.1 Sample Questions From Early Elementary and High School Students

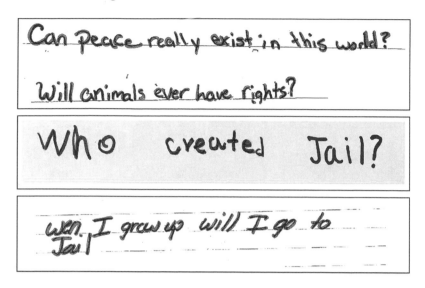

Can peace really exist in this world?

Will animals ever have rights?

Who created Jail?

wen I grow up will I go to Jail

Table 9.1 Social Studies Guides

Nathan Bowling

2016 National Teacher of the Year Finalist

2016 Washington Teacher of the Year

2013 Milken Educator

Lincoln High School

Tacoma, WA

AP Government, AP Human Geography

Follow Nate on Twitter @nate_bowling and on his website: www.natebowling.com

Sydney Chaffee

2017 National Teacher of the Year

2017 Massachusetts Teacher of the Year

Codman Academy

Dorchester, MA

Humanities

Follow Sydney on Twitter @SydneyChaffee and at her blog: www.sydneychaffee.com

(Continued)

Table 9.1 (Continued)

Jahana Hayes

2016 National Teacher of the Year

2016 Connecticut Teacher of the Year

Kennedy High School

Waterbury, CT

History

Follow Jahana on Twitter @JahanaHayes

Compare these to the questions suggested by the ten overarching themes in the humanities suggested by the National Council for the Social Studies (2010) that follow at the end of the chapter.

Four Takeaway Ideas That You Can Put to Work in Your Classroom

1. Make the Content Relevant to Students' Lives Even if It's a Difficult Topic

Bowling: When students walk into my class, on the board there's an infographic, or a pulled quote from the news, or tweets—all a connection to what they've read about the night before. What we're trying to do is make meaning of what we're learning and how it connects to what they already know. I start almost any lesson with a contextualized provocative pitch—for example, the power of government. Federal government and state governments are endowed to take away your life, liberty, and property; determine who you can and can't marry; determine whether you serve in the military.

We spend some time talking about a question like this: How does the killing of Mike Brown connect to the Fourteenth Amendment? Well, it connects because we're guaranteed equal protection under the law. Was he given equal protection? It connects to the history of Jim Crow, it connects to police violence, it connects to the drug war, it connects to mass incarceration, it connects to the historical legacy of segregation and the original sin of slavery. That question isn't one thing; it could be an entire class period discussion.

Hayes: When Charlottesville happened, I started thinking about monuments. How do we evaluate them? Is it ever appropriate to remove a monument? How can we turn this into a teachable moment? A couple of my colleagues said, "I could never do that. I don't want kids arguing in class." If we can't have critical discourse in class, if kids can't feel safe to say these things in a class where they can get good information, where you can oversee the discussion, where you can make sure it's respectful and all sides are heard, how will they ever be prepared to do that in the world?

People are afraid, especially now, to approach a topic that's uncomfortable or to teach about difficult ideas. I started my career teaching U.S. History I. For the first six months, I talked about slavery. That was incredibly uncomfortable for me. But I had to learn to teach it in a way that was less about me and more about the greater picture—to really help kids understand that in that time and in that place, people believed it was the right thing to do. As we study history, we see that there are various ways to be and to think. And at certain times and in certain places, people believed they were doing the right thing. Teachers who are uncomfortable with that are the ones who focus on memorizing facts but don't step back to ask themselves the value of this information.

2. Create Opportunities for Students to Enact the Learning

Chaffee: We re-create the Truth and Reconciliation Commission (TRC) process that was used in South Africa for the murderers of Steve Biko, who was an anti-apartheid activist. The TRC was a restorative justice panel that the new government began after apartheid to allow victims to confront their abusers as a way to find justice. Our big question throughout is, What is justice?

They research and they learn everything they can about the case and the people. Some of them take the role of lawyers, and some of them take the role of witnesses, and they work together to write questions, witness statements, and cross examination questions. On the day of the hearing, we have an authentic audience, and people come in from the community to be commissioners, to hear the case. I'm asking them to think about, to make inferences based on everything that was left unsaid during this trial—trying to figure out the truth when there is no objective truth. And they jump into it. And you know, watching them huddle over their desks with these incredibly complex texts in front of them with their highlighters, color coding and talking to each other and trying to figure it out is just the most amazing thing to see.

3. The Person Doing the Work
Is the Person Doing the Learning

Bowling: I've always thought throughout my career that the hardest thing to do was to ask questions, and so writing tests took forever. Classroom conversations didn't go very well. I've gotten better at inviting bigger, more philosophical questions. The level of the engagement in the classroom has skyrocketed because more of the cognitive demand is on the students. Whoever is doing the talking is doing the thinking. But simple questions don't drive talking or thinking. Simple questions drive simple answers and shallow understanding. I try to hit my students as often as possible with complex questions and nuanced questions and questions that tap into and expose how our content affects their day to day.

Hayes: We always circle back to this: What is a problem in this community? And how does what we're learning apply in that situation? How can we apply that to the problem that we have in this community? I introduced the lesson from a point of history, but everything else we did was from a modern-day standpoint. My kids were able to flip back and forth. So as much as I did service learning and integration, we were talking about what happened after World War II in housing and urban development, and that's how I got my kids out into different communities. We looked at city maps to see how the different neighborhoods were arranged, and it really tied back to the history.

4. Stop Worrying About "The Test"
and if Students Can Discuss Topics Like Race

Bowling: When people talk about the work and it boils down to talking about how many standards they have to get through, what they're really saying is "I need to be in control." Students are most engaged when the teaching's most relevant. And the teaching is most relevant when it's tied to real events in their own lives, period. Saying, "I don't want to bring race into the classroom" is BS because race is in their classroom every day—particularly if you're a white woman, which most teachers are, standing in front of students of color, which is the norm at many schools. People of color aren't endowed with magical, mystical, racial knowledge. Talking about race is difficult for me as well. I just do it. I don't try to pep talk people into doing what I do. My results speak for themselves.

The thing for me is the job is hard and challenging and uncomfortable. And if you're not comfortable with difficulty and complexity, then get out of the profession. We're preparing students for very difficult lives, and their very difficult lives aren't going to be based neatly around learning targets, standards, and competency outcomes. Life is complex, and we need to prepare them to deal with opinions that are contrary to theirs. We need to prepare them to deal with rigors of a high stress environment—an environment where a lot's expected. That's what drives engagement. Nobody gets better at anything from doing easy stuff; you get better from struggle.

Chaffee: A lot of my students come in reading way below grade level, not really able to write a cogent essay. I want to get them there. But I'm not going to get there by memorizing an essay template and memorizing it over and over, and so I use this really relevant curriculum with these really interesting questions to drive them to building the skills. It drives me crazy when people are either/or, like, you're either going to teach to the test or you're going to do projects. No. You're going to teach the skills and build the skills that will help them on the test through the projects. That's why we do it.

Hayes: All of the standards go with different time periods. When you look at them in a much broader sense, you can apply them to any time period. I focus more on that—the impact on people. I always taught through a lens of how history applies to what is happening right now. Let's find a modern-day connection and superimpose this over the history.

> We have to change the way we teach. That is, radically change it. I would die of boredom, too, if I sat in our schools now. I saw how my daughter did AP U.S. History and I winced. We kill the love for Social Studies through AP U.S. History. I used to discuss that with her at home, and she would fall in love with it at home, and go to school and hate it all over again. Again, not the fault of teachers; they are probably dying of the same boredom. It is the overall endemic structure.
>
> **—REVATHI BALAKRISHNAN, TALENTED AND GIFTED SPECIALIST, ROUND ROCK ISD, 2016 TEXAS TEACHER OF THE YEAR**

It's always about history's impact on people. And you can pull that out of the standards. Some people look at the standards, and they view them so literally. When you deconstruct them, you see that the standards aren't inextricably linked to the time period that they're listed under. If it's a good standard, you can apply it to any period. It's about the application of the information more than just knowing it.

LESSON 9.1 Applying Leveled and Big Questions in Social Studies, Humanities, Government, and Economics

Early childhood text: *Cinderella Stories Around the World: 4 Beloved Tales* by Cari Meister (2014)

Summary: Children can compare and contrast the "Cinderella" tales from Canada, China, Egypt, and France in one short, easy-to-read book.

Level 1: What is the same in the story of Little Burnt Face and Yeh-Shen? What is different?

Level 2: Why are the characters mean to the youngest child in each story?

Level 3 (for debate or discussion): How does knowing someone's story help you care about that person?

Elementary text: *Abe Lincoln: His Wit and Wisdom From A–Z* by Alan Schroeder (2016)

Summary: This alphabetic look at history through the life of our sixteenth president is a great mentor text for students to use in crafting biographies.

Level 1: What did President Lincoln do that he said is "the one thing that will make people remember I ever lived"?

Level 2: Why is President Lincoln, who lived so long ago, someone whose life we study today?

Level 3 (for debate or discussion): Why does slavery continue in different parts of the world?

Middle school text: *Photos Framed: A Fresh Look at the World's Most Memorable Photographs* by Ruth Thomson (2014)

Summary: Twenty-seven of the most iconic photos are grouped into the categories of portraits, nature, art, and documentary, inviting students to begin discussions about primary sources.

Level 1: In the portrait section, which details are the same for each photo?

Level 2: Why do the photos of the Afghan girl and the Cuban girl with her doll appear in this book of memorable photographs?

Level 3 (for debate or discussion): How do our choices about the people and events we photograph reflect how we see ourselves and others? Dorothea Lange said, "The camera is an instrument that teaches people to see without a camera." With so many of us taking photos (some estimates are more than one trillion taken each year), what is worth paying attention to?

High school text: *March: Book Three* by John Lewis and Andrew Aydin (2016)

Summary: The congressman's firsthand account of the civil rights era makes the complex historical realities understandable while delivering an emotional call for citizenship.

Level 1: In Dallas County, Alabama, how many African American adults were registered to vote? What were some of the African Americans asked to do when they tried to register to vote?

Level 2: Why did Fannie Lou Hamer and John Lewis continue in the civil rights movement even after they were attacked by state and local police?

Level 3 (for debate or discussion): What is important enough that you would be willing to suffer for it? What is the relationship between fear and justice?

EXTENSIONS FOR SPEAKING AND LISTENING (IN-CLASS DEBATE HANDOUT IN THE APPENDIX)

- Should people who committed a crime when they were a minor be given the death penalty?

- How do you make sure a rule is fair?

- Is it ever okay to use violence?

- As a way of preventing terrorist activity, should the federal government have access to your e-mail, library records, and other personal information? Should they be able to unlock your phone?

- Should the United States follow the lead of Australia and institute a fine for those who are registered to vote but don't?

- Should nicknames and mascots based on indigenous people be banned in sports at all levels?

- Should parents be punished for their children's mistakes?

EXTENSIONS FOR ACADEMIC WRITING PRACTICE

Students complete a debate reflection (handout in the appendix). ●

Standards Met by Activities, Strategies, and Practice in This Chapter

National Council for the Social Studies Standards

Civic competence rests on this commitment to democratic values, and requires the abilities to use knowledge about one's community, nation, and world; apply inquiry processes; and employ skills of data collection and analysis, collaboration, decision-making, and problem-solving.

College, Career, and Civic Life (C3) Framework for Social Studies State Standards summary:

- Social studies should maintain disciplinary integrity but should be rooted in an interdisciplinary inquiry approach.

- Social studies should prioritize deep and enduring understandings using concepts and skills from the disciplines. (Swan & Griffin, 2013)

Ten Thematic National Council for the Social Studies Strands and Their Questions

Culture: What is culture? What roles does culture play in human and societal development? What are the common characteristics across cultures?

Time, Continuity, and Change: How do we learn about the past? How can we evaluate the usefulness and degree of reliability of different historical sources? What are the roots of our social, political, and economic systems?

People, Places, and Environments: Why do people decide to live where they do or move to other places? Why is location important? How do people interact with the environment, and what are some of the consequences of those interactions?

Individual Development and Identity: How do individuals grow and change physically, emotionally, and intellectually? Why do individuals behave as they do? What influences how people learn, perceive, and grow?

Individuals, Groups, and Institutions: What is the role of institutions in this and other societies? How am I influenced by institutions? How do institutions change?

Power, Authority, and Governance: Under what circumstances is the exercise of political power legitimate? What are the proper scope and limits of authority? How are individual rights protected and challenged?

Production, Distribution, and Consumption: How are goods and services to be distributed and to whom? What are the best ways to deal with scarcity of resources? How does globalization impact local economies and social systems?

Science, Technology, and Society: How can we cope with the concern that technology might get out of control? How can we manage technology so that the greatest numbers of people benefit? How can we preserve fundamental values and beliefs in a world that is becoming one technology-linked village?

Global Connections: What are the benefits and problems associated with global connectedness? How might people in different parts of the world have different perspectives on these benefits and problems? What influence has increasing global interdependence had on patterns of international migration?

Civic Ideals and Practices: What is the balance between rights and responsibilities? What is the role of the citizen in the community, nation, and world community? (National Council for the Social Studies, 2010)

Resources for Further Exploration and Enrichment

Annenberg Foundation's Action Methodology Workshop for K–5 teachers (but is useful to all social studies teachers) that begins in inquiry: www.learner.org/workshops/socialstudies/session1/index.html

Nicky Case's site for "explorable explanations" of voting, gerrymandering, systems of segregation, and other topics: http://ncase.me

(Continued)

(Continued)

Canada's *Indian Residential Schools and Reconciliation Teacher Resource Guide* with activities for students: www.fnesc.ca/wp/wp-content/uploads/2015/07/PUB-LFP-IRSR-10-2015-07-WEB.pdf

South African Truth and Reconciliation lesson plan for middle grades: www.ncpublicschools.org/docs/curriculum/socialstudies/middlegrades/africa/southafricanlesson5.pdf

Stanford University's Reading Like a Historian inquiry model with lessons: http://sheg.stanford.edu/?q=node/45

CHAPTER 10

Fine Arts

The aim of art is to represent not the outward
appearance of things, but their inward significance.

—ARISTOTLE

A great teacher writes truth on your heart that circumstance can't erase.
That's been the case for me with Marshall Ganz. In his class, he taught us a
truth I can't forget: In this world, it's *probable* that Goliath will win, but it's
possible that David will win. Knowing that gives us hope. As I think further
about it, I believe that it's a truth for creatives of any kind. If you create,
no matter your medium, you are constructing a hope for yourself, a belief
that you have something to offer the world. For children who are shuttled
through school days full of worksheets and test prep, this idea can seem as
radical as David defeating Goliath.

Teachers, regardless of our content area, must be advocates for arts education. To the extent that we take away opportunities for children to participate
in the fine arts, particularly in the mistaken notion that we need to use the
time and space for more "college and career readiness" preparation, we blunt
their path to the resilience that the arts illuminate. To create is to participate
in the most deeply human act available to us.

Practically speaking, our ability to construct beauty is one of the things
that separates us from machines and protection from one day being
replaced by a robot. Steve Jobs credited his college calligraphy class with
inspiring Apple's design ethic: "It was beautiful, historical, artistically subtle in a way that science can't capture, and I found it fascinating," he said
in his Stanford commencement address. "None of this had even a hope
of any practical application in my life. But ten years later, when we were

designing the first Macintosh computer, it all came back to me. And we designed it all into the Mac" (Stanford University News, 2005).

Beyond its connection to hope, art is a language that crosses boundaries of individual countries, ages, and abilities and allows us to make concrete the abstractions of our experience. Through movement, breath, and voice, the mind joins the body. Aristotle, a student of Plato (who was himself a student of Socrates), saw the arts as a way to help us to bring our insides to the outside in a way that expresses the complicated nature of our emotions.

As my daughter, who began playing piano at three years old and the cello in elementary school, said to me, "Mom, music lets me say things I don't have any language for." This was true, I also saw, for the boys who calmed themselves by drawing when they came to class roiling with the strong feelings threatening to overwhelm them, and true for the girls who sang to each other to communicate their joy.

The arts are a bridge between the content areas, but I also think they're a pathway for critical thinking. This idea became clearer to me in the most unlikely teaching situation I ever found myself in: on a stage in front of an audience in China.

STUNT TEACHING IN CHINA

Education officials in Jinan, China, invited me in 2016 to visit the Shandong province, and I understood my role to be a visiting lecturer. However, my host turned to me, a half hour before I was to speak in front of an auditorium holding more than one thousand teachers and administrators, and asked if I could do a "demonstration." He explained that they had rounded up twenty middle school–aged children who would act as a "sample class" and sit in desks that they would bring onto the stage with them. The officials wanted to film the lesson, and they were fine with whatever I wanted to teach. This would follow my one-hour keynote, he said.

I shuffled my brain like a deck of cards, trying to figure out exactly what I would teach students who were likely at intermediate levels of understanding English, whom I'd never met nor likely had any experience with the kind of experiential teaching so many of us do in the United States. During stress, you tend to fall onto your bedrock practices. If ever philosophical inquiry were to be road-tested, I thought, now was the time.

My introduction to creating questions has always been through story, music, or art, and for this experience, I knew that art was my best bet.

Luckily, I had been working on a presentation for a conference in Georgia and remembered that I'd saved a Rembrandt painting of Jacob wrestling an angel. With that painting projected on a gigantic screen, the students eagerly followed me through a Socratic discussion of it.

This was particularly notable because I had to give them the words *angel* and *wrestle* and define them. But they were able to articulate the central idea of conflict, struggle, and confrontation in the piece, which helped them think about how they had faced difficulties in their lives and what they learned from it. From there, they generated questions like these: Is it allowable to make mistakes? Should we be happy for difficulty? And then they answered them in a quickwrite that they read into a microphone to the audience.

◇◇◇

Art crosses the gap between what we know and how we feel. This synthesis expresses the head and heart through performance. In some respects, it is enacted contemplation and therefore touches the boundary of what we typically refer to as soul or a spiritual sense. The fine arts help us to understand the intersection of our mind, body, and spirit in a way no other discipline can. An artistic practice helps us uncover and infuse meaning into the everyday experience. Artists call us to what some have called a sacred pause.

Much like coaches teach their athletes to "read" offenses, defenses, and fields of play, teachers of the fine arts train their students to read music, scripts, and visual and physical grammar. They must simultaneously teach skill and content while encouraging expression of their burgeoning aesthetic senses in the theater, visual art, music, or dance. In this regard, teachers of the fine arts support the development of the whole child. See Figure 10.1.

Figure 10.1 Sample Question From a Second Grader

Table 10.1 Fine Arts Guides

Mairi Cooper

2016 Pennsylvania Teacher of the Year

Fox Chapel Area High School

Pittsburgh, PA

Orchestra, Advanced Placement (AP) Music Theory, Piano, World Music

Follow Mairi on Twitter @patoy2015

Chris Gleason

2017 National Teacher of the Year Finalist

2017 Wisconsin Teacher of the Year

Patrick Marsh Middle School

Sun Prairie, WI

Band, Instrumental Music

Follow Chris on Twitter @GleasonCMP

Sia Kyriakakos

2017 National Teacher of the Year Finalist

2017 Maryland Teacher of the Year

Mergenthaler Vocational Technical High School

Baltimore, MD

Visual Arts

Follow Sia on Twitter @SiaKyriakakos and Instagram @siakyriakakos

Four Takeaway Ideas That You Can Put to Work in Your Classroom

1. The Fine Arts Are a Natural Source of Inquiry

Kyriakakos: I tried to figure out how to teach these kids who have absolutely no background in the fundamentals or language of art. Or even the language of mark making and aesthetics. They have nowhere to start. So I started with self-portraits because they're teenagers. So in asking that first question—*Who am I?*—I got a response that I didn't expect.

So who are they? Baltimore city kids who come from very poor families. They didn't know, when they came home, if there would be food or if there would even be a home or a parent. And then them exploring this question and trying to share them with each other was extremely difficult, but it was a great way to start making art. And then to revisit that question and see how it changed them: Who am I? Where do I come from? Who do I want to be? Where do I want to be and how am I going to get there? Those became my questions. Art lends itself to thinking about these things in a very safe space. We can talk about them and explore the possibilities.

Because they have never been given the experience of art, they've never learned to trust their voices, their abilities, their hands, their instincts. They don't know how to quiet the outside world that's screaming at them. We start slowly pushing the outside world away and bringing the inside world up.

Art gives them an opportunity to start believing in themselves. I don't know if they fully do before they leave—I only have them for three months. It gives them an opportunity to believe that somebody cares about them.

> I don't see school so much as a means to an end—to literacy, to numeracy, to graduation, to a secure job. I see it as an end in itself, the place where kids spend more waking hours during the week than they do at home, as a place that should feel good to their bodies, minds, and spirits.
>
> —JUSTIN MINKEL, FIRST- AND SECOND-GRADE TEACHER, SPRINGDALE, ARKANSAS

2. Empathy Is a Natural Complement for Inquiry and Can Be Taught

Gleason: We did "Salvation Is Created" by Pavel Tchesnokov this last year, and that's not one I'd done much ever before. It was a great tool to teach empathy because he wrote this beautiful piece, and he never heard it performed. And I asked the kids, "Can you believe that this beautiful piece, he never heard it performed in his life?" And to me, that's a really powerful thing that kids can learn from. In fact, I made that my kind of overall goal last year. My principal wanted it to be raising math scores, and I said that's important, but my goal's going to be empathy.

He challenged me: "How are you going to teach that?" And I explained the piece. He said, "How are you going to measure it?" That's the problem, I said. I'd rather aim high and fail than to aim low and succeed. I don't want to only work on the technical aspects of music, because at the end, what good is that? I'd rather aim super high and say every kid is going to grow in empathy.

My daughter is legally blind, visually impaired, and you know you take for granted the abilities you have like eyesight. So we did some stuff like lead your friend to the water fountain and try to get a drink blindfolded. The whole idea was to get them to put themselves in someone else's shoes: perspective-taking, the idea of empathy and of being vulnerable, and to get the kids to really go to that place. The final project was to find someone they don't know, spend the day with them, and to really empathize and gain perspective.

Kids came back with pictures of being with their uncle who had served in Afghanistan, some kids went out to the nursing homes and met all kinds of people, veterans, a business owner who was really important in our city and was retired and in a nursing home. Kids went on YouTube and found examples of others showing empathy and how powerful that is. There are a lot of artifacts that showed they were giving this a lot of thought and understanding.

Kyriakakos: That process of painting—it's so internal, it's like prayer. It's mindfulness. You're thinking about the work and somehow it clicks, that's you. You're powerful. You're beautiful. The kids start to see how beautiful and powerful they are. They start seeing, they start believing.

I'll put their writing with their portraits. And when it goes up, they stop. Everything in the hall stops. They start to look, they start to read.

3. Students Can Use the Arts to Create a Channel for Deep Thinking

Cooper: When I talk about a piece of music, I ask them what they think the music is about. Is it even relevant to today? Should we even be playing this piece of music? Then there are these things I structure, like the Grand Salon where there's an essential question that's also being asked in English class and in math class. Next year, we're doing *Carmina Burana*, and the composer, Carl Orff, was most likely a Nazi and certainly a sympathizer. So the questions are these: When are choices that you make to stay alive good or evil? What is moral? What is ethical? Can art be created by immoral people?

I'm not interested in answers. I'm interested in more questions and in getting them to think in layers. What is American? What is American culture? Those are the questions for Dvorak's *New World Symphony* and *Porgy and Bess*. Is the *New World Symphony* an American piece? A lot of these exercises are a way for students to begin thinking about and building their own values. I go back to teaching empathy with the thinking. Carl Orff forces people to be empathetic. He could die or save his life and compose this piece of music. The question from his life is this: In this instance, would I be brave?

Kyriakakos: There's this fabulous African American artist named Kehinde Wiley who asks questions about identity in his art. He takes regular, everyday people and poses them like famous paintings but in their cutoffs and jerseys and high-tops. We do the whole process like him. They have to pick a pose, talk about why they picked that pose and why it triggered something in them. It's really about a representation of power: What does power look like to you? How do you want to portray yourself as powerful?

They have to talk about how they define power—not in the dictionary but in images and people in their lives. Now, how would you represent yourself as powerful—strike a pose. So they take the photos. Extremely interesting work. They do two or three papers—one about Kehinde Wiley, another that answers this question: Who am I?

One student, when I asked, "Who do you want to become?," said, "I don't want to be my father. I don't want to be the man who doesn't take care of his family. I don't want to be the man who doesn't provide for his kids." And he made this really somber photograph of himself with half his face fading into the darkness, but that's the photograph he chose. You can see the darkness that surrounds him, and hopefully the light will take over. When you make art, you're making instinctual decisions that talk to implicit associations. So he may not have even known he was doing it—that's very high-level thinking, but emotionally, he's already there.

Gleason: For each piece of music, I write my skill outcome, my knowledge outcome, my affective outcome. In that is an essential question for them to understand. I'm really looking at Bloom's and Costa and thinking about the depth of that question. Questioning is the most powerful strategy we have as educators. It's our most used tool.

When I've seen education do the best, it's teachers who don't tell but who ask. It's this idea of uncovering and constructing learning. That's just magical. That's when I kind of geek out. If you were to come to one of my concerts, you would see the students talking about the piece before the piece was actually performed. You would hear a trombone octet with an arrangement that one of the students made of the main theme or main melody. Or you might see a video presentation of different projects kids did based on the music, as we're working toward an outcome. Instead of a performance, I call it an "informance." The parents see that we're not there to just entertain; we're there to show learning through music and the beautiful things that happen during the course of preparing. My goal is to show them that process and get a peek inside the classroom at what goes into the performance so they become part of what we do.

4. Giving Students Voice and Choice Is the Best Way to Prepare for Deeper Learning

Cooper: At the base of everything, the two most important things, from me to them and them to me, is trust and respect. And honesty. I tell them that I make mistakes all the time. I choose my words very intentionally with them. In talking about safety, that's the first thing I do. The second is building a classroom of empathy, so building a classroom, where there is strength in other people's opinions and people challenging you.

A student teacher asked me, "What would you say about classroom management?" And I said, "You have to know what your philosophy of teaching is. And then you have to constantly go back to it, and that what has to drive all the decisions you make in your classroom." My philosophy is that I want to create lifelong musicians who are respectful and listen and bend. Because, ultimately, that's what you have to do to be a world-class orchestra and a world-class human being. I want them to do that in all walks of life: to be eager and hungry to think more deeply.

Gleason: It really shouldn't work, if you think about it. I've got 110 kids in seventh-grade band; they all have instruments. They shouldn't listen at all. I think the thing is you've got to engage their curiosity. If they're curious, then they're engaged. Then, you've sparked something. I think kids are naturally curious.

They have to know more than just the notes. It can't just be about training kids. And every time I hear the word *training* like training teachers or training students, I get the heebie jeebies because we train dogs, not humans. We need to educate them. They need to have voice and choice and more autonomy in the classroom. So ever since that moment, my goal has been to provide them with opportunities to have intrinsic motivation built and for them to have more ownership in the process.

LESSON 10.1 Applying Leveled and Big Questions in the Fine Arts

Early childhood text: *No One Saw: Ordinary Things Through the Eyes of an Artist* by Bob Raczka (2006)

Summary: Simple rhyming texts introduce modern art to young children and highlight the way each artist looked at the world in their own unique way.

> **Level 1:** How many details can you find in the painting *A Sunday Afternoon on La Grande Jatte*? What is going on in the painting?
>
> **Level 2:** Why do you think Mary Cassatt decided to paint a picture of the woman and the little girl? What did she want us to see?
>
> **Level 3** (for debate or discussion): How does art help us think about the world and the people in it?

Elementary text: *Joyful Noise: Poems for Two Voices* by Paul Fleischman (2005)

Summary: Poetry, art, and choral reading blend together in this engaging book perfect for vocal performance, music and dance improvisation or composition, and as a mentor text for writers and artists.

> **Level 1:** How does the author use the design of each poem to signal which lines should be emphasized?
>
> **Level 2:** How does the rhythm of using two or more voices change your thinking about each insect? Why do you think the author chose certain phrases to emphasize doubled lines?
>
> **Level 3** (for debate or discussion): How does art help us care about the world around us?

Middle school text: *Six Kids and a Stuffed Cat* by Gary Paulsen (2017)

Summary: Six middle school boys are stuck together in the boy's restroom and bond despite their differences in this short novel, followed by a script of the novel's story perfect for reader's theater performance.

> **Level 1:** In the script that follows the story, how does the author show who is speaking and how they should move?
>
> **Level 2:** How does the script change how you think and feel about the characters? How could you add a song or a dance to the play?
>
> **Level 3** (for debate or discussion): Mr. Rogers said, "If you know someone's story, you can't help but love them." Do you agree? Why? How does performance help us understand someone's story?

(Continued)

(Continued)

High school text: *Steal Like An Artist: 10 Things Nobody Told You About Being Creative* by Austin Kleon (2012)

Summary: Practical advice and ideas are given for any creative endeavor, including visual art, graphic design, user design, writing, and other work.

Level 1: What does the author believe about creative ideas and where they come from?

Level 2: Why did Picasso say, "Art is theft"? Is remixing a form of plagiarism or closer to what Picasso meant?

Level 3 (for debate or discussion): Is creativity the natural state of humanity? Is art possible for other forms of life? Would art created by artificial intelligence be valid?

EXTENSIONS FOR SPEAKING AND LISTENING (IN-CLASS DEBATE HANDOUT IN THE APPENDIX)

- Certain artists, musicians, actors, comedians, and filmmakers have confessed to or credibly been accused of sexual harassment. Is it possible to separate their creative contributions from their offenses? Should we? Does knowing what they've done change how we should view their art?

- Is it ever okay to tell someone else's story or use their likeness without their permission?

- What is the artist's responsibility to society? Can you be both a good artist and a good citizen?

- Certain YouTube creators have been criticized and/or had their accounts deactivated for controversial material (showing the body of a suicide victim, hate speech, inappropriate inclusion of children and minors). Is this censorship valid or invalid? Why?

EXTENSIONS FOR ACADEMIC WRITING PRACTICE

Students complete a debate reflection rubric (handout in the appendix). ●

Standards Met by Activities, Strategies, and Practice in This Chapter

National Core Arts Standards

The standards are framed by a definition of artistic literacy that includes philosophical foundations and lifelong goals. Philosophical foundations include the following:

> **The Arts as Communication:** The arts provide unique symbol systems and metaphors that convey and inform life experience (i.e., the arts are ways of knowing).

> **The Arts as Culture, History, and Connectors:** Understanding artwork provides insights into individuals' own and others' cultures and societies, while also providing opportunities to access, express, and integrate meaning across a variety of content areas. (National Coalition for Core Arts Standards, 2014)

National Assessment of Educational Progress: NAEP Arts Education Framework

> **Creating:** This may include, but should not be limited to, the expression of a student's unique and personal ideas, feelings, and responses in the form of a visual image, a character, a written or improvised dramatic work, or the composition or improvisation of a piece of music or a dance.

> **Performing/Interpreting:** It means performing an existing work. . . . However, it does suggest the engagement and motivation involved in creating a work of art.

> **Responding:** The response is usually a combination of affective, cognitive, and physical behavior. Responding involves a level of perceptual or observational skill; a description, analysis, or interpretation on the part of the respondent; and sometimes a judgment or evaluation based on criteria that may be self-constructed or commonly held by a group or culture.

Resources for Further Exploration and Enrichment

"Visual Thinking Strategies for Improved Comprehension": www.colorincolorado.org/article/visual-thinking-strategies-improved-comprehension

National Association for Music Education: https://nafme.org/the-4-cs-critical-thinking

Drama strategies from David Farmer: https://dramaresource.com/drama-strategies

Critical Thinking In Dance Education: Do an online search.

The Feeling Wheel, a diagram of emotions: Do an online search.

Russel Tarr's online guide for suggestions of how to use the Feeling Wheel in the classroom: www.classtools.net/blog/using-plutchiks-wheel-of-emotions-to-improve-the-evaluation-of-sources

CHAPTER 11
Career and Technical Education

For the things we have to learn before we can do, we learn by doing.

—ARISTOTLE (1893/2004), *NICOMACHEAN ETHICS*

The photo showed a group of mostly white, mostly middle class, and mostly female teachers and it was meant to motivate and empower students. The teachers posed with one hand holding pens high in the air and another holding hammers in another hand that was dropped to their sides. "See? It's pens up, hammers down!" the photographer told me. Someone in the process stopped the photo from going forward onto the school's website, sensing that it could be misinterpreted. But in that photo I saw a visual argument that continues in education, particularly in communities that push "no excuses" for why all of their children aren't constantly thinking of college or being prepared for college. By "college," they mean four-year university. Rarely are community colleges or professional certificates mentioned, which is a disservice to students who are talented in career and technical education (CTE).

Apprenticeship is an ancient form of experiential learning that cultures used to teach technical and artistic knowledge to the next generation. Greek and Roman society seemed to have had the same tensions in preparing their young people as those we argue about when we push for all students to attend college. The ancients likewise debated whether to groom their children for the ruling class or the labor that ensured the stability of their trades.

Xenophon, a student of Socrates, preferred to prepare the aristocrats for leadership, which broke with his teacher's natural empathy for the working class. Socrates was himself a member of the working class, and in his view of teaching, when he "speaks of 'competent instructors' in the mechanical arts he probably has in mind not special teachers of the crafts but ordinary master workmen" (Anderson, 1912, p. 195). Socrates's other student, Plato, wrote in Book I of *The Laws*, "According to my view, he who would be good at anything must practice that thing from his youth upwards, both in sport and in earnest, in the particular way which the work requires."

Closer to our time, the colonists brought the apprenticeship model with them to the New World, and it was how most children joined society. It gave them an opportunity for learning when their parents couldn't pay for an education. The Industrial Revolution upended this arrangement as machines began doing more and more of the work. Early attempts at the lyceum model, which would "include the cultural needs of the artist, the farmer, and the mechanic," rose in the 19th century to meet American schooling needs. At the same time, "manual labor academies" formed for students to supplement academics with a job "in a shop or factory owned by a local business man who paid the institution for the student's services." This meld of school and work seemed to cause "distinctions between rich and poor . . . to break down [and contribute] to the development of better citizens" (Barlow, 1976).

Colton, a student in my middle school classes, wrote an opinion paper in answer to his own question about work that links with these ideas:

> Today I am thinking about all the pressure that is put on kids my age. One thing that is a little weird that makes me think is how in the "old" days when kids had to do all kinds of work like milking cows and getting eggs from chickens. I wonder if we're not all spoiled. If like Abraham Lincoln came and saw the world today what would all of the old timey people who had to actually start from scratch think? I don't think they would see an improved society. I think they would be disappointed in people. I think they would think we weren't even the same species.

Patrick Foster (2017), a construction technology professor at Santa Barbara City College in California, believes that vocational education creates well-rounded individuals and should be our model because "[n]o human problem is purely 'mental' or purely 'physical.' This has been a political dichotomy and not a natural one, and with it we have created a world of lop-sided people and institutions and careers."

Steve Elza, a master mechanic, sees a range of students in his automotive classes, from those in poverty to those who come from privilege. He told me that they discover personal meaning in vocational classes like his: "The fun part is when these kids who go to English, math, science, history, and they ask these questions: Why am I here? What is my purpose for being here? And all of a sudden, they walk into automotive class and it's their passion, whether it be the TV shows they watch or the magazines they read. It's a hobby in their family or their living, so they're able to express themselves in this way." See Figure 11.1.

Figure 11.1 Sample Questions From Early Elementary and Middle School

why dont kids have jobs?

why do some kids get more responsibility then others?

Table 11.1 Career and Technical Education Guides

Steve Elza
2015 Illinois Teacher of the Year
William Fremd High School
Palatine, IL
Automotive, Applied Technology
Follow him on Twitter @autoteach211

Jaclyn Ryan
2015 Virginia Teacher of the Year
Signal Knob Middle School
Strasburg, VA
Agricultural Education, Future Farmers of America Adviser

Four Takeaway Ideas That You Can Put to Work in Your Classroom

1. Discovering Their Own "Why" Helps Students Understand Themselves

Elza: When I was in high school, I didn't want to be there. I literally slept an entire semester in math class. The bell would ring, and I'd wake up. It wasn't that I couldn't do the work; it was that I didn't know *why* I was doing the work. And so I didn't. I was at the point of failing, and my counselor said, "You need to go to the tech center." And she said it, like "I want to get you out of school because you're causing trouble and doing poorly." So, for her, the technology center was a dumping ground. Little did she know that that was the turning point that really saved my life. It was a place I wanted to be. Making a connection to those teachers there gave me a reason to want to do math. Now I understood why.

I had a kid, Randy, who built his first engine at eleven years old in his kitchen. There was no other place to do it in the small condo where his family lived, so he built it there. He came to high school and found automotive class, and it was his passion. He started coming to my Auto Club when he was in seventh grade. He and his dad would come seventh, eighth grade, freshman year, and now he's finishing up his sophomore year and he's a fantastic student. It's great to see someone who has that hands-on knowledge, but he can work with Ray, who's a special needs student, and seeing them work together and learn from one another is fantastic.

Ryan: Allowing students to research what they want has been amazing, and I've definitely learned a lot along the way. That is something agriculture offers. We give them what we call a "supervised agriculture experience," which kids are doing all over the country and even in Guam. It's based on the students' interests, and they choose what they want to learn. It's really neat because it can be in plant science, animal science, leadership, community service, natural resources, agricultural mechanics—the list goes on and on.

The students record their hours and what they're doing to gain the skills in that area, and then they fill out an application for a proficiency award.

I've seen kids start these in middle school, and then all of their hours and experiences go on with them to high school; then they can use those applications to get scholarships. I had two students who were just named national finalists in their areas. It was all just them carrying on what they started in middle school.

2. Career and Technical Education Classes Are a "Lab for Life Skills"

Ryan: In the agricultural leadership class, we teach parliamentary procedure, how to actually use Robert's Rules of Order to conduct a meeting. I've seen kids come in, and they're not confident, they can't think on their feet very well, and they really struggle with formulating those thoughts before they speak—one in particular . . . did not excel in other areas. He had a learning disability, but he worked so hard. There's a contest in FFA called Conduct of Chapter Meetings, and this boy, we worked to develop his skills so that when he stood up, he was able to speak so fluently that he was actually named the all-state reporter. He was the top one of all the other reporters in the contest, and he got a medal.

They're learning life skills in those experiences. Later in life, they'll most likely conduct a meeting, and they'll be using parliamentary procedure. If they are going to be on a board or supervise others, they'll need those skills. That's true even if you're just standing up and being able to speak on your feet, you'll utilize this skill. I'm trying to help them see the relevance behind it and how it will work into their lives.

Elza: I had a kid who was special needs—his parents were very protective of him. He started my class freshman year. He had two aides with him. And by his junior year, he told them, "I don't need you anymore." The aides stayed there and watched him, hands off. And by his senior year, he didn't have any aides at all. So you see these kids, the task completion is very small, but the growth is huge. He graduated. He came in after he graduated and said, "My car's making a noise. Can I use the lift?" So he starts diagnosing it, and he found the problem. [School staff] were just trying to put him somewhere, find something for him to do—and he flourished in this class. He began learning on his own. All these kids grow, and then they have a skill they can take with them when they leave.

A lot of these kids wouldn't have graduated, wouldn't have gone on without CTE. Even if they don't take my class, they can take woods or foods or electronics courses. How great is it that they learn how to do things like change their oil in my fundamentals class or learn how brakes work? When they take their cars in, how powerful is it that they can negotiate? That's life skills; that's problem solving.

I have six girls in my class now, and they're incredible. They bring such diversity. It causes everyone to step up their game. I have an eleventh grader now, she's AP and honors, the high-achieving student. She wanted to take automotive, and her mom had to get involved, get her changed to another counselor because the first one was so against her being in the class. It's that mindset that if you're an AP student, if you're college track, then why would you ever need automotive, or construction, or CAD, electronics, family and consumer science? What they don't understand is whether you're working on cars or designing cars, you're still preparing for the automotive industry. You're better having that background.

3. Confidence and Competence
Are the Outcomes of Applied Learning

Elza: I had a kid whose brother went to medical school, so this kid, his parents put him in community college. He tried accounting, he tried business, he tried medical—all these different things. Five years he does this. He comes back to me and says, "Elza, I know what I want to do: automotive." He'd failed and failed, not because he wasn't smart enough but because he didn't have a passion for it. So he went to Southern Illinois University for automotive. Mind you, the whole time he's in college, he's working in a shop where they build BMW race cars. So, he's supporting himself doing this thing he loves, but he had been studying and trying to build a life on something he doesn't.

He entered with really bad grades but graduated with a 4.0. He's getting job offers for over $80,000 a year. He got a job offer at GM in Michigan for $83,000. He turned them down because he wanted to be close to home. Now he's working for a local alternative fuels place, and he's making over $60,000, and he's close to his family, and he's happy. There are a number of my students making over six figures.

Ryan: So many kids are graduating from college and realize they don't want to do what they've spent so much money to study. That's the beauty of CTE because it lets them explore and figure out what they're good at. It lets them figure out what they're interested in. Even if you go to college and get a degree, I think you shouldn't be afraid to learn a trade you can fall back on. Kids can go and get fundamental skills and then learn about it at a higher level if they want to. And it also gives them something they can do if they choose to go to college, to help them pay for it by working a trade like cosmetology or construction on the side.

We need plumbers, we need electricians. I've sat in so many meetings where we have industry-based people, and we want to know what skills they need us to prepare the kids to learn. And the biggest one is work ethic. It's hard for them to find people who are willing to work and put forth the effort and be willing to sweat a little. As a plumber or electrician, you can make really good money. Here in Virginia, we really see the importance of CTE. The numbers speak for themselves. The kids who graduate with industry certification are amazing. They can make good money doing what they want to do.

4. Matching a Student's Interests to Content and Connecting Them to Mentors Deepens Their Learning

Elza: This class helps them read a technical manual and be able to translate it into a hands-on piece. When they don't match up, then there's a problem-solving piece that brings in higher-level thinking. Unfortunately, we do have that huge divide between academic and technical classes. They really need to be integrated.

In our district, we have one school that's combined an English class with an automotive class. It's not on the books that way, but all the kids in the Autos 1 class are in an English 102 class together. The data that we have from the first two years is off the charts. The ones that do have the class together and the ones who don't, it is amazing how much better the ones who have the class together are doing. I mean, they're meeting all the Common Core State Standards, but meeting them in something they enjoy. They read tech manuals. So if we're doing cooling systems, they'll read about that. I answer questions, the English teacher brings her expertise, and we meet in the middle and these kids flourish in the process.

Geometry and construction is a big thing right now, so we're starting a geometry and construction class where there's a geometry teacher and a building construction teacher together, and they're using geometry to build these houses. It is a huge loss when we start minimizing these classes.

LESSON 11.1 Applying Leveled and Big Questions in Career and Technology Classes

Middle school text: *What Color Is Your Parachute for Teens: Discover Yourself, Design Your Future, and Plan for Your Dream Job* by Carol Christen and Richard N. Bolles (2016)

Summary: This is an engaging, easy-to-read guide for teens to help them match their skills and interests to possible careers.

> **Level 1:** How does the author explain what a transferable skill is and why it's something to think about for your future?
>
> **Level 2:** Why are self-management skills so important?
>
> **Level 3** (for debate or discussion): Many cultures believe in the power of dreams—that what we say we want to be, we become. Do you agree? Why?

High school text: *Shop Class as Soulcraft: An Inquiry Into the Value of Work* by Matthew B. Crawford (2010)

Summary: The author, a philosopher, mechanic, and electrician, writes eloquently about the value of making and fixing things and why everyone shouldn't be forced to become a "knowledge worker."

> **Level 1:** What are the "useful arts"?
>
> **Level 2:** The introduction of the book makes an argument that students today know how to bubble circles on a standardized test but they can't "do anything." Do you agree? Why?
>
> **Level 3** (for debate or discussion): What is a craft? Is there something uniquely human about our ability to make tools or work with our hands to fix, build, mend, and grow things?

EXTENSIONS FOR SPEAKING AND LISTENING (IN-CLASS DEBATE HANDOUT IN THE APPENDIX)

- Do we put too much pressure on students to go to a four-year university? Should everyone go to college? Should we value professional certification as much as a college diploma?

- Many economists predict that robots, automation, and artificial intelligence will replace many human workers. Are there things that only humans can do that robots will never replace?
- Some countries, like Germany, allow students to begin choosing technical and vocational training as young as middle school. Is this a good idea? Do you think it's possible to know what you want in middle school?
- The Harvard professor Howard Gardner says there are different ways of being smart that he calls "multiple intelligences." Two of them, visual spatial and bodily kinesthetic, are the kinds students in career and technical education (CTE) classes use the most. How do you respond to that? Have people ever talked to you about mechanical and technical skill being an intelligence? Why do you think that is?

EXTENSIONS FOR ACADEMIC WRITING PRACTICE

Students complete a debate reflection (handout in the appendix). ●

Standards Met by Activities, Strategies, and Practice in This Chapter

The Common Career Technical Core

- Consider the environmental, social, and economic impacts of decisions.

- Demonstrate creativity and innovation.

- Utilize critical thinking to make sense of problems and persevere in solving them.

National Consortium for Product Quality Curriculum Quality Standards for School to Work

School-to-work curricula, through active and applied learning experiences in school, community, and work-based settings, must enable students to acquire problem solving, communication, and reasoning strategies.

The SCANS Foundational Skills for Entering the Workforce

- Thinking skills: creative thinking, decision making, problem solving, seeing through the mind's eye, knowing how to learn, and reasoning

- Personal qualities: skills concerning responsibility, self-esteem, sociability, self-management, and integrity/honesty

The SCANS Competencies

Systems: understanding systems (e.g., complex interrelationships), improving and designing systems

Resources for Further Exploration and Enrichment

Center on Education and the Workforce at Georgetown University: https://cew.georgetown.edu

FHI 360: Resources for teaching and learning college and career readiness: www.fhi360.org/explore/content?f[0]=field_expertise%3A137

Association for Career and Technical Education online seminars: www.acteonline.org/seminars/#.WgO8YBNSxBw

Linked Learning resources from ConnectEd: The California Center for College and Career: www.connectedcalifornia.org/ideas_resources/overview

Teacher leadership training for career and technical education (CTE) educators from the National Center for Innovation in Career and Technical Education: http://ctecenter.ed.gov/training_center/single_training/professional-development-and-teacher-preparation

CHAPTER 12
Special Populations

I set to [each] one of you, individually . . . what I hold to be the greatest possible service. I tried to persuade each one of you to concern himself less with what he has than with what he is, so as to render himself as excellent and rational as possible.

—SOCRATES

THE CLASS FROM "HELL"

Sixteen-year-olds who looked like they were answering a casting call for "high school kids" trickled into my classroom after the tardy bell rang: Tyreek, the size and shape of an NFL linebacker, put both hands into one of the only spaces on Clemente's shirt that wasn't stained with paint and cement mix and pushed him forward, causing him to stumble; Stacie, perfectly coordinated from her ponytail holder to her gold lamé tennis shoes, rolled her eyes and kept talking on her cell phone; Angie, the lone white girl in a nondescript blouse and jeans, kept repeating "excuse me, excuse me, excuse ME" as she stepped around the mass of bodies at the door.

Tanshia, already seated, smiled at me. Her hair was meticulously swept into a perfect updo to show off a serious set of hoop earrings, and they bumped against her face as she shook her head and said, "I bet you're sorry you got all these clowns in here."

Because it was my first year to teach high school, I watched this parade as if I were watching a movie, unable to fully process that I was supposed to teach it. Teachers will talk about a "class from hell," but until you actually experience one, you have only your worst images from the movies to construct a definition. It's even worse when the class is scheduled after lunch because the kids are understandably resentful for being pulled away from some of the only choices they have all day. This was true for my sixth period.

Also true was the span of the letters and phrases after their names on my attendance screen: ADHD, BIP (behavioral intervention plan), diabetic, 11RR (each R representing a repeated year), ELL, SPED, and GT. Some were athletes, one was transitioning back into classes from jail, one was in band, and one had that morning decided to drop out of her AP English class and into what she felt would be a much easier regular class.

Sixth period was my master class in differentiation but also the one that convinced me that Socratic inquiry and discussion were not only possible with regular classes but also any type of learner. To teach them, I worked up some of the processes I've described earlier, so their introduction to this final content-area chapter is fitting.

Because behaviors were one of the most distracting obstacles to teaching the class, I spent most of the first six weeks trying out and discarding all kinds of management systems. One week, I decided to "get tough" and run the class like it was in-school suspension. Students would read out of a textbook, answer the questions at the end of each chapter, and I'd have control. The next week, I'd try a little bit of choice, but then Jamie, lost without the structure that came from the boring yet soothingly predictable book work, began acting out. But with Jamie under control, one third of the class slept or otherwise tuned out of the forced curriculum.

The lurch between control and choice dragged on until two separate resources banged together in my head: a DVD packaged with a professional book and a video camera the size of a cell phone that I could plug into the computer to show content. The DVD had clips of a high school class working together in pairs, small groups, and whole group discussion. I used it as a visual text for students, asking them what they noticed. Then, I told them I would have a volunteer film our next class, and we'd watch it the same way.

The comparison of the well-ordered class with the video of their own class's chaos worked like a coaching session: They saw the possibilities of where they could go but were forced to reckon with the reality of where they were. And they didn't like where they were. Using the video, we were able to cocreate norms for the class, set discussion goals, try them out, then film the results. This protracted learning was a necessary tilling of the ground—a practice in patience that is critical for creating cohesion from so many differences.

In this class, students were able to practice critical thinking using song lyrics and short videos (a list of songs and videos we used for this is in the appendix) and then generate their questions for use in discussions and then their own projects. Angelo, an English language learner (ELL) who received special education services, created an in-depth proposal for a video game;

Jamie read a book for the first time: *Monster* by Walter Dean Myers (2004); Clemente wrote a resume to get a job paying him enough to pay half his family's bills.

But what the class seemed most proud of was their ability to think together in discussions every Monday. We picked Mondays to practice Socratic discussion because it was a natural way for them to reconnect after the weekend. They were particularly pleased by their decision to discuss race in a way that helped everyone feel heard and respected yet pushed everyone to think more deeply about differences, prejudice, and identity. These "race circles" of discussion happened at least once every six weeks, at their request, and helped me to understand equity through their voices and experiences in a way that hours of professional development never could.

◇◇◇

Students are capable of so much more than we trust them to handle. Six of my colleagues who take this idea and deepen it are included here to deepen your own thinking about what's possible when differentiation becomes more than a static concept we perform and more of a mindset we encourage. See Figure 12.1.

Figure 12.1 Sample Questions From Middle School

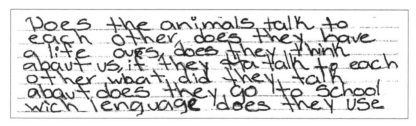

(Continued)

Figure 12.1 (Continued)

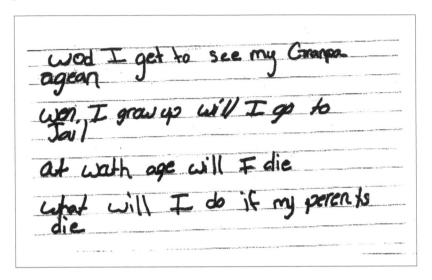

wod I get to see my Granpa
agean

wen, I grow up will I go to
Jail

at wath age will I die

what will I do if my perents
die

Table 12.1 Guides for Special Education

Brett Bigham
2014 Oregon Teacher of the Year
Special Education (Life Skills)
Portland Public Schools
Portland, OR

Megan Gross
2017 National Teacher of the Year Finalist
2017 California Teacher of the Year
Special Education (Autism) Del Norte High School
San Diego, CA

Two Takeaway Ideas That You Can Put to Work in Your Classroom

1. Rethink What's Possible for Students With Special Needs

Bigham: Just like with any student, you don't make a decision about what they can do in their life at one grade, what their goals are and make that for their whole life. But in special ed, we tend to do that. We make them this little program, and if it's successful, we'll do that for the next sixteen years. I want to know what they're interested in and what makes their eyes light up. If I can find that, I can create something around what makes their eyes light up.

I had a little guy with Down syndrome, and he was this gentle soul. He had been trained to do things like put poker chips in a blue or red cup, and that's awesome for five times, but it's so repetitious. Don't make him do that for four years. We started looking at outside jobs, like at the food bank, where he could extend that skill, and he was such a good helper. He had mastered the skill of putting things where they were supposed to go.

He's eighteen, and he's going to be out in the world soon, and he needs those kinds of experiences—those things that will prepare him for a job he can do. With the food bank, he could match colors and load boxes of food. He understood the principle. And when he got there, people knew him and talked to him and hugged him. Instead of having him sit at a table in a classroom, he was with people who cared about him. When he leaves, he will have a chance to do something and not sit at home.

Gross: As long as parents are happy, people don't care as much what you do in the classroom, which is a weird, strange, nebulous place to live. Because if you do the right things for kids, that's great because you have autonomy. If you do crappy things for kids, like nobody cares, which I think is horrible. I'm like: What *can* we do?

Right now we're reading the novel *The Thing About Jellyfish* (Benjamin, 2017) and talking about, in addition to the science aspect of it, the following ideas: What do you think about friendship? Have you ever been in a situation where you didn't read the situation correctly, as the character in the story does? Have you lost a friend? Have you gotten angry at friends? Half of my caseloads are nonverbal and the character in the story chooses to not speak, so I thought that would be an interesting connection for them. We ask this: How else do you communicate with the world besides verbally?

2. Create Access to Community Both Inside and OUTSIDE the Classroom

Gross: My room looks like a typical high school classroom. The only homework assignment I give kids is that every weekend take photos of what you're doing so we can talk about it on Mondays. They put the photos on Google Slides, and we just talk and share answers to this question: What did we do this weekend? I feel like that's really improved the culture in my classroom.

We've given them question frames to meet the requirement that you have to ask questions of the person presenting to try and get more information out of them and try to make connections. You can make comments like, "Oh, I like to do that too." The interesting thing is while we've been doing this, we've found out that one of our students is really interested in time. And I wouldn't have known that otherwise because he's really super quiet. But he likes to ask, "What time did you go? How long were you there?" It's like this insight into how he probably plans and categorizes his days.

Bigham: I have students who are Life Skills students, so my students are not the ones who are going to be at the library checking out a book. I'm going to go with them and help them find a book that's pretty that they want to look at. So there's a different level even in special education. There are kids that can do inquiry with assistance, or with modifications, or maybe not modified but done in a way that works for them. What I do with my kids in my classroom is adapt curriculum, like if they're studying Egypt in another class, since my kids often don't read, I create my own curriculum.

I always asked my students what they're interested in, and for me one of the most important things is community access. And I base that on what their interests are. They're going to graduate out of the system, so if they have an interest in trains or an interest in art, then I need to teach them how to go to those places and access those things that they really like. For those eighteen- to twenty-one-year-olds, I made work for the purpose of helping them access the community.

Table 12.2 Guides for English Language Learners

Dorina Sackman-Ebuwa

2014 National Teacher of the Year Finalist

2014 Florida Teacher of the Year

ESOL Language Arts Consultant

Greenville, FL

Dania Vazquez

2017 Barr Fellow

Founding Headmaster

Margarita Muniz Academy

Jamaica Plain, MA

Two Takeaway Ideas That You Can Put to Work in Your Classroom

1. Understand Who Your Students Are

Vazquez: Of all the decades of work I've done in bilingual education, there's this misunderstanding and fear of what we perceive as the "other." In this country, there is a misconception about people who speak another language—that they're unintelligent because *we* don't understand them. There is some need to reshape people who don't look or sound like you or me so we feel better. My students who represent linguistic, ethnic diversity and more are actually really, really smart kids. Many of my students have come as immigrants and ELLs and who do better and outshine those who've grown up here. They have a little skin in the game. They're here because of some sacrifice their families had to make.

We also need to recognize that the Latino community is not monolithic. We can't treat all Latinos the same because they're not. In our school, we have many Dominican students—that experience is very different from students in other Caribbean, Central, and South American countries. They're very different kids. We need to be attuned to that diversity—the real cultural differences, the different histories, and the different entry points.

Sackman-Ebuwa: My initial academic relationship with students begins with a survey, ten questions that help me get to know more about them before coming to the States. I need to know my students' stories before I teach them so I may infuse all that I learn into each lesson. It helps them connect to the content and to each other. After they finish the survey, yes, I ask them to use Google Translate or Reverso. I know it's not perfect, but it helps me see how well they can (a) manipulate a computer, (b) write, and (c) create sentences in their native language. It's my first observation of their work besides an entrance exam that can help me prepare my differentiated lessons. And that's also their pretest. Showing that to the student one year later is magical, as they see the linguistic before and after right before them! After they complete the survey, a family member and community member has to do it as well. You find out a lot when you ask this of your child and their family. It's my way of letting them know they matter, I care, and I want to get to know them beyond the four walls of the classroom. I want them to feel valued, safe, and loved. Once you have this relationship, you not only have actual phone numbers from parents and engaged students but you have trust, and there is no better compliment than to have people coming from other countries, cultures, and challenges trusting you implicitly. It is an honor and a responsibility—one that I don't take lightly.

The minute an ELL enters a classroom, many teachers go into panic mode. "I don't speak Spanish!" they'd say, even if the child is from Syria. I call it the innocence of ignorance and the arrogance of ignorance. I see both in my twenty-one years of teaching ELLs strategies to teachers. Either you are innocently ignorant of what to do when ELL children arrive in your classroom—and that's okay—you know not what you do or you are arrogantly ignorant—and that's not okay—you know exactly how you feel about a child coming from another country entering your classroom, your world. The latter is the hardest to break, as they only see the child through one lens, their own. It takes time and a lot of culturally relevant professional development, patience, empathy, and listening to know why the teacher feels the way they do. Yet, once you empower them with everything from differentiated instruction to scaffolding to model lessons, they wind up asking for all the newcomers to join their class! I won't deny it; teaching ELLs is hard. Some say it is simply "good teaching" used in "lower reading levels," but there is so much more to teaching ELLs. There is a growth mindset, a shift in thinking, and a revisiting of teaching you never had to do with students who have English as their heritage language. You teach, but with ELLs in your classroom, I call it "Teach Plus One." You have to realize that for every ELL, one must give ten minutes of more time to prepare. So if you have four or five students, you've got to give yourself another hour for your planning. That can be frustrating at first, but the beauty of that is you are actually reflecting on your lessons and practice, perhaps saying to yourself, "Did Anac get that? I wonder if I needed to explain it better. Maybe I need more visuals or do more group work." Working with ELLs is constant reflective practice, so you will find teachers who embrace ELLs become stronger teachers.

And that is what it takes. After all, it is your civic responsibility. You have a child in your room, regardless of your political or religious or philosophical ideologies, who needs to have an equitable education. So in order for that to happen, you have to think of all the ways your "equal" teaching of all children who speak the same language has to shift. If not, it becomes linguistic inequity and that's not right. Sure, it isn't easy, but that's the beauty of what an ELL does to a teacher: They challenge teachers with what they are comfortable with, with what they are used to, with what they have been "doing for the past ten years" and makes that monolith educator uncomfortable because they must change with the change that has occurred in their classroom—different children speaking different languages from different education systems and levels of education. You can't go from good to great without acknowledging and facing some discomfort from change. If you choose not to, are you really teaching? Change is inevitable in a classroom with ELLs; the growth is optional. Without the growth, in comes that linguistic inequity again!

So as the world shifts and as the political turmoil shifts, the biggest thing that must be understood through cultural relevance and one's own bias, one's own privilege is that you have to be aware of the historical aspects of why kids are coming here in the first place. A lot of it has to do with the intervention of the United States. It's a moral issue and a world issue. So Teach Plus One doesn't just mean differentiated instruction and strategies; it means to learn about the world around you, the history of the countries of the students and the relationship to the United States. Get conversations going with parents and community members and ask questions. Get vulnerable. Get uncomfortable so your ELLs can feel comfortable with you.

2. Actively Work to Reduce Fear

Sackman-Ebuwa: People's unconscious biases are affecting the way ELLs learn. Learn the difference between equality and equity. Know your ELLs' stories. Find out what their academic and linguistic levels are to help drive instruction. That's the first thing. A "label" of ELL doesn't mean the same, so know where they are in the linguistic acquisition journey. Assess them in their first language. Assess their computer skills. Know their pen to paper skills, favorite subjects and abilities in the arts. Go into their folders. Know where your students are from, and look at it on a map (that would be nice to show in your classroom—especially how far they have traveled). Study a little: Teach Plus One. Find out their first language. As obvious as that may sound, there are many teachers and counselors who hear a name or country and automatically assume it is one language over another. There are students from Mexico who do not speak Spanish and students from India who have no desire to speak Hindi because Tamil is their language of choice.

What I am saying is that a teacher cannot simply welcome an ELL into their classroom and think they can just start to teach. If you do, however, let it be with a welcome video and packet—for example, "Welcome! I'm Miss Dorina. I'm your English teacher. You are safe here. You are respected here. You are loved here by all of us. Here are some things that you need to know. Here are some questions. Can you answer these for me?" And then, somewhere on your wall should be in big bold letters, "English is not my first language." That is the first assignment for each child that comes into my classroom—to never say, "I don't speak English." Rather, it's to be empowered to say, "English is not my first language." It is transforming. Other things to have ready in a classroom with ELLs are word walls, visuals, sentence frames, and my favorite academic language power phrases. I put about ten a week on 3" × 5" index cards. My newcomers may be shy to speak, being in their "silent period," so they simply put the card on the top left corner of the desk, and I see how they feel or what they need. They are given phrases such as "I don't understand, YET," "Speak slower please," "Please help me," "I understand everything!," and "May I go to the bathroom?" It sets the tone of "I got you, kiddo. I got your back."

Moreover, placement is key. It's kind of like, "Nobody puts baby in the corner!" Nobody puts ELLs in the corner! ELLs in the back sets a tone. ELLs in the back with a paraprofessional sets another. Students who are new to the class should always be near the teacher, as comfort and a form of welcoming and security. Placing an "ambassador" with a newcomer ELL is a strong way to build empathy and comfort. After all, the success of an ELL is based on community and confidence, not isolation and question.

The point to all of what I am saying is that ELLs deserve the best education. Language should not be the reason an ELL is not successful. ELL students bring such a beauty, drive, story, and resilience to any classroom. If innocently ignorant to what it takes to reach and teach ELLs, teach with the best place to start, the heart. But be tough. TLC, in my book, is not tender loving care; it is tough love culture. Push ELLs to give them strength in their language acquisition and content mastery. Our job as teachers of ELLs is to empower them to empower themselves, to fuel them with knowledge, and to arm them with a voice that will inevitably be heard in two or more languages. It is their human right. It is our civic responsibility to ensure ALL children have that right.

Vazquez: My philosophy about this is that we need to create schools and places of work that are welcoming to the whole person, whoever you are. It's not just about the kids bringing their whole selves to the table; the teachers have to do that too. I also have to do that for it to work. It's not a one-sided deal. Although I am a progressive educator, it's not about coddling kids but about being authentic in our engagement. We need to be constructivist and creative and open to a lot of possibilities.

Table 12.3 Guides for Gifted and Talented Education

Revathi Balakrishnan

2016 Texas Teacher of the Year

2011 Region XIII GT Teacher of the Year

Talented and Gifted Specialist

Patsy Sommer Elementary

Round Rock, TX

Fifth-Grade Language Arts and Social Studies

Charles Giglio

2015 New York Teacher of the Year

Adjunct Professor, State University of New York at Albany

Gloversville High School

Gloversville, NY

Latin

Two Takeaway Ideas That You Can Put to Work in Your Classroom

1. Students Need Teachers to Guide Them to Rich Content

Balakrishnan: One of the misconceptions about gifted and talented (GT) learners is that they know everything. They do not know everything; they just have the capacity to absorb at a faster rate. It seems like they know everything because they can pick up a book about anything and absorb it at a very fast rate. They can learn a concept in three days that would take three weeks in a regular classroom. Just because they get it faster doesn't mean they already know it—you still have to expose them to it.

If they make a mistake, it's like, "You're gifted, you should know this." Well, they're just like any other kid. Kids in poverty who are gifted need more background knowledge. If you give them the opportunity to read a wide variety of text, they will take off. All they need is for you to point them in the right direction. Gifted children are highly interested in one topic, and they will pursue anything on that topic.

Here, too, in the GT classroom, there needs to be differentiation. There is a wide range of GT kids. You have the one who is slightly gifted to the one who is profoundly gifted. And everything that goes on with differentiation in the regular classroom has to go on in the GT classroom: the handholding and the guiding, the interest surveys, the books you pull. That's what you do for the gifted student. Again, I go back to if you're not a master of your subject, then direct teach works because it's very scripted. It kind of works as a guide for a first-year or second-year teacher. After that, you've got to ask questions based on where the students come from.

All the behavior problems arise because things come easy to them. They don't have good study habits, typically. Even a gifted student will maximize at some point in terms of knowledge and drive. In third and fourth grade, when the curriculum is easy, that's when you should build the study habits. Even if you can do the problems in your head, you need the practice of writing them down and showing your ideas.

2. Children Flourish When Learning Includes Their Inner Lives

Giglio: I love Plato's *Allegory of the Cave* and the question of "What is truth, and how do you know it?" I want the kids to start asking those questions on their own. But I present them first from the masters. We'll listen to Mozart's *Requiem*, for example, and link it to the life of a serf in the Middle Ages and why resting in peace was so enticing for people who worked all their lives.

They looked forward to *requiescat in pace* (RIP; means "may he or she rest in peace"). We even get the idea of resting from the fact that people worked all the time—and we do too. We may not do physical labor, but we're under the gun to produce every day for someone else, whether it's as a teacher, a principal, a boss, a parent. And you think, where can I get some respite? How did the ancients do it?

We'll do a module on *De Amore*, on love, and we'll start with Aristotle. We have a set of six questions we came up with. I try to get them to interview their grandparents. They are so surprised to find out that grandma fell in love with grandpa. Then we share the answers with the class.

The questions are as follows:

- What is your definition of love?
- When did you first fall in love?
- What is their advice about love?
- How did you meet your love?
- What do you think about love now?
- What would you recommend to other people about falling in love?
- What advice would you give to me?

You don't have to be religious to realize that there's a spiritual part of us that needs to be fed. Don't be afraid to say the word *soul*. People are so afraid that you're talking about God—and by the way, so were the Greeks and the Romans and everybody else, but it's part of our culture. It's how the ancients explained the world. Be inquisitive about how other people defined our universe. Don't you want to find out how you fit into and make contributions?

Standards Met by Activities, Strategies, and Practice in This Chapter

Council for Exceptional Children

Special Education Professional Ethical Principles

1. Maintaining challenging expectations for individuals with exceptionalities to develop the highest possible learning outcomes and quality of life potential in ways that respect their dignity, culture, language, and background

Special Education Standards for Professional Practice 1.4

Create safe, effective, and culturally responsive learning environments which contribute to fulfillment of needs, stimulation of learning, and realization of positive self-concepts. (Council for Exceptional Children, 2015)

Council of Chief State School Officers
English Language Proficiency Standards

Guiding Principles

1. Potential: ELLs have the same potential as native speakers of English to engage in cognitively complex tasks. Regardless of ELP level, all ELLs need access to challenging, grade-appropriate curriculum, instruction, and assessment and benefit from activities requiring them to create linguistic output (Ellis, 2008a; 2008b). Even though ELLs will produce language that includes features that distinguish them from their native-English-speaking peers, "it is possible [for ELLs] to achieve the standards for college-and-career readiness" (Council of Chief State School Officers, 2017, p. 1).

2. Multimedia, Technology, and New Literacies: New understandings around literacy (e.g., visual and digital literacies) have emerged around use of information and communication technologies (International Reading Association, 2009). Relevant, strategic, and appropriate multimedia tools and technology, aligned to the ELP Standards, should be integrated into the design of curriculum, instruction, and assessment for ELLs.

National Association for Gifted Children

Standards 3.1.3 and 3.1.4

> Educators adapt, modify, or replace the core or standard curriculum to meet the needs of students with gifts and talents and those with special needs such as twice-exceptional, highly gifted, and English Language Learners.
>
> Educators design differentiated curricula that incorporate advanced, conceptually challenging, in-depth, distinctive, and complex content for students with gifts and talents. (National Association for Gifted Children, n.d.)

Resources for Further Exploration and Enrichment

Equity resources from FSG and the Aspen Institute for Community Solutions: http://collectiveimpactforum.org/resources/equity-resources

Insights Into Inclusive STEM High Schools from the National Science Foundation: https://inclusivesteminsights.sri.com/resources.html

Omniglot Online Encyclopedia of Writing Systems and Languages: www.omniglot.com

ELL and bilingual resources from Colorín Colorado (WETA): www.colorincolorado.org

National Association for Gifted Children resources: www.nagc.org/resources-publications/resources

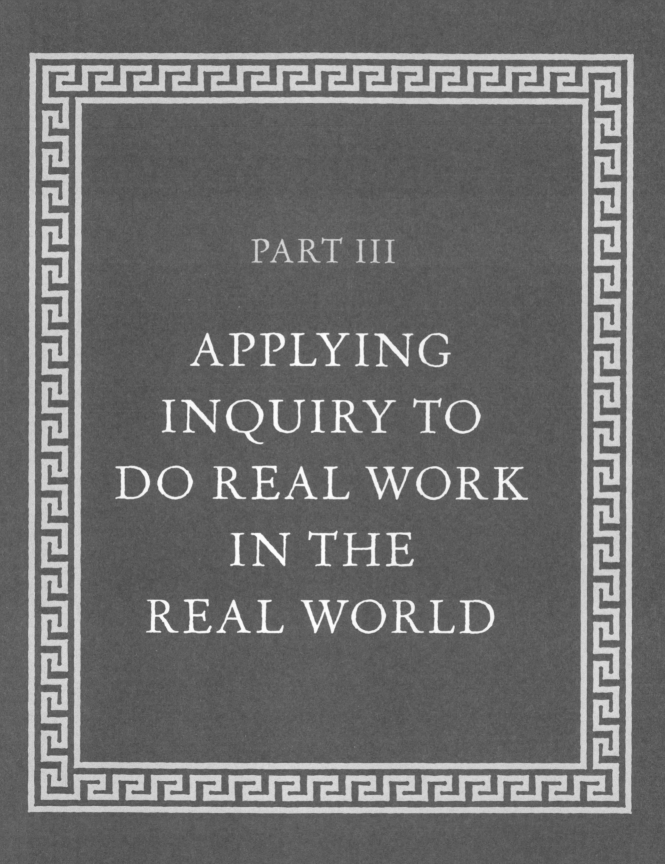

PART III

APPLYING
INQUIRY TO
DO REAL WORK
IN THE
REAL WORLD

> Socrates . . . is the first philosopher of life. . . . Thinking serves life, while among all previous philosophers life had served thought and knowledge. . . . Thus Socratic philosophy is absolutely practical: it is hostile to all knowledge unconnected to ethical implications.
>
> **—FRIEDRICH NIETZSCHE**

TESTS CAN'T PREDICT THE FUTURE

Tuan looked like a seventh grader's version of a gangster—skinny as a minute, practice tattoos from a friend dotting his knuckles, he laughed at everything. He wore lots of red: a flat-brimmed baseball cap pulled low over his eyes, a red basketball jersey over a white T-shirt, red shoes, his neck roped with silver chains.

"Hey, hey, Miss Gangsta Teacher, what's up?"

His laugh was high and silly. And charming. I found myself looking forward to the fact that he would laugh at even my worst jokes.

"Mrs. Loughlin IS a gangster," I said, laughing with him, teasing my friend and colleague, Elaine, who'd brought me over to the high school to help her teach night class.

"I'm not Miss Gangster Teacher. I'm Mrs. Loughlin," she said, thoroughly unamused.

"No, you Miss Gangsta because you teach me to pass the test."

And we wanted him to pass. My pride wanted him to pass to prove that what we were doing in our classes worked on even the most seemingly hopeless cases like Tuan. At eighteen, Tuan was down to his last try on the test for graduation. I told him that if he passed I'd take him to dinner at the most expensive steak house in town. He laughed and said I could just bring it to him takeout.

We sat with him night after night, giving him various test hacks to help him get to the magic numbers that would give him the barest passing minimum. We helped him think in Vietnamese, then translate that over into English by drawing pictures as a form of annotation.

Elaine pushed him—and me—to stay focused. Between us, we struggled to find a narrative he could use to crack the writing portion. He only needed to get fifty-two lines of a workable story, written in basic grammar and legibly printed, to pass.

"Me and my friend, we like to go and have fun," he told us when we probed his memory for noteworthy stories. Rounds of clarifying questions uncovered a thin anecdote about how he and his friend Phuong liked to go bowling. Torturously, he transcribed this story over and over, memorizing it so he could repeat it on the test and make it fit whatever prompt he faced.

Miraculously, all of this worked, and Tuan passed his test.

Beyond proud, my ego used this information to fill a hole that the difficult school year had cratered into me. *Super teacher*, it said, troweling flattery over all the emptiness. *You're a super teacher who can get kids to pass when nobody else can.*

But there's a coda to this neat arc of success: shortly after his testing victory, Tuan was arrested and held on $500,000 bond for armed robbery.

"He and his friend are the ones behind all those robberies on the boulevard. They're both in jail," our principal explained, interrupting us as we sat planning how to get Tuan that steakhouse meal. "He put a gun in a woman's face right after she drove home from closing the restaurant. Can you imagine?"

Elaine and I looked at each other. What was there to say? That our boy was going to get his diploma in jail? The next day, I couldn't eat my lunch as I read the details in the newspaper. The facts of the case made me feel like someone shoved an icicle into my stomach. Tuan, according to the timelines, was walking out of our tutorials, meeting up with his buddy Phuong, and executing a string of robberies.

All I'd picked up on was his silliness and how hard he worked on his test prep. His goofiness kept me from paying attention to anything else about him. Over the summer, scenes from our classes played in my head. I believed I was complicit in enabling an alibi for him. These feelings coalesced into a deep doubt about teaching. Why, I wondered, should I even keep teaching when this was what happened? "You're a super teacher all right," my brain said. "Super naive."

Eventually, I came to view Tuan as a caveat for teaching in an era where its metrics of achievement are measured with test scores and branded with qualifiers like "effectiveness." When I've prompted people to define what effectiveness as a teacher means, many have answered with various takes on what we call college and career readiness. But pushing harder on this answer reveals that most of what we consider as readiness is a high score on a standardized test.

No test can tell you with any accuracy what will become of the tester once he or she leaves the testing center. At least in Tuan's case it couldn't. Tuan failed the most basic test of humanity, but according to his scale score — and to some of the rhetoric from reformers and consultants — he's a model of how a focus on "the test" yields results. Elaine and I were amazingly successful with him in that regard. We gave him no excuses. We insisted on hard work.

My experience with Tuan caused me to spend time asking myself and my colleagues to reflect on this idea that seems to be watermarked into not only our contracts but the current conception of what "good" teaching is. We asked ourselves this: Is the test really all we want for our own kids? Should we cooperate with a system that forces it as the main sorting of students—and particularly students of color? What unforeseen consequences might result from an overfocus on test-based curriculum?

My story—*Tuan and Phuong, Instead of Bowling, Commit Armed Robbery After School*—is a powerful narrative for me and characterizes how I view successful teaching. For me, it is based on structuring learning experiences giving students practice in situations that strengthen their ability to become good people. Our success as teachers, in this measurement, is everything we do to help kids with those old-fashioned ideas of citizenship, of courtesy, kindness, and decency.

"His parents, they call him dust boy," one of my other students told me about Tuan, using the Vietnamese expression for the term. She clapped her hands together in demonstration, pulling them apart and puffing against them as if she were blowing on a dandelion. "It means he is nothing."

◇◇

What might have happened if I'd focused more globally on Tuan and his abilities? That's a question that keeps me thinking years after Tuan began serving a decades-long probation for his crimes. What if I'd resisted the tunnel vision that pushed me to see only his test-taking prospects? Tuan's legacy is that he pointed me toward becoming a better teacher by connecting kids to their communities in positive ways that would give them the opportunity to do real work in the real world. I'm far from the first to have this idea. It's often described as service learning or project-based learning, but for me it is the way to truly personalize learning in a meaningful way.

Creating those experiences for students who are typically shunted into test prep became a moral imperative for me as well. Researchers from Georgetown University found that "each year, there are 111,000 high-scoring African-American and Hispanic students who either do not attend college or don't graduate. About 62,000 of these students come from the bottom half of the family income distribution" (Carnevale & Strohl, 2013).

The reasons for that are complex, containing strands of fixed mindsets in college recruiters who overlook poorer schools, white racial privilege, and variabilities in "soft skills" like executive functioning and motivation. Often, I suspect, we simply don't present a compelling reason for students to persevere in school beyond needing to pass a test. That works well for the adults whose career aspirations hinge on a demonstration of raising test scores but not so well for students who need much more support beyond just test-taking skills.

Using Student Questions as a Base for Real Work in the Real World

My newer focus on authentic learning began to take shape for me as I listened to my students and noted their obsessions. Lucy, a junior in my fifth period AP Language class, was livid with annoyance over the craze for the silicone "I Heart Boobies" bracelets sprouting on wrists all over school.

"Guys are just wearing those so they laugh that they're wearing the word *boobies*," she said. "They don't have a clue of what those are for." She decided to start asking boys if they knew anything about the plastic band's connection to breast cancer awareness and then film their answers. "I wanted them to realize how dumb they were, but then even when I started asking girls and adults, no one really could tell me anything about why they were wearing them. They didn't know anything about breast cancer like how to check yourself or that even guys get it."

She wondered why, in an age of nonstop social media campaigns and public service announcements, no one knew much about breast cancer. Her questions coincided with a brand-new unit I'd created. It used student questions as the basis for doing a project to build rhetorical skills for work and school and aimed to affect the community. (See Protocol III.1.)

"Do you think I could do something on that?" she asked as we conferenced about ideas. "Nydia, Addy, Anakaren, Cynthia, and Mariah want to do the same thing." All of these girls shared some things in common: They were bilingual in Spanish and English, they were interested in helping people, and were seriously thinking about careers in the medical field. They shared Lucy's question about why there was so little consciousness of breast cancer in their north Amarillo neighborhood.

Their group formed around questions that came from learning in their science class that Potter County, Texas, has one of the highest breast cancer mortality rates in the state. They found research showing that the disease heavily affects disadvantaged women of color who live in culturally rich communities (Clayton, Brooks, & Kornstein, 2014). One of their discoveries led them to a hypothesis that language was a barrier for many women needing access to information and screening.

"We need to go to their house and tell them this in Spanish," Nydia said. Because the assignment required them to partner with a social service agency, I helped them contact the Amarillo Area Breast Health Coalition (AABHC), which, in turn, supplied them with training and informational resources in Spanish to share. The AABHC also helped to mentor the students into the creation of a bilingual breast health presentation.

Their project was honored at the "Kiss Cancer Goodbye" Breakfast of Champions later in the year. Because they had a desire for this work to live after them, they sought out a sponsor to help create the extracurricular club Women Inspiring Serving and Educating (WISE).

"We know of at least one woman who, because she attended one of these meetings, was connected to mammography services where a cancer was found and she could begin treatment," Denise Rayford, WISE sponsor, told me. She said that the club eventually grew to import many of the more than thirty languages spoken at the school through the membership of Somali, Burmese, Karen, and Kenyan students.

When I reached out to one of the students, Nydia Sotelo, to get her recollections of the experience, she remarked on the fact that their work continued after they graduated. "I was just really surprised how the girls the following year continued the group and expanded it. I remember us going to different classes and talking about it. I thought it was interesting to see girls talking to other girls about a topic we never think about," she said.

Currently, Nydia is finishing a master's degree in social work and can see a connection between the breast cancer project and the work she does today as a counselor. "I remember how confident we all felt. I always knew I wanted to help people, but I never really knew how that was going to look for me. Thinking back to my junior year, I think it helped me to do those presentations. To say, 'You know it's uncomfortable to check yourself for cancer, but it's important.' It's like how I deal with difficult issues. Like right now, I have very difficult conversations with my clients. And I felt more prepared to do that. I can see now, even though I wasn't even thinking this then, that I was practicing helping others."

Nydia Sotelo, third from left, is pictured with Lucy Castanon Murguia, far right, and the other girls in the group who created a bilingual breast health presentation that won recognition from the Amarillo Area Breast Health Coalition.

Source: Photo provided by Lucy Murguia.

That practice in possible futures also helped Lucy, who's also completed a social work degree, and Cynthia, who became a teacher. Other students found that their projects tied into their future education plans. Viet, who cocreated a group of high-achieving seniors to work as tutors for students with language issues and learning problems, used an essay about the project to write a successful admission essay for Harvard.

Yen's group created an ad campaign for Big Brothers Big Sisters of America that was so good she used it as a portfolio piece in her application for the prestigious advertising program at the University of Texas. Oscar, who created a working antibullying video game based on the comic character Scott Pilgrim, used the digital portfolio of his game specifications to gain a scholarship to the Rochester Institute of Technology.

Kelly, whose original documentary was of the difficulties of second-generation Laotian immigrants in maintaining their culture, relied on the skills and confidence she gained in the project to join student government at the University of North Texas. Alex replicated the same experiments in the relationship between gratitude and happiness from the University of Pennsylvania's Martin Seligman's research; Jasmine and Karen worked together to create and teach writing workshops to struggling students at the elementary school they'd both attended as young children.

Using students' own questions as a way to guide projects became a way to "flip" classes in a manner that didn't necessarily require technology but did require students to interact with their communities. Inquiry-based projects became the method for personalizing learning for students, drawing out their assets, like bilingualism, and helping them to use those skills in service of others.

PROTOCOL III.1   Creating and Implementing Inquiry Projects

SUGGESTIONS

- Help students group their questions into bigger categories. For example, questions about justice, unfairness, or equity would be grouped together. Other groupings may be love, relationships, and friendship. These bigger categories will help students begin to focus on the issues they feel most drawn to as projects.

- Present the possibilities for student projects as one of three areas: (1) a change in school policy, (2) a support for underserved students at school, or (3) a partnership with an existing social service agency to work on a community problem. This makes the projects more concrete. For example, students who choose to work on a change in school policy may want to petition administrators for a student advisory board to give student input on decisions. Students who want to work on a support for underserved students at school may decide, as one of my former students did, to create a school spirit organization to build student morale. Those who are interested in community-based issues can generate a list of social service agencies that are already working on a problem they're interested in, such as the Coalition for the Homeless.

- Group students by the problems or areas they're interested in working on (e.g., school-based or community) so they can help each other think through and decide on an area of focus.

CONDITIONS

- Opportunities for directed small group brainstorming and creativity

- A respect for and nurturance of student motivation to create real value for their communities

- Curiosity about the issues that surround them; respect for the people in their environment who struggle and need help

- Comfort with teamwork. For detailed help on creating and supporting teams, see Kahn's (2009) *The Student's Guide to Successful Project Teams*.

MATERIALS

- Curated student questions from previous lessons or writing

- Pack of 3" x 5" cards

- Access to the Internet for researching community issues

- Access to knowledgeable adults in the school (e.g., counselors) who may advise students about needs they could address

- Chart paper to capture ideas

- Handout of the assignment (see the appendix for a model of what I used with advanced placement [AP] students)

TIME

Six to eight weeks

INTRODUCTION

Each of you has a talent or skill that can benefit those around you, and school rarely gives you the opportunity to find true purpose and meaning for your abilities. In this assignment, you will be able to find and focus on an issue you really care about and create a real and workable solution. You will also get the chance to work with adults as equals in solving those problems.

PURPOSE

This project will help you to focus on the kinds of skills people use in businesses, nonprofit organizations, government, and college. These include public speaking, research, technical writing, and problem solving. But you'll also get practice in what employers say are some of the most in-demand skills they look for when they hire people: leadership, collaboration, ability to focus, persistence, and ability to learn from mistakes.

(Continued)

(Continued)

PLAN

1. Give students one class period to work in their shared interest small groups. Set the end of class as the deadline for their first-draft ideas. You may have students write these ideas on individual 3" x 5" cards or one for each group that decides to work together. Groups should not be more than five members.

2. During the second class meeting, give students assignment handouts and answer questions. Lead students through the rubric, and be sure that they understand the level of work required and how they will be assessed. Next, have students decide on roles within the group; they will turn in this role sheet at the end of class. Give students the rest of class to begin working on their project proposals.

3. For the third class meeting, go over the timeline with students, and help students think through their schedules. Decide on a day when you will check in with students to assess progress each week. Students should finish their proposals either as homework or by the end of this class meeting.

4. For the fourth class meeting, have students identify adults to whom they can turn for help and advice. Hand back student proposals and confer with groups, giving feedback on their ideas as needed. Allow students to begin calling on adults who will help them. For younger students, you will act as the main adviser and liaison with anyone needed from outside the classroom.

5. The rest of the class meetings will be at your discretion, but it's easier for students to spend one class day a week working in their groups. Help students navigate meetings outside of class time for when they may want to visit a social service agency or visit with an administrator or possible adult sponsor for in-school activity.

6. The final class period will be used for group presentations of their problem and solution that follow the PechaKucha format of twenty slides (PowerPoint or Google Slides) using a timer of twenty seconds per slide. This gives everyone the same parameters of space and time in their presentation while also allowing for most groups to present during one typical class period. More information about PechaKuchas is available at www.pechakucha.org.

MODIFICATIONS

- You may shorten and narrow the assignment as needed for younger students or struggling students.

- Alternatively, you may choose to invite a panel of community experts to judge group presentations on the assignment rubric and include a question and answer period. If you choose this option, you will need to ask administrators for extended class time to make sure everyone can present to the same panel. (I did this the first year of the project, and it was an enjoyable experience for everyone. Plus, students were able to receive feedback from community experts. The community members had a positive experience in the school and were able to see the abilities of students framed in a way that showcased skills beyond mere test-taking.)

EXTENSIONS

- Gifted and talented (GT) students, pre-AP, AP, or International Baccalaureate students may write individual documented essays to accompany their projects, complete required reading from two or more books for the college-bound reading list that is tied to their topics, and complete an annotated bibliography of their books and research.

- Students may decide to keep documents related to the project in a digital or physical portfolio for use in applying for a job, college, and/or scholarships. ●

CHAPTER 13

Using Student Questions for Project Ideas at All Levels

Do not train a child to learn by force or harshness;
but direct them to it by what amuses their minds,
so that you may be better able to discover with
accuracy the peculiar bent of the genius of each.

—PLATO

One of the ironies of American education is our insistence on "getting kids ready for the real world" yet rarely giving them time and opportunity to interact with it. As a teacher in Title I schools, I felt tremendous pressure to focus solely on test preparation, and any deviation from that was viewed with suspicion at best and meetings with administrators at worst. The theory behind the pressure seems to be that if we can get kids to pass standardized tests, the test scores will get them into college, college will get them into a job, and then the job will get them a good life.

But what if we are brave enough to help our students look up from bubble sheets and workbooks? What would happen if we take them to the windows of our classrooms and have them look outside? Is it possible to connect what they see in the world to what they wonder in their hearts and think in their minds? If we, to paraphrase T. S. Eliot, really want to disturb the universe that's set up to systematize a culture of testing, then we will need all of our courage.

The good news is that it's possible to take our students' questions into the world and allow them to contribute our common good. Making space for that was worth whatever it cost me because it opened so many possibilities for my students and for who and what they might become. As a side benefit, when they generated answers for their questions, they found that they became better readers; mathematicians; thinkers; planners; and learners.

Karen Vogelsang, an elementary teacher from Memphis, Tennessee, became a promoter of questioning for teachers in early childhood classrooms after finding inspiration at Harvard Graduate School of Education's Project Zero.

"It's all about making thinking visible and one way you do that is by encouraging student questioning both orally and in writing," she said. "It's also about using questions to deepen student thinking. Through the progression of the lessons, they discover the answers to their own questions, thereby owning and retaining their learning," she said.

Her work often involved students with significant learning disabilities, and they responded well to her invitations to pose questions.

"Every child feels included and valued. These aspects develop critical thinking and problem solving skills. There is no way to know what skills will be necessary to be successful in life when my new crop of third graders graduate high school. However, critical and creative thinking and problem-solving skills will always be necessary to solve the questions of tomorrow," she said.

"Early childhood teachers must cultivate a culture of curiosity in their students. They are more than capable if teachers will release control to their students. If they don't, they are doing a huge disservice to their students."

A Business Built on What's in Kids' Hearts

Students as young as five or six years old are capable of relating to their communities and the wider world if their ideas are valued and they're given choice, said Ann Marie Corgill (personal communication, March 21, 2017), a first-grade teacher in Birmingham, Alabama. "If we're giving them all the ideas and we're telling them what to write, then there's no engagement. They've got to have choice. They've got to have understanding that 'what I have to say matters'—so every opportunity for them to have choice, whether it's learning how to write poetry or writing about tornados or losing your dog: whatever matters to you in your heart," she said.

She gives her students authentic audiences through work that's displayed inside and outside school and in a blog that the class publishes. Her most ambitious project came from her students' wishes for the world shortly after the 2016 elections. She asked students to think about this question: What are we going to do to get people thinking differently about how we can be human and kind to each other?

"I recorded what they said because I knew I wouldn't get their words exactly if I didn't. It blew my mind. We transcribed it, and they wrote it and we did an illustration study," she said. Students' illustrated wishes went onto a website that Corgill built for them to share their work. From this collection, she and the students created and published a book that sold out. That experience prompted Corgill to guide her students in building their own business to sell kindness-related creations like bookmarks and magnets. The proceeds from www.kindkidscreate.com go back into the classroom to supply more projects or a charity chosen by their school.

Beyond just teaching entrepreneurship and business skills, the project gives her students a sense of purpose. "This matters, and we might change things. They go around the school saying, 'We're going to change the world,'" Corgill said. "We might change somebody's mind. Somebody might not kill anymore. Somebody might not bully anymore. There might be somebody who wants somebody who's a different color as their friend."

A Message Magnet Created by Corgill's Students

Source: Photo provided by Ann Marie Corgill.

Using Questions to Build Connection in Middle School

An easy entry point for teachers who want to try on student-led projects is to have them attach their questions to issues they see in their immediate surroundings or in the schools that feed into theirs. This was how I started with that group of middle school students who were so mean to each other.

In looking for ways to extend their questions into authentic work that would create the conditions for them to practice empathy, I asked them to work with groups of questions in their writing circles to see if they could find patterns in them. The students sorted them into big ideas about feelings, the environment, space, friendship, and other categories. They used these categories to generate ideas for writing.

"What if we used these ideas to write books for the little guys in the elementary school where you used to go to kindergarten?" I asked them. They loved the idea, and the thought of real readers prompted them to see their writing as purposeful.

"We can't just slap this out," Jeremy said. "This is for kids and for them to learn, so we have to make sure it's right."

As students worked in their writing circles to help each other think of ideas, they naturally connected to the idea of audience and decided to focus on high-interest nonfiction topics like tornadoes, spiders, and how to be a good friend. We studied children's books and made anchor charts of what we noticed and could use in this project. While they composed drafts, I conferred with students; others read their work to others for feedback. Because the project was for a real audience and had an authentic purpose, students worked harder on it than anything else I'd seen them do.

Another colleague used PowerPoint as a way of helping students create study guides, and I modified the process to compose and publish student books. We agreed to use ten pages for each book to standardize them for the young readers. The middle school authors worked with the librarian during one class period to learn how to search for usable images to illustrate their books. Each slide became a designed page, and the deck was easy to peer edit. They helped each other catch mistakes as I checked in with each author as a final editor.

We received special permission to print out each slide deck because they were ink intensive, but my principal saw the value of the work. Each slide was laminated, trimmed, hole-punched, then bound together with plastic rings. As they finished putting the books together, I worked with administrators to find the right time to present and read the books.

We decided to use the day right before Thanksgiving break, and I secured an assistant principal and paraprofessional to help guide classes of students to the school, which was in easy walking distance from ours. The plan was for students to read the books one-on-one to kindergarteners and first graders, then leave the books for each class to have as a gift.

Julio, a dyslexic student whose learning challenges caused him to be a behavior problem in most classes, eagerly read his book to child after child. Because Julio had attended this school when he was younger, the staff knew him well.

"I can't believe what I'm seeing," his former counselor said. "I honestly didn't know what would become of him because of all the trouble he's had and how hard it is for him at home. To see him be so gentle, so patient with these kids—I just have no words," she said, pressing her fingers to the corners of her eyes to keep tears from blurring her mascara.

LESSON 13.1   Lesson Plan
Creating Easy Shareable Books

The conditions you need are as follows:

- Good relationships with administrators and other staff
- Shared understanding of the workshop model of literacy with students and administrators
- Knowledge of what resources such as computers and printers are available and how you can access them

(Continued)

(Continued)

- A rationale for the use of time and resources to create a shared literacy experience that benefits all learners involved
- Dedicated time for students to plan, research, revise, and edit

MATERIALS

- Children's books to act as mentor texts (good ones are single-subject nonfiction books on weather, insects, and other phenomena. Ask your librarian to find a range of nonfiction topics that also touch on ideas like families, friendship, and other subjects of interest to younger readers.)
- Computers (we booked time in the computer lab once we had our paper drafts done.)
- PowerPoint or Google Slides
- A color printer
- A laminator
- A three-hole punch
- Half-inch plastic rings (available at craft stores); enough for three rings on each finished book
- Time to print and laminate student slides outside of class time

TIME

Twelve fifty-minute class periods

One day to visit classes where you will share books

PLAN

1. Students revisit their journals and question cards to find themes and ideas for books and capture them on chart paper. They will work in their writing circles to narrow their idea to a topic they want to research, like tornadoes or friendships.

2. Use one class as a genre study, helping students to pull out elements of the mentor texts that they can use for their own books.

3. Students spend one or two class periods researching their topics and working with the librarian to find fair use images to save in digital folders for use in their books.

4. Students then begin drafting their books, making sure to note where they got their information, paraphrase it, and cite their sources. (Children as young as third grade are able to do this with guidance.) They can return to the anchor charts about the genre and consult the mentor texts to see how authors make information interesting for readers.

5. Students share first drafts in writing circles and confer with teacher for feedback.

6. Use one class period for revision.

7. Two class periods will be needed for composing and editing the final drafts.

8. One class period will be needed to assemble books.

9. One class period will be needed to visit the classes where students will share books.

10. You may choose to use one more class period to debrief the process.

MODIFICATIONS

Struggling students can work with a paraprofessional or complete sentence stems created with guidance and help from the special education coordinator or English language learner (ELL) coordinator.

EXTENSIONS

- I modified this assignment and extended it for use with my ELLs and refugee students when I began teaching high school. Because I had no books in Swahili, Somali, or Arabic, the students created them. For languages like Thai, Burmese, and other languages, we couldn't access a keyboard for composing; students wrote the first language by hand and then took pictures of the sentences to include on each page. Students who had no written language or who were illiterate in their first language worked with a peer or adult language speaker to compose their stories.

- Students used the same process as I described previously to create bilingual books that told a simple story (based on a well-known saying from their countries such as, "Be patient and you'll get what you want") in their first language and in English. They then illustrated them with their own drawings. Students uploaded photos of these drawings into the slides. As a final step, they recorded themselves reading the books in their first language and in English. The MP3 audio files were housed on our class website for access to parents, siblings, or anyone else who wanted to hear and read the book in two languages. ●

Projects as a Way of Helping Students Identify Their Guiding Principles

Members of Mairi Cooper's (personal communication, November 18, 2017) orchestra at Fox Chapel Area High School in Pennsylvania and in Richard Ognibene's (personal communication, August 5, 2017) chemistry class at Fairport High School in New York share one thing in common: teachers who push their students to think beyond the content into what kind of people they want to become.

"If I make 100 kids into chemists, but they're bad people, that's not a win," Ognibene said. "Selfishly, I want them to be good people, and I think that's why we live. You talk to somebody twenty years after graduation, they never remember the content, they remember the humanity. They remember those things that made them happy or feel loved, or encouraged them to be a better person. The physics they'll remember until June for the test, but if I want to be a teacher with impact, I've got to teach more than physics or chemistry."

Similarly, Cooper asks big questions of her music students: What is your philosophy? What are your guiding principles? In thinking through what they valued and wanted to leave as a legacy of their learning, her students decided to create four pillars to help them put their philosophies into practice:

1. **Have access to music**—Regardless of barriers like socioeconomics or ableness

2. **Give education**—Reaching out to underserved potential musicians

3. **Build audiences**—Performing in unusual spaces where they can cocreate, like museums

4. **Encourage joy and the love of playing**—Extending creativity and generativity into thematic multimedia presentations

After students created and agreed on the four pillars, Cooper led them through a brainstorming session of deciding where they could create pop-up concerts to match each pillar. Students then voted on which pillar and pop-up concert they would begin planning first. All orchestra students worked on the design of the concerts but were required to play only one of them. She was most surprised by the concert they planned for access at a local school for the blind.

"They want to play for them, but then they want to break out into stations, and they want to teach them how to play the instruments," Cooper said.

"But they also want to pair with students who will teach my students to read music in braille. So they want it to be a back-and-forth, because we spent a lot of time talking about when you're giving you're also receiving."

Students decided to plan concerts at a middle school for education, a flower-based multimedia show at Phipps Conservatory to encourage the joy of playing, and a cocreated science performance at the Carnegie Science Center to build their audiences.

Ognibene's students have created a gay-straight alliance at the school and helped plan celebrations for Brotherhood/Sisterhood Week to build community. These larger projects begin with small decisions about how he begins classes each fall. He requires students to interview each other during the first week of school along with participating in small ice-breakers to get his students comfortable with talking to people different from themselves.

"The expectation in my room is that any child can ask any other child for help. That's nonnegotiable," Ognibene said. "If you have the ability to answer a question that somebody asks you, that takes the barriers down around the fear. They appreciate being forced to sometimes go outside of their comfort zone because in the teen moral code, you don't do that."

Other choices he makes includes an authentic discussion during Red Ribbon Week of substance abuse and the people they know who are affected by addiction. During Brotherhood/Sisterhood Week, they discuss the various "isms" that divide people like racism and sexism, then write a personal narrative about their own experiences of being targeted for their differences from the dominant culture.

"I started it twenty-two years ago. Another teacher and I were called by the principal to a meeting with a group of parents, mostly parents of color, about how we could make our school feel more welcoming," he said. "When you're 93 percent white, it can be really daunting to be a student of color. We have very few Jewish or Muslim kids. And what about the black shirt robotics kids who just want to look at their calculators? So we came up with this idea of 'Fairport Family' and this theme of we all belong. And we try to make people feel loved. It's become the ethos of our district. It makes it a much better place for kids to show up, a much better place to work."

But this kind of connection doesn't come without risks. Creating community is hard and takes time. For many teachers, they don't understand the connection between working on the climate and culture of their classrooms when there's so much content to cover.

"But that's what they remember," Ognibene argued. "They're not used to teachers sharing a little bit of humanity and caring. It's not that other people don't have it in their heart. It's just that it's never crossed their minds that this would be important. You know, 'I'm teaching algebra. Why should I have to compliment Timmy on the basketball game?' Because to Timmy, it's the most important thing in his world right now."

He stressed that the process is helped by having good classroom systems in place as well as good relationships with administrators. "It's not, you walk in and say, 'Hey, we're just going to talk about feelings all day long.' Because yeah, they'll walk all over you. I think that balance of structure and love—at the secondary level, we focus so much on the structure that we lose sight of the love. Because, jeez, we've got the state test and we've got to do this or that. So finding that balance of what works for you as a person and what meets the needs of your students is hard."

Using Current Events as Easy Entry Points Into More Student Engagement

Another small step in allowing my students to try on autonomy, research, and connection came through an old required reading whose volumes were literally covered with dust in the English storeroom: *Walden and Civil Disobedience* by Henry David Thoreau (1849, 1852).

I wondered if Thoreau, a person I view as not only the original hipster but also one of the first people to perform a kind of reality show, could cause shifts in thinking about technology.

The bigger questions to frame the reading were these:

> What is our relationship to technology? How much of our relationships with humans have we given over to machines, especially the small ones we carry around as phones? What do we gain and what do we lose from staring at screens all day?

Children increasingly struggle with the consequences of technology, and helping them interact with each other face-to-face is becoming critical.

Social media leads many of us, not just students, to mistake likes, comments, and retweets for relationship. Experiences that disrupt this relationship can help them see their own difficulties in sitting in undistracted quiet. Unshackled from their phones, they begin to look around them. Projects and service learning opportunities then become a meaningful way to satisfy deeper human needs for purpose, connectedness, and worth.

When my students read Thoreau and Emerson, we played with the idea of the "Walden challenge," where students tried a tiny bit of Thoreau's deliberate withdrawal from society. During one full class period, they agreed to lock up all of their electronics in my cabinet and note what happened to their brains without the constant distraction.

Next, we went outside and spent time in silence, noticing the natural environment. I asked students to note what they responded to, whether we went out onto the front lawn or took a walk across the baseball diamond, soccer field, or around the track. Many of them became anxious for the first part of the challenge, then more peaceful. Most reported experiencing "phantom vibrations" from their absent phones, which always startled them.

As a closing activity, we wrote about these noticings and then reentered Thoreau's essays. Students played with the famous quotes, substituting their current tech for parts of the sentences. For example, "We do not ride upon the railroad, it rides upon us" was altered to "We do not play XBox, it plays us."

Nate Bowling breathes new life into older texts for students in his after-school book club. Almost two dozen of his government and geography students gathered for ninety minutes to compare Ayn Rand's objectivist philosophy with the current policies of the Republican majority in Congress. He's helped students to channel their thinking into concrete actions like drafting a petition for the Tacoma City Council to increase funding for homeless children and public transit. His students also lobbied state legislators to provide funding for low-income students to attend college.

"I think about government as a language, so I think about it like Spanish class," Bowling said. "If you only think about Spanish in Spanish class, you'll never improve your Spanish. But if you're thinking about Spanish all the time and practicing it and reading in it, you'll be better off. So I push my students to immerse themselves in the world of government and to be thoughtful observers of government."

Creating a Space for Students to Engage With Community Outside of School

When things go wrong in a class, it's tempting to abandon deeper learning projects. It took me years to understand the power of moving toward the trouble rather than away from it. What I mean by that is a deliberate decision to become curious about procedural and behavioral problems rather than become annoyed by them. This can be as simple as taking a student aside and privately asking about what's going on for them.

Jahana Hayes (personal communication, September 24, 2017) decided to try this after seeing her freshman history students tune out day after day. She discovered that seven of them shared one thing in common that she'd missed in the early weeks of school: Each had lost a parent to cancer. Those students had formed a support network around another girl in class who'd recently lost her father and whose mother was in hospice.

"I was devastated. First of all, how do I not know that? And then second, these kids don't care about anything I'm saying. How do you teach kids who are in crisis?" Hayes said. "I was so focused on the lessons that I forgot that there are people in the room who are dealing with life."

In response, she began asking students these questions:

- What is important to you?
- If you could change something in this community, what would it be?
- How can we get involved in changing the things that are happening around us?

With seventeen of her students, Hayes cocreated an after-school club that they named Helping Out People Everywhere, eventually growing it to 130 students. Their first collective action was to participate in a Relay for Life as a way to respond to the cancer affecting them. The club's next focus became their neighborhood as they planned, made phone calls, and organized volunteers for a cleanup and repair campaign.

"Kids started out saying, 'Well, this is a problem that's too big for a fifteen-year-old to work on,' to then taking a great amount of pride that a group of fifteen-year-olds got together and began to address this problem. They illuminated it in such a way that adults who were positioned to help joined them," Hayes said.

To give her students experiences beyond their neighborhoods, she partnered with Habitat for Humanity and set the group's sights on New Orleans, which was thousands of miles away from their homes in Connecticut. Because they were an independent after-school organization, the club would need to raise its own money to travel. Hayes signed them up with a grocery chain's loyalty card program and encouraged staff and parents to designate the club as beneficiaries of the program's charity, giving whenever they shopped. Students contacted local professionals and businesses to get donations, enlisted parents in working a pancake breakfast for a staff development day, and baked pies for sale at Christmas.

Once students were onsite for Habitat, the ones who were sixteen and older could build the homes, but younger students volunteered at a local school where they brought books and school supplies. Returning home, students found ways to give back even if their schedules were heavy with class work, jobs, or extracurricular activities. For example, a student who wanted to help the women's shelter but couldn't volunteer during regular hours decided to bake desserts and pair them with books to deliver for the residents. This became the Tuesday Book Club at the center.

"It was one of those things where we tried to figure out how she could be involved even though she didn't have much time," Hayes said. "You know, 'Let's take what you love, what you're good at, and turn that into a service project.'"

This kind of personalized volunteering gained parent support, and the district's superintendent took notice.

"And then in the end, you get improved student performance. My superintendent would say, 'Show me how this is quantifiable, how this is measurable.' And it's one of those things where you just have to trust that you've given students the tools to be inquisitive, critical thinkers and problem solvers, and now we need to let them use those tools. I taught students about democracy or the voting process, and now I need them to demonstrate to me what it looks like in the community to be a citizen."

PART IV

USING OUR OWN QUESTIONS TO TRANSFORM OUR PRACTICE

> Our society has been prepared to appreciate nothing but ostentation: nowadays you can fill men up with nothing but wind and then bounce them about like balloons. But this man, Socrates, did not deal with vain notions: his aim was to provide us with matter and precepts which genuinely and intimately serve our lives.

—MICHEL DE MONTAIGNE

Every teacher I know has a professional development story that stands out from so many numbing experiences as a truly awful example of how bad it can be. Here's mine:

Because of the rise in school shootings nationwide, my district, like others in the United States, added mandatory "active shooter training" for teachers into the two days before classes began in the fall.

For this particular training on my campus, we were herded into our school's auditorium. On the bare stage, a lone male police officer paced under a spotlight, holding a microphone. To me, it looked like the set of a 1990s-era stand-up comedian. It must have seemed that way to our speaker as well. He cracked himself up, especially when he found ways to insert sexist commentary into whatever information he presented.

"Now, ladies," he said, his deep Texas accent drawling out the vowels. "Y'all are the worst in the world when it comes to a lock and secure drill. Y'all need to get off your cell phones when that's going on. It ain't a time to call your husband and ask him what you need to make for dinner."

He continued his presentation, holding up a hammer.

"Ladies, y'all know what this is? It's a hammer, and it ain't gonna mess up your manicure. In fact, it'll save your life because you can break a window and escape," he said.

This was the most informative part of his talk. Wielding a hammer was the summation of what we should know and be able to do in the event of a violent person on our campus. The presentation not only was a complete waste of time but it also managed to generate extra work in the form of complaints several of us wrote afterward.

While most professional development isn't as egregious as this example, much of it follows a pattern of being

- Mass produced for an entire faculty
- Passive
- Mandatory
- Irrelevant to individual teachers or whole departments
- Hierarchical—one or two described experts dispensing knowledge
- Canned or scripted
- Unengaging—mostly lecture

Sometimes I worry that we've helped encourage shallow and insipid "trainings" by asking for more "tips, tricks, and techniques." If we're honest, we know many of us have whole file cabinets full of these that we've never looked at again. Our insistence on these quick fixes is fueled by the stress around us, which encourages us to react rather than reflect. Also, it's much easier to tune in and out of these kinds of sessions, both physically and intellectually. That's why I often preferred them to deeper, more collaborative experiences where I might be asked to trust my ability to think and create with other teachers.

Talking with Parker Palmer helped me understand the relationship between the separateness reinforced in so much of our in-service days and the professional silence it creates.

"When you are able to isolate people from one another, you prevent them from effectively resisting the worst of the rules and the most toxic of the institutional structures," he said. "I think what part of the power of the courage to teach does for teachers is that it gives them the firsthand experience of the power of community."

The teacher retreats he founded at the Center for Courage and Renewal slow down the process of personal and professional development, spreading it over two years. During that time, teachers attend three-day retreats five to eight times.

"The first thing they learn is that they're not alone with their concerns," he said. "I think it's an ancient reality that if you have a concern about a big issue and you are cut off from other people in a way that makes you think you're the only one with the concern, you pretty soon start thinking you're the crazy one instead of holding on to the rightful belief that the world is crazy."

A Fear of Losing Control

No other experience makes me feel more empathy for my students than being ordered to attend a meeting or session where someone uses the time to read PowerPoint slides, lecture us about school rules, or worse, hold us hostage to their performance. It makes me feel powerless, invisible, and disrespected. If you feel the same way, it's because these kinds of terrible meetings are the rule rather than the exception. Surveys of U.S. teachers report that 90 percent of teachers attend similarly ineffective experiences every year. Seen in light of the $3 billion allocated to professional development from Title II funds, this is not only an expensive problem but one that calls on us to change how we teach teachers (Darling-Hammond, Wei, Andree, Richardson, & Ophanos, 2009).

In debriefs and evaluations of sessions I've either facilitated or helped to facilitate, teachers and administrators report learning more when they had many opportunities to do the following:

- Talk to each other.
- Share resources and practical ideas specific to their context.
- Take part in experiential learning.

Even though this approach is backed by research and makes sense to most practitioners, it's not the norm in the United States. Why is that? My sense is that it's for the same reason that the kind of learning I've argued for in this book is not the norm: power issues. Just as many teachers are uncomfortable with the power they must necessarily cede in order to invite student curiosity, creativity, and collaboration into their classrooms, many administrators struggle to give teachers similar trust. To give teachers autonomy seems like an abdication of their role and an erosion of their authority. This creates a cycle of pressure and explains why so much professional development exists as a frayed patchwork stitched together from habit, familiar faces, and promotional flyers fished out of a folder.

Giving teachers a daily collaboration time doesn't help if a hierarchy outside of classrooms controls what happens in the meetings. When you require teachers to fill out forms as "evidence of work" done in the meeting, that's no better than a classroom where students do nothing but worksheets. In my experience, administrators mean well but aren't allowed to be instructional leaders. They often find themselves required to sit in on teacher collaboration where they make all the decisions and do most of the talking.

The cycle continues at the district level as leaders, who answer to a board, are required to account for the time given to these meetings. It's easier to label these a "professional learning community" than complain about the inability of staff to change their practice. Board members must account to community, state, and federal departments that fund schools with tax dollars, while pressured to show evidence of student gains.

> The major characteristic of this age is fear and it's being cultivated by fear of the other, fear of the poor, fear of the immigrants, fear of refugees, fear of Muslims. It's always what leaders do to get some power. They get us to be terribly afraid of others so they can then guarantee our safety, which of course is a false promise.
>
> —MARGARET WHEATLEY

"I think it's a consequence of our obsession with outcomes and results," Palmer said. "One of the things I constantly talk about with my audiences is that if we remain obsessed with outcomes and results and don't have any higher standard than that, what's going to happen is very predictable: We're going to take on smaller and smaller tasks. Because they're the only ones you can get results with. Which means, in education, we're no longer interested in educating a child; we're interested in getting kids to pass tests, and that's a very different task. It's one where we enjoy the comfort of the illusion that we're getting results that matter."

Even those principals and superintendents who feel that they've encouraged or given permission to teachers still need to make sure they equip teachers with structures for giving and receiving genuine feedback—some of which I share in the next chapter. This is a step toward creating the kinds of conversations that move teaching and learning forward.

CHAPTER 14

Using Teacher Questions to Guide Staff Meetings and Plan Professional Development

Employ your time in improving yourself by other men's writings, so that you shall gain easily what others have labored hard for.

—SOCRATES

LA MAESTRA

My first week of teaching was disastrous: I cried every day driving home and grabbed the phone to call my editor to beg for my job back at the newspaper more than once.

The only job opening at the time was for a seventh-grade writing teacher, and I took it with the kind of hubris that only a nonteacher would. Any delusions of being like a teacher in the movies were quickly dismantled by the realities of facing streetwise and suspicious twelve-year-olds.

About two months into daily ego erasures courtesy of the boy sitting in the first seat on the first row, I ginned up my courage to make my first parent phone call to express concern about Juan.

Juan, a jittery, hormonal, bored boy, spent his time drawing genitalia on his desk and ignoring our reading to work on writing love notes to the girl two rows over. During read-alouds, he coaxed other boys into wrestling and shadow boxing. When I asked most anything of him, he responded by rolling his eyes and making a sucking noise with his teeth.

"Man, I hate this class," he said as he commenced to carving *U SUK* into his desktop.

You suck.

This critique, one I'd thought of myself so many times, was enough to snap me out of the fear of calling his parents. With the school counselor's translation, I was able to detail all of Juan's crimes against my authority into vivid Spanish.

"His father is very upset and wants you to know he will handle this," Olivia said, hanging up.

And that was that, I believed. Nothing more would come of it. To soothe my still-trembling self-image, I imagined some possible scenarios where Juan would have his Nintendo locked away or be made to mow every lawn on his block for free.

The next day, I was surprised when he and his father came to my room after school. Juan's father stepped in, bent forward from stoop labor, his hands raw, his face lined from years of squinting.

I was afraid that he had come to tell me that I was a fraud and to demand that his son be transferred to another class. But my defensiveness quickly dropped when he took off his snap-back ball hat, speaking to me in the tones usually reserved for those in power.

"Ms. Peeples," he began, "I come to apologize for Juan's disrespect to you." He pulled Juan forward and looked at him. "This lady is one you respect. This is *la maestra*. She is teaching you so you don't be like me. You respect *la maestra*, and you apologize."

La maestra.

I'd never heard the term before. He called me *la maestra*.

The teacher.

Whether he knew it or not, Juan's father reversed all my resentment and self-pity. All I could do was respond by smiling and thanking him profusely.

"No, I thank you," he said.

I stood, staring at the door after they'd left, feeling my heart squeezing inside me. Juan's father gave me a title and an identity that I carry to this day as an honor, as a burden, as a responsibility, as a noble title, as the description of my life's work.

Source: Peeples (2017).

◇◇◇

This anecdote was forgotten to me until a colleague invited me to think deeply about a question of calling and identity. We were together in a small group attempting to use our own questions as topics for professional development. We'd each written several questions we wanted to explore on cards and then distributed them among ourselves, choosing which one resonated with us. I chose this one:

> I don't feel like a respected professional anymore and it's hard to be here, but I love the kids. If teaching is a calling, is there a way to get back to that idea that feels authentic? Is there a way to think about our identities as teachers that will help us when we feel burned out?

Once we chose a question, we decided to sit with it for a minute of silent reflection, then "write into the question," putting down whatever thoughts, stories, or ideas came to mind within a ten-minute window of writing. The anonymous question above helped me to think deeply about a time when I first started to think of myself as "a real teacher."

Until we are able to reclaim our own stories, we adopt the stories of others, allowing ourselves to adopt their definitions of us, their purpose for us, their meaning of what school and education are about. When we share them with each other, we are practicing a form of professional development that is personal and sustainable. Marshall Ganz (2009) calls this the "power of public narrative and the art of leadership storytelling" (p. 19). He writes that we "have to claim authorship of [our] story and learn to tell it to others so they can understand the values that move [us] to act, because it might move them to act as well" (p. 19).

Both the easiest and the most profound practice I adopted as a department chair and staff developer was to welcome teachers to write as a way to begin meetings, then find a partner and read to each other.

When I began with the question protocol I'd been using with students, that small opening reshaped our time together, creating depth and connection more quickly than silly icebreakers or other getting-to-know-you exercises. We have fear and hesitation around speaking with each other this way. I think our profession's implicit demands to be up and be on creates the same kind of loneliness and isolation for teachers as it does for students.

> We can't expect those few who are well-served by the current reality to give us time to think. We need time to develop clarity and courage. If we want our world to be different, our first act needs to be reclaiming time to think. Nothing will change for the better until we can do that.
>
> **—MARGARET WHEATLEY**

Teaching is personal in the way that medicine is personal. Like the unguarded nature of illness, submitting yourself to learning from another is a vulnerable process. It's a risk to say, "I don't know" or "I'm hurting," and trust in another to hold it in a way that helps us. That's why it's safer to fill our days with "administrivia," arming ourselves with checklists and objectives against the daily crush of so much responsibility with so little say about what happens.

Taking the lead in designing our own professional development as an embedded, iterative process helps us to reclaim our identities as teachers, as learners, as people with agency and expertise. We don't have to wait for a group or wait for permission. All that's necessary to begin is a belief that your best work comes from the alchemy of honest and brave conversations between human beings. No one will applaud you for doing this or make it easy for you to do, it's important for me to add. If you want this, you will have to take it for yourself and your colleagues. That's why you have to affirm each other and why you have to create the space and time necessary to do this work.

With even one other person, we can give each other the grace that comes when we answer those implicit questions that cause us to suffer because we believe we're alone in having them.

PROTOCOL 14.1 Generating Teachers' Authentic Questions

PURPOSE

To begin, use an adapted form of Protocol 1.1: Generating Students' Authentic Questions in Chapter 1. This works best with groups that have already established a bit of trust with each other and with a facilitator who models his or her own questions.

It's critical to make sure everyone understands the need for distraction-free quiet. My worst experiences with this protocol have happened when someone breaks the silence, giving in to the temptation to talk rather than write.

You'll need the same conditions as you need with students:

- A sacred space for writing and thinking, whether physical or virtual
- An attitude of respect, kindness, and openness to new ideas
- A comfort with and trust of discussion as a way of thinking together
- A belief in the expertise of people and their power to solve their own problems
- A willingness to listen deeply to others

MATERIALS

- A reading to open the session (try using any of the quotes in this book)
- Some reflective writing from yourself with the questions that haunt you or nag at you
- A timer
- Quiet, both internal and external
- A copy of this protocol for each member
- Index cards (enough so that each person gets one)

TIME

Ten minutes is enough if you are using this in a typical planning period, but it's short enough that you may decide to use more time for any part and/or try an extension of the protocol.

INTRODUCTION

Socrates said that the unexamined life is not worth living, yet we don't make it easy to do this within our profession. Part of the problem is time pressure, part of it is professional pressure for certainty, to always appear competent and in control. Questioning undermines this and feels threatening. We often try to manage these risks with distraction and distance but wind up isolating ourselves from our own motivation for this work. Giving ourselves the space, time, and courage to reclaim our questions is the first step back to finding personal meaning and our truest purpose.

This welcoming of our questions is meant to break the isolation that happens not just between teachers but between all human beings. As a culture, we are increasingly distanced from each other, overwhelmed by the pace of technological change, the brutality of the world made manifest in our social media feeds, twenty-four-hour news cycles, and the steady stream

(Continued)

(Continued)

of notifications and text messages. It is hard to be quiet, to sit in quiet, and to listen to our own thoughts.

In the 17th century, Blaise Pascal suggested that so many of our problems stem from an inability to sit in a room quietly. We're afraid of what we might hear if we listen to our own hearts and minds. This, he observed, is why we crave distraction, live in hurriedness, and cram our lives with busyness. If we allow ourselves time with our own thoughts, we might find that the questions underneath them sound like these:

- Does this work matter?
- If I do this, what are the consequences?
- Apart from all of my labels, who am I?
- Why do I stay here? What is my responsibility to others?

As Krista Tippett (2016) writes, these kinds of questions begin "to give voice to those raw, essential, heartbreaking and life-giving places in us," but if we allow ourselves to bring them into our consciousness, we can "live what they teach us and mine their wisdom for our life together" (p. 8).

PURPOSE

To help teachers think about the questions that really matter to them, to draw out those questions and make them explicit, then use those questions as a base for professional thinking and learning

From these questions, you can help yourself and each other link what you are deeply curious about to your practice. Connecting to your own questions changes the context of your teaching on a personal level and helps you uncover your deepest motivations for engaging in the difficult work of teaching.

DIRECTIONS

Turn off and put away all distractions. Don't write your name on the cards—these are anonymous so you can write honestly. Write down the questions that you would like to ask the smartest person in the world, or maybe the best therapist, or even God. Write as many questions as you can. Don't stop to talk about them, worry about them, or try to answer them. Just write the questions as fast as you can. If you feel you can't do this or find yourself finished before time is up, please sit quietly.

- **One minute**—Read the introduction and directions.
- **Five minutes**—Members write. Encourage them to keep writing questions, but if someone is having difficulty writing, it's okay to sit

silently. It's *not okay* to talk, or get on a device, or otherwise interrupt the mental and physical quiet of yourself or others.

- **Three minutes**—Debrief. Ask teachers to answer questions about the process of writing questions: What was hard? What was easy? What surprised them?

- **One minute**—Ask them to fold cards in half for privacy and then collect them.

EXTENSIONS

You may decide to read a few questions as a discussion starter or as a reflective writing prompt. Alternatively, you may wish to let the questions "marinate" for a while and come back to them as an opening or closing activity in another meeting. You may choose to let the questions guide the group as you plan other gatherings or use them with the inquiry groups I explain later in this chapter. ●

Parker Palmer suggested using them as a way of prompting people to tell stories:

> You give them fifteen minutes to tell a story, and then you give the folks that that person is sitting with fifteen minutes to ask honest open questions, and it becomes a different kind of conversation.

> For one thing, it may be the first time in a very long while someone feels listened to. And it does that thing we say we want to do in education—it draws out the inner teacher, the person's inner wisdom as they get honest, open questions that cause them to think about what they themselves are saying in new depths and new ways.

> You hold that kind of space over an extended period of time, people start realizing that theirs is not the only experience, that there are other ways to look at things they've experienced because they're hearing them from their peers. A group like this helps us do that. What we teach, instead of fixing, saving, advising, and correcting each other, we teach others to ask open and honest questions.

As teachers, many of us are adept at facilitating deep discussions within our classrooms but don't have structures for complex discussions with our

> Ischomachus, I am disposed to ask, "Does teaching consist in putting questions?" Indeed, the secret of your system has just this instant dawned upon me. I seem to see the principle in which you put your questions. You lead me through the field of my own knowledge, and then by pointing out analogies to what I know, persuade me that I really know some things which hitherto, as I believed, I had no knowledge of.
>
> **— XENOPHON, QUOTING SOCRATES**

colleagues. For example, race matters in education, but it is a topic where entry points for discussion are difficult. When 82 percent of U.S. teachers are white, it's also a discussion many of us don't realize we even need to have.

"Why do we have such high expectations around students and their learning, but we are so uncomfortable with our own? We have no expectations of adults as the learners," Jose Vilson told me in a recent conversation. "We expect students to be lifelong learners but yet we don't do that for adults. It's almost as if we're trying to say that adults shouldn't learn after a certain period, or that we as teachers have nothing to learn or we're not humble enough to accept that. That's a deeper thing and I think especially when it comes to very uncomfortable things."

This is where inquiry within an environment of trust can help teachers talk to each other about the realities in our work that we feel but don't have a way of examining. Even asking the question Who am I? begins to uncover all the forces that have shaped us if we think about the dimensions of gender, race, age, socioeconomic status, sexual orientation, religious belief, language, and disability in ourselves.

How might our professional lives deepen if we are daring enough to make a space to think together around these kinds of questions? Each time I've been lucky enough to join a group of teachers willing to be curious and vulnerable at this level, it has been the most enriching professional growth I've ever experienced.

Using Questions to Develop Inquiry Groups Around Common Questions of Practice

In Chapter 2, I mentioned that a team of teachers created the Socratic circle protocol and refined it over a year. The process and structure for that work was a result of reworking the way we used time within the school day. Districtwide, a recent adoption of a daily collaborative hour within the school day for all secondary campuses (weekly for elementary) helped us think about how to use the new resource of time. Our principal changed the school's master schedule to add inquiry group meetings two times each six weeks for a total of twelve meetings over one school year.

Every faculty member was assigned to an inquiry group according to our answers on a simple survey of what we wanted to know more about (e.g., student engagement). The survey collated responses and grouped teachers, cross-content, into smaller groups and tasked them with working together to investigate a topic and report our findings to administrators.

My group formed from an interest in increasing student engagement. Members included the social studies department, almost all of whom were also athletic coaches, along with members of my own English department. Our initial meeting was supposed to help us find a topic and then investigate it with an even smaller group (six to eight teachers) made up of colleagues from our content area.

After only a few minutes, it was obvious that we had no way to talk to each other and no way to approach such a task. We also had no way to find our commonalities or ways to talk productively toward the goal of shared inquiry. Without this, the loudest voices in the room, which belonged to the coaches, used our time together to complain.

One teacher, new to our campus, dominated the time. Without a protocol to create a structure and purpose for our meeting, we were reduced to functioning as an audience for her monologue of grievances. The dissatisfaction radiating from her rippled out to the rest of the group, causing everyone to feel demoralized.

This isn't uncommon. Kristy Cooper, an associate professor at Michigan State University, was hired by my principal as a consultant to the process of forming and managing inquiry groups. She led an in-service meeting, sharing Horn and Little's (2010) research about the five problems inherent in "teacher talk":

1. Making tacit knowledge explicit for the group
2. Avoiding confrontation
3. Avoiding disagreement
4. Making assumptions or granting assumptions power
5. Having a sense of urgency (time squeeze)

All of these plagued our small groups, threatening to torpedo collaboration and make it into "one more thing we have to do" in an already-overloaded day. The only way out of the mess, I thought, was to risk a bit of authenticity with the smaller group of English teachers.

"I hate these kinds of forced meetings so much that I'm going to do something crazy right now," I said, which caused them to look at me for a second.

Holding my phone in front of me, I switched it off and put it under my desk. "I'm going to keep myself present in this meeting, and I'm inviting you to try it with me."

Then I stopped talking. The next seconds were excruciating as I forced myself to sit silently in front of five other adults, waiting to see how they'd respond.

As department chair, I had no real power with which to threaten or force them to do anything. They were free to ignore me, leave the meeting, or laugh in my face. However, I did have the power of my own vulnerability, which those of us who are leaders often don't think of as a form of power.

When you allow yourself to be real, it makes a space for others to join you there. And the truth is, many of us want to be there. Much of the temptation toward technological distraction seems to arise as a response to an internal distress over our increasing disconnection from each other. The connections promised by technology give the illusion of human contact just as playing a video game gives the illusion of movement. The drive for relationship is powerful, and when given support, it feeds our creativity and helps us find solutions to difficult problems.

None of this happens unless someone is willing to lead it from their own authenticity. That leader can then invite everyone to create shared behavioral norms. Writing helps to lessen the sense of exposure for people beginning to work together. I know this from teaching writing to younger and older audiences. Leaning on this knowledge, I asked the group if we could write for a couple of minutes about the worst meetings we've ever had to sit through. We used our senses to help us search our memories:

- What do you remember seeing, hearing, feeling?
- Can you remember the smells in the room?
- Can you remember the taste of the food and beverages offered?

From this writing, we were able to develop an idea of what we didn't want our time together to be like. Then I asked the opposite questions about the best learning experiences they could remember with a similar emphasis on sensory details.

Overall, this took about ten minutes, but it focused us for creating norms, which was the next step. "We have the opportunity to keep this from being something 'they' do to us," I said, "and decide instead to use it on a real problem. But that won't happen if we can't agree on a couple of ground rules for this time." Using our writing, we talked through what kinds of behavior we wanted to avoid but also those dispositions we wanted to encourage. Norms are easy to glide right past with adults because it's easy to think you don't need them. That's just not true, especially when it comes to personal devices. Cell phones, for example, are problematic, and the norms agreed to about their use make learning experiences much better for everyone.

Because many people are connected to their children through texting, it's hard to demand that they don't have their phone on during the meeting, but it's also hard to have a deeper discussion if one or two people in a group are always looking down at a screen, swiping and tapping. In this group, we agreed to keep our phones facedown, not checking them during a discussion, and agreeing that if someone needed to attend to someone with texting or a call, they would leave the room.

When I talked to Parker Palmer about the difficulty of teachers being able to meet together during the school day, he said that teachers need to organize internally the way a community organizer would for a "neighborhood in bad need of transformation."

"When teachers gather together in intentional forms of community, and incidentally it doesn't have to be every teacher in the building or the district . . . I'm a big believer in working with what I call pockets of possibility," he said.

"Small groups of people model things and then other folks get interested . . . because they see some of their colleagues be given new life, and they want to get some of that for themselves. That's how mutual support works and spreads. Not to despair if you're starting out with three or four colleagues. You can still plant some good stuff and grow some possibilities for other people."

We realized, in our small group, that we could be friends rather than competitors—that we didn't have to compare, as a friend of mine says, our insides to each other's outsides or our "chapter one to someone else's chapter twelve." A guidepost both to and through that kind of conversation is to develop a routine that helps everyone to speak, uncovering ideas that suggest how to move forward.

Research on teacher talk revealed these steps, which our inquiry group, in our most productive sessions, had seemed to move through without this information (Horn & Little, 2010). Dr. Cooper, in consultation with our principal for sustaining the work of teacher-led inquiry groups, summarized Horn and Little's findings, which she shared as six bullet points for consideration (see Protocol 14.2).

PROTOCOL 14.2 Conversational Routine for Any Professional Learning Community

1. Identify a problem of practice. (For example, kids are tuning out in class, don't do the homework, and won't participate in discussions.)

2. Normalize the problem of practice ("we've all had this happen . . ."). This helps teachers to have commonalities with one another, creating a sense of membership and affiliation.

3. Further specify the problem; analyze what happened to get at the root problem. (Video helped us see and hear that in our classes it was the teachers who were doing 90 percent of the talking, and when they talked, they gave all the answers to the homework.)

4. Revise the description of the problem (What was it like? What did you notice? What were the possible causes?). (For example, when we do all the talking, we're creating passive learners. They're watching us like bad television. We're not showing them how to take ownership of their learning, giving them choices, or giving them experiences to practice their thinking and discussion.)

5. Create general rules or guidelines from what you noticed. (For example, student voice and choice increases engagement; teacher-centered learning creates passivity and disengagement.)

6. Have discussions not just for tips and tricks but as ways of investigating student responses (What are students doing in our classroom specifically? What patterns are we noticing?) (Cooper, 2013).

Armed with this scaffold, groups may find it easier to mitigate the problems that often occur with small groups of teachers thinking together. A routine helps to lower defensiveness but also provides a useful plan for finding a group's purpose.

Guidance for addressing these issues came from research about productive teacher groups, which Dr. Cooper also shared with our staff (Garmston, 2004). Her summarization of this work is as follows:

Leaders must clarify the group's role at the outset by giving members all the steps in a process the leader envisions and clarifying the group's role at each step.

-   Anticipate issues: Address common obstacles to productivity.

-   Provide protocols (especially for topics that are hard to talk about): Protocols determine the type of thinking required, place boundaries around conversations, and provide psychological safety.

-   Use a "paraphrase passport," in which each new speaker must paraphrase the preceding speaker as a passport before he or she can speak, to assist listening.

-   Explain processes: Tell everyone why you are using a particular process. It focuses on the content or purpose of the group's work.

-   Build understanding: Ask, "What are some factors contributing to this problem?"

-   Follow meeting standards. Try doing the following:

    1. One topic at a time

    2. One process at a time

    3. Balanced participation

    4. Safe engagement in cognitive conflict

    5. Understanding of meeting roles

-   Generate compelling conversations—use visuals—seeing helps people think; when you're tired, auditory systems are the first to fade.

Source: Cooper (2013). ●

Another roadblock appeared as we began thinking about how, with our different teaching schedules, we might give each other feedback and support and also how we might observe each other. Our principal wasn't keen on the idea of hiring substitute teachers—already notoriously difficult to secure—to watch classes so we could observe each other. From working with my mentor, I knew that video was a way to solve the problem of how to observe each other. One member of our group used grant money to buy video cameras and offered to share one of them with the group. With this logistical problem solved, we turned to the more difficult work of cocreating our own observation and evaluation protocol.

PROTOCOL 14.3   Observation, Debrief, and Iteration for an Inquiry Team

PURPOSE

To provide an efficient, repeatable, rigorous, and engaging lesson cycle for other group members to modify for use in their own classroom

DIRECTIONS

Designate a facilitator and first-time presenter.

- Decide on strategy to study: BE AS SPECIFIC AND NARROW AS POSSIBLE.

- Topics that are too big or vague (e.g., motivation or technology) will frustrate everyone and cause you to waste time and energy. For example, we studied Socratic circles and how to make them more engaging for students, both intellectually and behaviorally.

- Allow each member to voice concerns and questions. Hold each other accountable for beginning on time with necessary materials, and attempt to create a safe and supportive environment for each other.

- Dedicate yourselves to achieving collective success, not just showcasing each other to "look good" in front of the group. Be open to suggestions. Be committed to improving learning for everyone, students and teachers. Attempt to share failures and successes without fear, because no one has this figured out and we're all learning together.

DIRECTIONS

- **Five to eight minutes**—The designated presenter gives a brief overview and explanation of the process being studied.

  o The presenter gives each member a handout containing this information:

    1. Materials used
    2. Goal of the lesson, strategy, or technique
    3. What you modified in planning for your specific classroom
    4. What you altered from previous presenters (after first person has videoed himself or herself)
    5. Basic outline of lesson
    6. Problems, issues, and/or difficulties
    7. Reflection on successes, student understandings, what you will try next

- **Ten to twelve minutes**—View video of the students or teacher using lesson or process from presenter's classroom.

- **Ten minutes**—Debrief the video by giving feedback on student successes noted. The presenter may share what wasn't on video or other material "left on the cutting-room floor."

- **Ten minutes**—Discuss the lesson with suggestions for modifying, adjusting, and improving the lesson, as well as planning for technical issues and/or other ways to structure for maximum success.

- **Five minutes**—Decide on who will be presenting next and what they will video. ●

Creating this protocol together gave each of us a sense of empowerment. That's not a surprise, Palmer told me, because teachers don't often think of themselves as people with power to solve their own problems or make their own decisions. To the extent that we grant ourselves the time and space to wrestle and resolve our own issues, we create a force multiplier effect where the good we do ourselves is magnified and spreads to other areas.

Working together effectively creates energy, a critical resource for teachers who spend so much of their time helping others.

"I think *empowerment* is a big word here because most of us who are in the serving or helping professions, we don't think of ourselves as people with power or people who engage in power struggles," Palmer said.

Many of our problems are really a problem of fear, he said. It feels safer to say that we're helpless against the system, that our kids and ourselves are just cogs in the giant bureaucratic system. "For years, I've listened to faculty in colleges and universities tell me how powerless they are," Palmer said. "I finally got so impatient with that talk that I would say: 'Powerless in comparison to whom? You've got tenure, you've got easily a salary that you and your family can live on. Compared to whom are you powerless? Aren't you really saying that you're afraid to use your power? To acknowledge it?' I think we really need to challenge each other in that way."

How Teachers Can Take Their Questions Into the World

Questions, I learned in Peru, can change a community, and I believe there are lessons for those of us who work in schools. Jane Gavel, a young Australian on holiday nearly two decades ago, found herself drawn to helping the people in Pumamarca, a village on the outskirts of Cusco near Machu Picchu. The village, like many others, suffered the weight of poverty's consequences: malnutrition, domestic violence, addiction, little education, and lack of access to health care.

Gavel founded Peru's Challenge, a small, nongovernmental organization, from two questions: (1) What do we have? (2) What can we do? The questions drew out the native intelligence, skills, and talent inside the community and helped them create their own solutions.

Asking the question What do we have? produced this answer: land. And the question What can we do? created this answer: make it more productive with an irrigation system powered by gravity, a technology created by their Incan ancestors.

From this beginning, crops were planted and harvested. What the village didn't eat, they sold. The money from that allowed them to build a greenhouse to grow flowers and add to Peru's position as the second-largest exporter of fresh flowers in the world. This, in turn, financed cookstoves, which reduced the respiratory illness plaguing the village from the inefficient and dangerous eucalyptus log fires in their dwellings.

The villagers, Gavel told those of us visiting in the summer of 2016, began to help each other build homes, intentionally practicing the deep Peruvian value of reciprocity: "The saying is, today you work for me and I work for you; tomorrow, we work together," she said.

Most impressively, Pumamarca dramatically cut its addiction and domestic violence rates by creating female entrepreneurial collectives to market and sell native crafts. Profits go to build onto the school and other village infrastructure.

"Ten years ago, the school didn't exist," Gavel told us as we stood near the building housing the Pumamarca preschool. "It started with two classrooms and classes in the summer. Everyone showed up to build, and it took six days to build the first building."

Teachers, recruited from throughout Peru, teach kindergarten through seventh-grade classes. The school supports itself from selling bread made at the school and six greenhouses tended to by each grade, which supplies their school kitchen, leaving the excess to sell.

When any community, in or out of school, asks itself questions like those in Pumamarca—What do we have and what can we do?—it is operating from a place of strength and agency. The answers uncover the intelligence in the people around us, whether they are colleagues or students. This is also true of a school's wider neighborhood.

Margaret Wheatley, who has helped communities struggling with poverty to see themselves as wise councils, told me that the power underneath these forms of change is a belief in people.

"You're not there to fix them," she said. "You have to give up this paternalistic idea of 'I'm here to help you.' It's a place of 'I'm with you, I'm not here to fix you, you can help yourself. I'm here to bear witness. I'm a companion.'"

She advises teachers to begin by choosing one or two things to do differently.

"Think small, think immediate," she said. "This we can do. It's not putting in a new curriculum or putting in a new program. It's changing the atmosphere in the classroom. My greatest lesson is relationships are all."

Sydney Chaffee echoed the need for collaboration and talked to me about her work with the Boston Educators Collaborative. It brings together educators from public, public charter, and parochial schools in Boston to teach and learn from each other. Her experience with a fellow teacher who was overwhelmed by the pace and depth of change taught her to start small.

"He's been a teacher for a long time and he feels a lot of despair, and he's like, 'I just don't know how I will ever get my kids to do this,'" she said. "'This seems like Level 20, and my kids are on like Level 3. How will I ever get them there? It's too big of a jump.' So we've been talking about what's the first step. What's the first little step?"

In talking to him, she said she realized that teachers can do for each other what they've always done for their students: break bigger ideas into smaller thoughts that are easier to put into action.

"What's the little thing out of this teaching that you're going to try? Just start there," she said. "So maybe you try that for six months or maybe a year. And then the next year, you bite off a bigger piece. Starting something new, when you don't have that support network in your building, it's going to feel so overwhelming to you."

Chaffee's experience is one with the potential to spark conversations across a district but seems particularly helpful for teachers in rural areas to concentrate regional expertise and support.

Inviting Parents Into the Process

The rich potential of authentic parent engagement built around a celebration of storytelling and shared inquiry first became clear to me in the work of my mentor and teacher partner, Elaine Loughlin. She modified a side-by-side writing project demonstrated by an elementary teacher to make it inviting for high school students (Dowling, 2003).

Students invited an older sibling, friend, caregiver, or parent with them to a themed writing night in Loughlin's classroom over five months. The prompts were questions to help participants search their memories around topics like family traditions. After each pair wrote, they would then talk and write about their memories.

Working with her principal, the migrant coordinator, and the parent involvement liaison, Loughlin applied for funding from several sources to provide food and door prizes as well as publish a book of collected stories for each person attending.

"This project, which was for kindergarten kids, a logical high parent interest group, was something I thought might work with our kids since I thought this was one more thing missing in the school experience," Loughlin told me. "And it did translate. Some of the parents, specifically Hispanic and Asian, came to school at night and shared their stories. Many kids had never heard these stories before from their parents."

What started in her classroom eventually moved to the cafeteria as more people heard about the event. Loughlin said she had more than sixty people participating and then even more when other teachers began inviting their students and parents.

From her model, I created an event embedded in the school day where I taught middle school, creating a "coffee house" for invited parents to our classroom to hear their children read or perform a work written during the year. Families insisted on providing the food, which became a multicultural feast attracting faculty and their students as audience members.

After I began teaching high school, the coffee house concept wasn't workable, so students asked if we could talk more specifically about philosophy together after school. Using Christopher Phillips's (2010) model of what he called the *Socrates Cafe*, I invited faculty, parents, and students to meet at a coffee shop after school to discuss their choice of questions. People from the community who weren't affiliated with the school or my students sometimes joined in as speakers or audience members. This had the side benefit of changing the community's perception of my students, seeing them as high-level thinkers who loved intelligent discussion.

Extensions of this idea can be created by teachers at any level around any theme. For example, I see the potential for parent involvement within Nate Bowling's in-class workshop on civil liberties. His government classes examine their civil rights through the lens of relevant current events.

"I do an entire lesson looking at the Black Lives Matter movement and Campaign Zero and what the actual policy changes they're looking for are,"

Bowling said. "And my kids understand their rights a hell of a lot afterward. It's way more meaningful to say to a kid that the Fifth Amendment means you don't have to self-incriminate, and this is why you shouldn't talk to the police and should ask for a lawyer."

By inviting others to ask questions, we can create an intentional community that begins to discover its power to solve problems, invent solutions, and revive the ancient wisdom evoked as we begin to think like Socrates.

APPENDIX
Resources, Recommended Texts, and Rubrics

Sample Weekly Schedule

Note: This is for forty-five- to fifty-minute English language arts (ELA) classes but can be modified and adapted for block schedules and content areas. Having a focus day for strand of skill helped both me and students to be intentional about our time and build consistency without being rigid.

MONDAY	TUESDAY	WEDNESDAY	THURSDAY	FRIDAY
Speaking and Listening Workshop	Reading Workshop	Reading Workshop	Writing Workshop	Writing Workshop
Sample activities: • Socratic discussion • In-class debates • Presentations	Sample activities: • Academic vocabulary • Genre study • Book club meetings	Sample activities: • Independent reading • Research • Conferences	Sample activities: • In-class essays • Direct teaching of modes and genres • Conferences	Sample activities: • Independent writing • Writing circle meetings
Rationale: Students eagerness to reconnect with each other after the weekend made this a logical forum for focusing on speaking and listening.	Rationale: Focused skills allowed for targeted interventions.	Rationale: In-class time to read and research allowed me to confer with students to assess their skill and personalize their learning while allowing them choice.	Rationale: Using this time to practice pressure writing helps students prepare for college and career writing demands. Direct teaching embedded within the process ensures that I'm meeting kids in their zone of proximal development. Conferences allow me to assess their skill and offer targeted feedback.	Rationale: Students spend part of class writing on their projects and then meet to get peer and teacher feedback. They can then return to their writing and revise it in light of feedback.

Peeples's Telemarketing-Inspired Template for Parent Calls

1. Before you call, have a documentation method so you can take notes for each parent called.

2. Document (a) date, (b) time, (c) number(s) called, (d) name of person you're talking to (the easiest system for me is to type while they're talking, then save the document by uploading to my Dropbox).

3. Whenever possible, just validate. It's magic. People really just want to be heard—for example, "I can really hear that you're frustrated/angry/tired of these kinds of calls." This will defuse angry parents 99 percent of the time. Just keep validating until they calm down.

4. Refer all difficulties to the counselors for a conference, and give them the school's main number to contact them. Referring to counselors also lowers the antagonism factor by not involving principals.

Here's my script for grades:

> Hi, this is (your name), (student's name's) (subject) teacher at (school name). Do you have a minute, or am I catching you at a bad time? I wanted to let you know that (progress reports/report cards) are coming out this week and (student's name) is failing (subject) with a (grade). I'm calling now so we can work together to get (student's name) to come to tutorials to fix this before it causes worse problems. He/she can make up missing work (give tutorial times/days). Thank you so much for your help. I appreciate parents like you.

Here's my script for behavior problems:

> (Same intro as above). . . . Could you tell me if (student's name) is having some difficulties at school or outside of school that I need to be aware of? I'm asking because he/she is really struggling with some issues in my class (describe behavior as clearly as possible without lapsing into commentary on the behavior—such as, he or she puts their head down on the desk during group work and won't participate in class. Just give the facts without elaborating to keep the conversation focused on the issue). I'm calling to let you know this before the consequences become more serious and to

give (student's name) the benefit of the doubt. I didn't just want to write an office referral and cause more problems for him/her without talking to you first. Thank you so much for your help. I appreciate parents like you.

These calls show good faith effort on your part and go a long way to creating partnerships with parents rather than conflicts. It's also good documentation to show during conferences or when administrators need more information about a student's difficulties in class.

Texts and Lesson Ideas to Practice and Extend Speaking and Listening Skills

Resources

"Teaching With Podcasts" from ReadWriteThink (National Council of Teachers of English, or NCTE): www.readwritethink.org/professional-development/strategy-guides/teaching-with-podcasts-30109.html

Beyond Penguins and Polar Bears: "Podcasts in the Elementary Classroom: Tools for Teachers and Students" (for younger students): http://beyond penguins.ehe.osu.edu/issue/polar-oceans/podcasts-in-the-elementary-classroom-tools-for-teachers-and-students

For Colleagues/Adult Teams/Administrators: Consultancy Triads

This is a powerful protocol, if done within an atmosphere of respectful listening. Teachers and administrators often find, in my experience of using this protocol, that the answers they've been seeking are already within them or their colleagues. I've used it as a coach within a small team of teachers, as staff development with teachers from different grade levels, and at the district level with administrators. Do a search for "consultancy protocol" to find one that will work for you.

Books

All Ages

- *Do Unto Otters: A Book About Manners* by Laurie Keller
- *Interrupting Chicken* by David Ezra Stein

Videos (on YouTube)

For Younger Students

- *Sesame Street*: "Elmo Knows How to Listen"
- Howard B. Wigglebottom series

For Older Students

- *Patch Adams* movie clip: "He at least listened"

TED Talks

- (7:42) Julian Treasure: "5 Ways to Listen Better"
- (32:04) Evelyn Glennie: "How to Truly Listen"

Podcasts/Audio

All Ages

- *Brains On!* by NPR

For Younger Students

- *But Why: A Podcast for Curious Kids* by NPR

Intermediate/Middle School

- *Kids Like You and Me* by NPR
- *The Radio Adventures of Eleanor Amplified* by NPR

Teens

- *Dayton Youth Radio* by NPR

Songs for Use as Texts for Thinking, Writing, and Discussing

In a public Spotify playlist titled "Critical Thinking," I've collected forty-one songs from genres as diverse as Broadway soundtracks to vintage blues based on these classic questions from philosophy:

- What can we know? How do we know what is real?
- Why do we suffer?
- Who deserves mercy?
- How should we use resources?
- How should we treat each other?
- What does it mean to be a man? What does it mean to be a woman?
- Who owns culture?
- Who am I? What is my purpose?
- How do we know what to do? How do we know what and who to trust?

Also included are songs (https://spoti.fi/2kvnuh/) that examine how stylistic changes affect meaning as well as the changes in meaning that occur when songs are recorded by artists of a different gender.

Inferential Thinking or Practice

In the song "Before He Cheats" by Carrie Underwood, what happened here? How do you know? What seems like a straightforward narrative is upended by a closer look at the lyrics, especially the word *probably* repeated throughout.

"The Man in the Long Black Coat" by Bob Dylan (Joan Osborne's version) with "Possum Kingdom" by The Toadies call on listeners to make inferences about what is happening or happened.

Why Do Bad Things Happen to Good People?
How Does Language Shape Our Perception of Events?

"Casimir Pulaski Day" by Sufjan Stevens shows how Stevens's understated delivery creates a reverent tone about his friend who died of bone cancer. Note how he pairs the ideas of faith and doubt in lines like "All the glory that the Lord has made" with "We lift our hands and pray over your body/But nothing ever happens." The lyrics use specific detail and nature imagery to explore grief, which helps the listener or reader to create the scenes Stevens sings about.

Who Deserves Mercy? How Do We Know When Someone Has Been "Reformed" From Punishment?

"Branded Man" by Merle Haggard, himself a former inmate, shows in the song's intro how shame can act as a prison long after a person leaves jail. In using the term *branded man*, he touches on this idea as well as the way American society struggles to reintegrate ex-convicts.

Why Is There a Double Standard of Behavior for Men and Women?

"The Wild Side of Life" by Hank Thompson paired with "It Wasn't God Who Made Honky Tonk Angels" by Kitty Wells highlights cynical misogyny from Thompson. The "clapback" rebuttal from Wells focuses on male hypocrisy and male complicity in the misery of many women like those he criticizes in his song. The songs were recorded within months of each other in 1952. Wells's version was actually banned by NBC and the Grand Ole Opry for trespassing traditional gender roles.

How Does Meaning Change When Style Changes?

"You're the One That I Want" by John Travolta and Olivia Newton-John contrasted with the same song reinterpreted by Lo-Fang: What are the tone or mood and meaning changes that result from tempo, phrasing, and other musical changes? See also the contrast of "No Diggity" by Blackstreet and Chet Faker and the pairing of "The House of the Rising Sun" (a folk song that musicologists believe may date to the 16th century) by Nina Simone with the popular version by The Animals. Also, the stripped acoustic contrast of "Mad World" by Gary Jules contrasted with the dance anthem original by Tears for Fears. What do these contrasts add to the meaning of the song? Which do you prefer, and why? Why do artists remix and reconfigure existing work? Is it just as valid, artistically, to remix the work of another artist? Why?

Who Owns Culture? What Are the Roots of Gender Bias in Performance?

"Whole Lotta Shakin' Goin' On" by Big Maybelle and Jerry Lee Lewis, "Hound Dog" by Big Mama Thornton and Elvis, and also "When the Levee Breaks" by Memphis Minnie contrasted with the version from Led Zeppelin look at the notion of cultural appropriation as well as the idea of female artistry. Why weren't these big hits from Black females, but they were from white men?

What Is the Right Relationship to Our Environment? How Should We Use Resources?

"Big Yellow Taxi" by Joni Mitchell creates irony for the listener by pairing the lyrics about environmental devastation and urban sprawl with a cheery pop structure. Mitchell uses the irony as a rhetorical device to underscore the lack of attention paid to things that we "don't know what we've got till they're gone." Notice also her use of consonance in the repeated "paved paradise and put up a parking lot" lyric—why might she have chosen this poetic device?

Does Gender Matter?

"Prove It on Me Blues" by Ma Rainey and "Masculine Women! Feminine Men!" by The Savoy Havana Band look at our social constructs of gender and sexual preference—why do so many people feel that they have to "pass" as someone they're not? Why do you think these songs were written? Who is the audience?

Who Owns Work? Who Owns the Products of Labor? What Is Our Ethical Responsibility to Undocumented Workers, Particularly in Light of America's Bracero Program in World War II?

Listen to "Plane Wreck at Los Gatos" by Joel Rafael (written by Woody Guthrie) and "Pastures of Plenty" by Odetta.

Woody Guthrie, outraged that victims of a plane crash in 1948 were identified only as "deportees," was inspired to write this song to grant humanity to migrant workers. He wrote this song in 1948, but what details in the song make it relevant to today? How does Odetta's song "Pastures of Plenty" create dignity for those who labor to convert our crops into the food we all eat?

How Should We Treat Each Other? Who Is an American?

"This Land Is Your Land" by Woody Guthrie has been called the alternate national anthem by some because of its commonplace rendering of the ideas in patriotic songs as well as those in Emma Lazurus's "Colossus" poem engraved on the Statue of Liberty. The song was seen as controversial in the 1950s because of its original lyrics: "As I went walking I saw a sign there/And on the sign it said 'No Trespassing.'/But on the other side it didn't say nothing/That side was made for you and me./In the shadow of the steeple I saw my people/By the relief office I seen my people;/As they stood there hungry, I stood there asking/Is this land made for you and me?"

How do the original lyrics change the meaning of the song? Or do they?

What Does It Mean to Be a Woman?
What Does It Mean to Be a Man?

"Unpretty" by TLC paired with "Try" by Colbie Caillat, "Video" by India. Arie and "Sit Still, Look Pretty" by Daya look at concepts of body image and what it means to be a woman. "A Boy Named Sue" by Johnny Cash paired with "Real Men" by Joe Jackson and "Fight Test" by The Flaming Lips ask listeners to think about what it means to be a man.

Can Art Change Society? Does Inequality
Matter? What Is Racism? Who Benefits From
Keeping Things the Way They Are? Who Suffers?

"Inner City Blues" by Marvin Gaye, "Living for the City" by Stevie Wonder, and "Hope in a Hopeless World" by Widespread Panic critique lingering social problems and the effects that income inequality and racial inequality have on the country. Why do these inequalities persist?

Who Defines "Normal"?
Who Are You? How Should We Live?

"Little Boxes" by Walk Off the Earth, "What Did You Learn in School Today?" by Pete Seeger, "You've Got to Be Carefully Taught" by William Tabbert, and "Follow Your Arrow" by Kacey Musgraves look at society's messages about what it means to be "normal" and "good" at the expense of who we might really be. Do we become who people say we are? How much weight should we give traditional forms of authority when trying to decide how to live?

Videos for Use as Texts for Thinking, Writing, and Discussing

Award-winning and recognized videos (shortest = 2:46; longest = 1 hr. 25 min.) in the genres of wordless animation, how-to, live-action short, animated short, documentary, and foreign short subject may be used as an entry point for discussing the eleven questions of the heart. There are nineteen films in a YouTube list titled "Using Video for Critical Thinking" (https://bit.ly/2GZNNoz), but the following titles are ones I've used in classes with English language learners (ELLs), remedial students, and advanced placement (AP) students, Grades 7 through 12:

La Maison En Petits Cubes

A widowed man remembers his life as he tries to save his house from rising water in this animated short film that considers the topic of love, grief, and memory.

Madame Tutli-Putli

Madame Tutli-Putli, the main character in this stop-motion animation, boards a night train for a mysterious and suspenseful journey that suggests death and the afterlife. (This is for older students because of topic and one obscene gesture made by another character.)

Critical Thinking Explained by ProCon.Org

This short how-to video on critical thinking comes from the highly recommended website that updates forty high-interest debatable topics.

The Children's March

This shortened version of the Oscar-winning documentary shows how the young people of Birmingham, Alabama, suffered police brutality—dogs and fire hoses—to protest segregation in 1963. It is highly recommended as a model of student community action.

Pixar Shorts

Knick Knack

A snow globe snowman futilely attempts to join other travel souvenirs in a party but is frustrated by unforeseen consequences.

For the Birds

A group of gossipy little birds bully a larger bird and face instant justice.

Presto

A rabbit gets revenge upon but ultimately reconciles with an egotistical magician.

Partly Cloudy

Storks get various assigned babies—animal and human—to deliver with some having easier deliveries than others. (**Note:** I've often used this film with teachers in professional development.)

Poetry, Flash Fiction, and Children's Books for Leveled Questions Thinking Practice

Secondary

- *The Three Questions* by Jon J. Muth
- *Zen Shorts* by Jon J. Muth
- *The Sneetches and Other Stories* by Dr. Seuss
- *The Red Tree* by Shaun Tan

Younger Readers

- *I Want My Hat Back* by Jon Klassen
- *This Moose Belongs to Me* by Oliver Jeffers
- *Tuesday* by David Wiesner

Poetry

Elementary

- *Where the Sidewalk Ends: Poems and Drawings* by Shel Silverstein
- *A Light In the Attic* by Shel Silverstein

Middle School

- "Write a Poem" by Olive Dove
- "Oranges" by Gary Soto
- "Poop" by Gerald Locklin
- "The Whipping" by Robert Hayden

High School

- "The Summer Day" by Mary Oliver
- "Out, Out" by Robert Frost
- "The .38" by Ted Joans
- "Porphyria's Lover" by Robert Browning

Flash Fiction

- "Thank You, M'am" by Langston Hughes
- "The Hit Man" by T. C. Boyle
- "Snow" by Julia Alvarez
- "Girl" by Jamaica Kincaid
- "The Last Night of the World" by Ray Bradbury

Sources for Art and Photography to Prompt Thinking

The National Gallery of Art (www.nga.gov) is a source of downloadable art and lesson plans that I used extensively with remedial learners.

The International Center of Photography (www.icp.org) is a rich source of photographic images for use in helping students use their comfort and facility with visual literacy (thanks to their use of Instagram, Snapchat, and phone cameras) as a bridge to textual literacy. I used these, as well as the collections in the New York Times Learning Network's "What's Going on in This Picture?" (www.nytimes.com). English language learners (ELLs) and struggling learners noticed and named the skills they used to make meaning with photos.

Handouts for In-Class Debates

Argument Planner

Please complete BEFORE the debate

DEBATE QUESTION:	PRO	CON
	List at least three arguments to argue FOR the question. For example, We think that . . . should . . . 1. 2. 3. 4.	What are the arguments AGAINST yours? 1. 2. 3. 4.
	List reasons for why you think this: We think this because . . . 1. 2. 3.	What do you think the other team will use as reasons and evidence?
	What evidence supports your argument? Include it by saying this: Our evidence comes from (state your source) and says . . . Source 1: Source 2: Source 3: Source 4:	How can you argue against them? Write your rebuttals here.

Scoring Sheet

Debate Topic: _____ **Date:** _____ **Pro** or **Con** (circle one)

Team Member Names:

1. _____

2. _____

3. _____

CRITERIA	PERFORMANCE POINTS			
	1 POINT	**2 POINTS**	**3 POINTS**	**4 POINTS**
1. Organization and Clarity: Viewpoints and responses are outlined both clearly and orderly.	Unclear in most parts	Clear in some parts but not overall	Mostly clear and orderly in all parts	Completely clear and orderly presentation
2. Use of Arguments: Reasons are given to support the viewpoint.	Few or no relevant reasons given	Some relevant reasons given	Many reasons given; fairly relevant	Most relevant reasons given in support
3. Use of Examples and Facts: Examples and facts are given to support reasons, with references.	Few or no relevant supporting examples or facts given	Some relevant examples or facts given	Many examples or facts given; fairly relevant	Most relevant supporting examples and facts given
4. Use of Rebuttal: Arguments made by the other teams are responded to and dealt with effectively.	No effective counterarguments made	Few effective counterarguments made	Some effective counterarguments made	Many effective counterarguments made

CRITERIA	PERFORMANCE POINTS			
	1 POINT	**2 POINTS**	**3 POINTS**	**4 POINTS**
5. Presentation Style: Tone of voice, use of gestures, and level of enthusiasm are convincing to the audience.	Few stylistic features used; not convincingly	Few stylistic features used but used convincingly	Most stylistic features used convincingly	All stylistic features used convincingly

Total: _____   **Score** = Total × 5 = _____

Comments:

You may use this reflection as a quiz grade or prewrite for a timed writing.

Debate Reflection Rubric

17 points each

_____ Heading: Your name, the date of the debate, and the issue you debated

_____ One paragraph reflecting on your individual performance

_____ One paragraph reflecting on the performance of your group

_____ A thesis statement for a possible essay on this text

_____ One paragraph explaining the main points of that possible essay

_____ One paragraph explaining the connections you made between the issue or topic and another source or yourself

_____ **Total**

Suggested Rubrics for Assessment

Note: These are rubrics cocreated with students and teachers at Palo Duro High School. In my experience, rubrics that are collaboratively negotiated build ownership and deeper understanding of target performances.

Presentation Rubric

	BELOW GRADE-LEVEL STANDARD	GRADE-LEVEL STANDARD	ADVANCED PLACEMENT STANDARD	COLLEGE AND CAREER STANDARD
Explanation of Ideas and Information	Does not present information clearly, concisely, and logically Argument lacks supporting evidence Inappropriate to the purpose and audience	Presents information in a way that is not always clear, concise, and logical Attempts to use a style appropriate to the purpose and audience but does not fully succeed	Presents information clearly, concisely, and logically; audience can easily follow Style appropriate to the purpose and audience	Presents information clearly, concisely, and logically Obvious effort has been put into designing the information for the audience's needs Audience can connect to and apply ideas and information to their own lives
Organization	Does not meet requirements for what should be included in the presentation Does not have an introduction and/or conclusion Uses time poorly; too short or too long; seems put together at the last minute	Meets most requirements for what should be included in the presentation Has an introduction and conclusion, but they are not clear or interesting; may spend too much or too little time on a topic, audiovisual aid, or idea	Meets all requirements for what should be included Clear and interesting introduction and conclusion Organizes time well; no part of the presentation is too short or too long	Includes supplemental items or other material that goes beyond required material Beginning grabs attention; conclusion is memorable; excellent timing and pacing; obvious effort involved in construction
Eyes and Body	Does not look at audience; reads notes or slides; does not use gestures or movements; lacks poise and confidence (fidgets, slouches, appears nervous)	Makes infrequent eye contact; reads notes or slides most of the time; uses a few gestures or movements but they do not look natural Shows some poise and confidence	Keeps eye contact with audience most of the time; only glances at notes or slides; uses natural gestures and movements; looks poised and confident	Engages with audience naturally throughout Doesn't use notes because the material is well-known and polished Poised, confident, positive, and energetic

(Continued)

(Continued)

	BELOW GRADE-LEVEL STANDARD	GRADE-LEVEL STANDARD	ADVANCED PLACEMENT STANDARD	COLLEGE AND CAREER STANDARD
Voice	Mumbles or speaks too quickly or slowly Speaks too softly to be understood Frequently uses "filler" words (*uh, um, so, like*, etc.) Does not adapt speech for the context and task	Speaks clearly most of the time Speaks loudly enough for the audience to hear most of the time but may speak in a monotone Occasionally uses filler words Attempts to adapt speech for the context and task but is unsuccessful or inconsistent	Speaks clearly; not too quickly or slowly Speaks loudly enough for everyone to hear; changes tone and pace to maintain interest Rarely uses filler words Adapts speech for the context and task, demonstrating command of formal English when appropriate	Speaks clearly with feeling, proper tone, and pace Speech is smooth, polished, and professional Uses academic vocabulary and formal English correctly
Presentation Aids	Does not use audiovisual aids or media Attempts to use one or a few audiovisual aids or media, but they do not add to or may distract from the presentation	Uses audiovisual aids or media, but they may sometimes distract from or not add to the presentation Sometimes has trouble bringing audiovisual aids or media smoothly into the presentation	Uses well-produced audiovisual aids or media to enhance understanding of information and to add interest Smoothly brings audiovisual aids or media into the presentation	Uses professional grade and effective audiovisual material; helps explain the information and/or make it memorable Seamless transitions demonstrate a practiced and polished presentation
Response	Does not address audience questions	Answers audience questions but not always clearly or correctly	Answers audience questions clearly and completely Seeks clarification and admits "I don't know" or explains how the answer might be found when unable to answer a question	Anticipates audience questions and includes information in the presentation Speech demonstrates depth of content knowledge and research beyond what was required

General Rubric for Writing Assessment

		DEVELOPMENT OF IDEAS	ORGANIZATION AND FOCUS	LANGUAGE AND CONVENTIONS	AUTHOR'S CRAFT
3	Meets standards for career and college readiness **Perfect score is 20 points**	**(5 points)** • All of the evidence and examples are well chosen, specific, and relevant. • The piece is thoughtful and engaging. • The student demonstrates a deep understanding of the task.	**(5)** • Form or structure is appropriate to genre. • The student establishes and sustains focus, which affects the unity and coherence of the piece. • The student controls focus and organization with transitions and sentence-to-sentence connections and establishes the relationship among ideas.	**(5)** • Word choice is thoughtful and appropriate to form, purpose, and tone. • Sentences are purposeful, varied, and controlled. • The student demonstrates a command of conventions; writing is fluent and clear.	**(5)** • The work is well tailored to the specific audience and purpose. • Conscious stylistic choices enhance the effect of the piece. • The student displays insight or unique perspective.
2	Meets basic standards set for grade level	**(3 points)** • Most evidence and examples are specific and relevant. • Some of the piece is thoughtful and engaging. • The student demonstrates a general understanding of the task.	**(3)** • Form or structure is mostly appropriate to the genre. • The student establishes and sustains focus with few lapses. • The student makes an obvious effort to control focus and organization with transitions and sentence-to-sentence connections and to establish relationships among ideas.	**(3)** • Word choice is appropriate to form, purpose, and tone. • Most sentences are well constructed, and there is some varied sentence structure. • There are some errors in grammar or spelling, but they do not distract from the content.	**(3)** • The audience appears to be limited to peer group. • Control of stylistic elements meets standards. • There is a general understanding of the subject matter, or the task is apparent.

(Continued)

(Continued)

		DEVELOPMENT OF IDEAS	ORGANIZATION AND FOCUS	LANGUAGE AND CONVENTIONS	AUTHOR'S CRAFT
1	Below basic standards set for grade level	(1 point) • Evidence and examples are not relevant and/or are nonexistent. • There is little or no attempt to be thoughtful or engaging. • The student has little or no understanding of the task.	(1) • The specific form or structure for the task is not evident. • The focus is lost or not adequately established and maintained. • Transitions between ideas are unclear or nonexistent.	(1) • There is poor word choice; purpose and tone are unclear. • The majority of sentences are not well constructed or varied. • There is a weak command of conventions.	(1) • The target audience is unclear. • There is little evidence of stylistic control. • The student has a superficial grasp of the subject matter.

Comments:

Suggested Books for High School by Major Topic Area

The Future

It Can't Happen Here by Sinclair Lewis

Out of the Silent Planet by C. S. Lewis

"In the Penal Colony" by Franz Kafka

A Clockwork Orange by Anthony Burgess

The Handmaid's Tale by Margaret Atwood

V for Vendetta by Alan Moore

The Children of Men by P. D. James

Super Sad True Love Story by Gary Shteyngart

Wool by Hugh Howey (an e-book on Amazon)

Faster: The Acceleration of Just About Everything by James Gleick

Tomorrow's People: How 21st-Century Technology Is Changing the Way We Think and Feel by Susan Greenfield

The Shallows: What the Internet Is Doing to Our Brains by Nicholas Carr

More Than Human: Embracing the Promise of Biological Enhancement by Ramez Naam

Nature

Silent Spring by Rachel Carson

Prodigal Summer by Barbara Kingsolver

The Snow Child by Eowyn Ivey

Into Thin Air: A Personal Account of the Mt. Everest Disaster by Jon Krakauer

Pilgrim at Tinker Creek by Annie Dillard

Life of Pi by Yann Martel

The Spider and the Wasp by Alexander Petrunkevitch

The Grapes of Wrath by John Steinbeck

A River Runs Through It by Norman Maclean

The Maytrees by Annie Dillard

Gender and Sexuality

Luna by Julie Anne Peters

Gay America: Struggle for Equality by Linas Alsenas

Almost Perfect by Brian Katcher

The Handmaid's Tale by Margaret Atwood

Middlesex by Jeffrey Eugenides

The Color Purple by Alice Walker

Oranges Are Not the Only Fruit by Jeannette Winterson

Giovanni's Room by James Baldwin

The Line of Beauty by Alan Hollinghurst

The Beauty Myth by Naomi Wolf

Race and Class

The Absolutely True Diary of a Part-Time Indian by Sherman Alexie

Between the World and Me by Ta-Nahesi Coates

Just Mercy: A Story of Justice and Redemption by Bryan Stevenson

The New Jim Crow: Mass Incarceration in the Age of Colorblindness by Michelle Alexander

Hillbilly Elegy: A Memoir of a Family and Culture in Crisis by J. D. Vance

The Prince of Los Cocuyos: A Miami Childhood by Richard Blanco

Born a Crime: Stories From a South African Childhood by Trevor Noah

The Kite Runner by Khaled Hosseini

Night by Elie Wiesel

Native Son by Richard Wright

Push by Sapphire

Germinal by Émile Zola

Food

The Omnivore's Dilemma: A Natural History of Four Meals
by Michael Pollan

Fast Food Nation: The Dark Side of the All-American Meal
by Eric Schlosser

Born Round: The Secret History of a Full-Time Eater by Frank Bruni

What the World Eats by Faith D'Aluisio

The Joy Luck Club by Amy Tan

Like Water for Chocolate by Laura Esquivel

The Particular Sadness of Lemon Cake by Aimee Bender

Babette's Feast by Isak Dinesen

Bread Alone by Judith Ryan Hendricks

Animal, Vegetable, Miracle: A Year of Food Life by Barbara Kingsolver

Kitchen Confidential by Anthony Bourdain

War

Blood Meridian by Cormac McCarthy

Where Men Win Glory: The Odyssey of Pat Tillman by Jon Krakauer

The Chocolate War by Robert Cormier

World War Z by Max Brooks

The Killer Angels by Michael Shaara

A Farewell to Arms by Ernest Hemingway

Belief and Spirituality

Life of Pi by Yann Martel

Letter to a Christian Nation by Sam Harris

God Is Not Great by Christopher Hitchens

The Screwtape Letters by C. S. Lewis

The Alchemist by Paulo Coelho

Siddhartha by Hermann Hesse

Mere Christianity by C. S. Lewis

The Art of Happiness by His Holiness, the Dalai Lama

Blue Like Jazz by Donald Miller

Zen and the Art of Motorcycle Maintenance: An Inquiry Into Values by Robert M. Pirsig

Jesus Freak: Feeding Healing Raising the Dead by Sara Miles

The Poisonwood Bible by Barbara Kingsolver

Jonathan Livingston Seagull by Richard Bach

The Book Thief by Markus Zusak

Fire in the Heart by Deepak Chopra

Everyday Struggles: The Stories of Muslim Teens by Sumaiya Beshir

Family and Relationships

The Glass Castle: A Memoir by Jeannette Walls

Naked by David Sedaris

The Joy Luck Club by Amy Tan

Parrot in the Oven: Mi Vida by Victor Martinez

Angela's Ashes by Frank McCourt

A Tree Grows in Brooklyn by Betty Smith

Caramelo by Sandra Cisneros

The Chosen by Chaim Potok

Growing Up by Russell Baker

That Old Ace in the Hole by Annie Proulx

Oddly Normal: One Family's Struggle to Help Their Teenage Son Come to Terms With His Sexuality by John Schwartz

A Heartbreaking Work of Staggering Genius by Dave Eggers

Silver Linings Playbook by Matthew Quick

The Lives of Girls and Women by Alice Munro

Men Are From Mars, Women Are From Venus by John Gray

The Relationship Cure: A 5 Step Guide to Strengthening Your Marriage, Family, and Friendships by John Gottman

Health, Disease, and Death

How We Die: Reflections on Life's Final Chapter by Sherwin Nuland

Stiff: The Curious Lives of Human Cadavers by Mary Roach

I Would, But My Damn Mind Won't Let Me! A Teen's Guide to Controlling Their Thoughts and Feelings by Jacqui Letran

The Hot Zone: The Terrifying True Story of the Origins of the Ebola Virus by Richard Preston

Autobiography of a Face by Lucy Grealy

The Man Who Mistook His Wife for a Hat and Other Clinical Tales by Oliver Sacks

The Immortal Life of Henrietta Lacks by Rebecca Skloot

The Curious Incident of the Dog in the Night-Time by Mark Haddon

Frankenstein by Mary Shelley

Never Let Me Go by Kazuo Ishiguro

The Plague by Albert Camus

For Advanced Placement, International Baccalaureate, or College-Bound Students

The Harvard Classics are a free digital collection of fifty-one volumes curated by Harvard University president Charles W. Eliot in 1909. Eliot argued that if you spend just fifteen minutes a day reading the right books, you could give yourself a world-class liberal arts education. His collection, originally titled *Dr. Eliot's Five Foot Shelf,* includes the following titles:

Vol. 1: *Autobiography of Benjamin Franklin* by Benjamin Franklin, *The Journal of John Woolman* by John Woolman, and *Fruits of Solitude* by William Penn

Vol. 2: *The Apology, Phaedo,* and *Crito* by Plato; *The Golden Sayings* by Epictetus; and *The Meditations* by Marcus Aurelius

Vol. 3: *Essays, Civil and Moral* and *New Atlantis* by Francis Bacon, *Areopagitica* and *Tractate of Education* by John Milton, and *Religio Medici* by Sir Thomas Browne

Vol. 4: Complete poems written in English by John Milton

Vol. 5: Essays and *English Traits* by Ralph Waldo Emerson

Inquiry Project Handout:
Independent Researching, Problem-Solving, and Presenting for Spring Final

Note: I used this with advanced placement (AP) and college-prep students, but it can be modified for use with Grades 7 through 12. (Adapted from Jim Burke)

Overview

Each of you has a cause or a passion that you believe in strongly that school rarely gives you the opportunity to work on. This assignment outlines the five requirements for an inquiry project of your own design. The purpose of this assignment is to allow you to investigate your own questions; generate real solutions; and prepare you for college-level reading, writing, and thinking, as well as career preparation in presentation skills. Also, this kind of project makes you very competitive in scholarship programs. In addition, however, I want each of you to leave this year having given your time and talent to a personal cause in depth, by using your own reading, viewing, and research.

Due dates: Proposal due by _____

Window for presentations opens _____ and closes _____. All work must be turned in by _____ .

Requirements

Each group **must** do the following:

- Investigate a real community problem and propose a workable solution.

- Submit a contract for each group member.

- Write a formal proposal for solving the problem and then a documented essay detailing your project that includes a works cited page.

- Investigate your problem using at least five sources, all of which must be included in your works cited or bibliography.

- Submit a typed reflection detailing your personal learning and growth from the project as well as how you can apply this learning to other situations.

- Present your final project; it must incorporate all reading, research, and interviewing. No longer than 10 minutes.

- Turn in a typed annotated bibliography of all sources that includes the following:

  1. Introduction that clearly identifies the problem you seek to solve in this project

  2. Brief explanation of why this subject interests you

  3. Identification (with bullet points) of the three main conclusions you drew from your study of this topic through your sources

  4. Title, author, publisher, publication date, city, and number of pages (i.e., complete MLA citation for each source; see Purdue University Online Writing Lab [OWL] website for help) for each print source; MLA citation for interview sources

  5. Approximately seventy-five words that explain not only what each source contributes to your problem or solution but also how it relates to your essential question

Proposal

Each student must submit a typed one-page proposal; it should include the following:

1. The subject of your project (environment, homeless, children, awareness campaign, tutoring force, etc.)

2. A statement of the problem and your proposal for solving the problem

3. A rationale for why you want to study this subject

4. A summary of what you know about this subject at this time

5. A prediction about what you think you will discover during your investigation into the problem

6. The sources you will research and the people you will interview in addition to the databases you plan on using for research

7. An explanation as to the importance of this subject (which answers the question "So what?")

8. Other possible sources (databases, websites, publications, people, and organizations) you might consult to satisfy the three "additional sources" requirement

Note: Students must read the printed sources and interview the people listed on their proposal; you may—if you learn of new and more relevant sources—revise, but please check with me first.

Samples of school and community problems:

- Peer mediation team to solve conflicts or act as peer assistance with personal problems
- Peer tutoring group to assist lower classmates who are failing core subjects
- Companionship for the elderly in a nursing home
- Recycling
- Animal welfare
- Homeless youth

Documented Expository Essay Requirements

To Review

Five sources minimum are required for this essay. More will raise your grade. **Five is the basic requirement** (a 70).

- This is **not a book review**. This is an essay where you explain your topic to a general reader in an interesting way, uncovering facts and other information about the subject that aren't widely known plus take a position on the subject and support it with your sources.

- The essay requires documentation in the text of the essay (MLA format) as well as a separate but attached annotated bibliography. Please see the Purdue University Online Writing Lab (OWL) for a sample documented essay and annotated bibliography.

For the Essay

- There is no length requirement, but three pages is a good minimum.

- Essays must be typed, double-spaced, 12 pt. Times New Roman font.

- Please include a formal heading (not header) on the top left corner of the first page.

- Please include an original title that is centered and double-spaced from the heading.

Please Note

- Waiting until the last minute will significantly stress you and ruin your waking hours—maybe even your sleeping ones too. You know you shouldn't procrastinate. Put that knowledge into practice.

- Your emergency is no one else's but your own. Please plan. Don't blame others for your lack of planning.

- Computers, printers, the Internet, and even a knowledgeable writer who can help you are here on campus for you every day until 6:00 p.m. Beyond the conferences we will have in class, you may schedule time to confer with me at all steps in the process.

Inquiry Project: Contract

All parties agree that academic success is the product of a cooperative effort. To ensure that _____ (Student) will benefit from this union, each party has the following responsibilities:

As a student, I will do the following:

1. Be respectful to my classmates—no loud talking, distractions.

2. Put my best effort into my schoolwork and meet deadlines.

3. Obey the student code of conduct in reference to cheating and plagiarism.

4. Submit original work with an academic honesty statement attached.

5. Spend at least thirty minutes a day reading, planning, or writing on my project.

6. Work with group members to keep myself focused and accountable. My group members are _____.

As a parent, I will do the following:

1. Spend five minutes per day checking in on my child's project and helping them plan for deadlines provided by the teacher.

2. Monitor my child's schoolwork and extracurricular activities.

3. Notify the teacher of any problems at home that might affect student work.

As a teacher, I will do the following:

1. Provide a safe, comfortable environment for my students.

2. Provide ample time for my students to receive extra help after school.

3. Enforce school rules about academic integrity.

4. Provide students with clear and concise expectations.

5. Work to make learning an enjoyable experience.

6. Be available for help with student questions.

Signed:

_____   _____   _____
Student Signature   Parent Signature   Teacher Signature

_____
Date

REFERENCES

Aliki. (2015). *My five senses*. New York, NY: HarperCollins.

Anderson, L. F. (1912). Some facts regarding vocational training among the ancient Greeks and Romans. *The School Review, 20*(3), 191–201.

Anderson, L. W. (Ed.), Krathwohl, D. R. (Ed.), Airasian, P. W., Cruikshank, K. A., Mayer, R. E., Pintrich, P. R., . . . Wittrock, M. C. (2001). *A taxonomy for learning, teaching, and assessing: A revision of bloom's taxonomy of educational objectives*. New York, NY: Longman.

Aristotle. (2004). *Nicomachean ethics* (F. H. Peters, Trans.). New York, NY: Barnes and Noble. (Original work published 1893)

Aristotle. (1926). Rhetoric (J. H. Freese, Trans.) Aristotle in 23 volumes, vol. 22. Cambridge, MA: Harvard University Press. (Original work published 1926). Retrieved from http://www.perseus.tufts.edu/hopper/text?doc=urn:cts:greekLit:tlg0086.tlg038.perseus-eng1:1.10

Bang, M. (2004). *When Sophie gets angry—really, really angry*. New York, NY: Scholastic.

Barlow, M. L. (1976). 200 years of vocational education: 1776–1976: Coming of age, 1926–1976. *American Vocational Journal, 51*(5), 63–88.

Bass, R. V., & Good, J. W. (2004). Educate and *educere*: Is a balance possible in the educational system? *The Educational Forum, 68*(2), 161–168. doi:10.1080/00131720408984623

Benjamin, A. (2017). *The thing about jellyfish*. New York, NY: Little, Brown.

Bennett, J. O. (2016). *A global warming primer: Answering your questions about the science, the consequences, and the solutions*. Boulder, CO: Big Kid Science.

Bloom, B. S., Anderson, L. W., & Krathwohl, D. R. (2001). *A taxonomy for learning, teaching, and assessing: A revision of Bloom's taxonomy of educational objectives* (Complete ed.). New York, NY: Longman.

Bordessa, K. (2006). *Team challenges: Group activities to build cooperation, communication, and creativity*. Chicago, IL: Zephyr Press.

Carnevale, A. P., & Strohl, J. (2013). *Separate & unequal: How higher education reinforces the intergenerational reproduction of white racial privilege*. Retrieved November 17, 2017, from https://cew-7632.kxcdn.com/wp-content/uploads/SeparateUnequal.FR_.pdf

Carroll, J. A., & Wilson, E. E. (1993). *Acts of teaching*. Englewood, CO: Teacher Ideas Press.

CBS SF Bay Area. (2016, August 11). *In-school laundry gives students clean clothes, academic success.* Retrieved December 04, 2016, from http://sanfrancisco.cbslocal.com/2016/08/11/in-school-laundry-giving-students-clean-clothes-academic-success

Centers for Disease Control and Prevention. (2013, May 16). Mental health surveillance among children—United States 2005–2011. *Morbidity and Mortality Weekly Report, 62*(2), 1–35. Retrieved from https://www.cdc.gov/ncbddd/childdevelopment/documents/CMH-feature20130514.pdf

Christen, C., & Bolles, R. N. (2016). *What color is your parachute for teens: Discover yourself, design your future, and plan for your dream job.* Berkeley, CA: Ten Speed Press.

Cirillo, F. (2011). The Pomodoro Technique. *Cirillo Consulting GmbH.* Retrieved May 5, 2018, from https://francescocirillo.com/pages/pomodoro-technique

Cisneros, S. (1992). Eleven. In *Woman hollering creek and other stories.* New York, NY: Vintage Books.

Clayton, J. A., Brooks, C. E., & Kornstein, S. G. (2014). *Women of color health data book* (4th ed., pp. vii–182). Washington, DC: National Institutes of Health. Retrieved from: https://orwh.od.nih.gov/sites/orwh/files/docs/WoC-Databook-FINAL.pdf

Cooper, K. (2013, February). *Inservice.* [Palo Duro High School session handout].

Council for Exceptional Children. (2015). *What every special educator must know: Professional ethics and standards.* Arlington, VA: Author.

Council of Chief State School Officers. (2017, April 1). *English language proficiency standards (ELPS).* Retrieved May 23, 2018, from https://www.ccsso.org/resource-library/english-language-proficiency-elp-standards

Crawford, M. B. (2010). *Shop class as soulcraft: An inquiry into the value of work.* New York, NY: Penguin Books.

Darling-Hammond, L., Wei, R. C., Andree, A., Richardson, N., & Ophanos, S. (2009, February). *Professional learning in the learning profession: A status report on teacher development in the United States and abroad.* Retrieved from https://pdfs.semanticscholar.org/27a2/ddcbbce4e24b6b9458976d3617237f1801f1.pdf

Dillard, A. (1989). *The writing life.* New York, NY: HarperCollins.

Dowling, K. (2003). *Side by side: A child/parent writing project.* Spring, TX: Absey & Company.

Duckworth, A. (2016). *Grit: The power of passion and perseverance.* New York, NY: Scribner.

Eggleston. R. (Director). (2000). *For the birds* [Motion picture]. United States: Pixar.

Ellis, R. (2008a). *Principles of instructed second language acquisition.* Washington, DC: Center for Applied Linguistics. Retrieved January 21, 2013, from http://www.cal.org/resources/digest/instructed2ndlang.html

Ellis, R. (2008b). *The study of second language acquisition.* Oxford, England: Oxford University Press.

Faste, R. A. (2001). The human challenge in engineering design. *International Journal of Engineering Education, 17*(4–5), 327–331.

Fisher, D., Frey, N., & Rothenberg, C. (2008). *Content-area conversations: How to plan discussion-based lessons for diverse language learners.* Alexandria, VA: ASCD.

Fleischman, P. (2005). *Joyful noise: Poems for two voices.* New York, NY: HarperTrophy.

Fleming, N. (2018, March 1). *Schools are using social networking to involve parents.* Retrieved August 17, 2015, from https://www.edweek.org/ew/articles/2012/11/07/11digitalparent_ep.h32.html

Ford, J. E. (2017). Student-teacher relationships are everything. *Education Week.* Retrieved from http://blogs.edweek.org/teachers/teacher_leader_voices/2017/01/relationships_are_everything.html

Foster, P. (2017). The philosophy of vocational education. *Journal of the Krishnamurti Schools, 12.*

Fromm, E. (1994). *The art of listening.* New York, NY: Continuum International.

Ganz, M. (2009). Why stories matter: The art and craft of social change. *Sojourners Magazine, 38*(3), 16–21.

Garmston, R. J. (2004, March). Group wise. *National Staff Development Council, 25*(3), 65–66.

Gelbach, H., Brinkworth, M. E., Hsu, L., King, A., McIntire, J., & Rogers, T. (2016). Creating birds of similar feathers: Leveraging similarity to improve teacher-student relationships and academic achievement. *Journal of Educational Psychology, 108*(3), 342.

Gottman, J. M. (2014). *What predicts divorce? The relationship between marital processes and marital outcomes.* New York, NY: Psychology Press.

Graff, G., & Birkenstein, C. (2009). *They say, I say: The moves that matter in academic writing* (2nd ed.). New York, NY: W. W. Norton.

Hart, B., & Risley. T. (2003). The early catastrophe: The 30 million word gap by age 3. *American Educator, 27*(1), 4–9.

Hattie, J., & Yates, G. C. R. (2013). *Visible learning and the science of how we learn.* New York, NY: Routledge.

Henkes, K. (1996). *Lilly's purple plastic purse.* New York, NY: Greenwillow Books.

Horn, I. S., & Little, J. W. (2010). Attending to problems of practice: Routines and resources for professional learning in teachers' workplace interactions. *American Educational Research Journal, 47*(1), 181–217.

International Organization for Standardization. (2015). *Ergonomics of human-system interaction—Part 210: Human-centered design for interactive systems* (ISO/DIS Standard No. 2010). Retrieved from https://www.iso.org/standard/52075.html

International Reading Association. (2009). *New literacies and 21st century technologies*. Newark, DE: Author. Retrieved August 18, 2013, from http://www.reading.org/general/AboutIRA/PositionStatements/21stCenturyLiteracies.aspx

Jarrow, G. (2016). *Bubonic panic: When plague invaded America*. Honesdale, PA: Calkins Creek

Kahn, W. A. (2009). *The student's guide to successful project teams*. New York, NY: Routledge.

Kessler, R. (2001). Soul of students, soul of teachers: Welcoming the inner life to school. In L. Lantieri (Ed.), *Schools with spirit: Nurturing the inner lives of children and teachers* (pp. 107–131). Boston, MA: Beacon Press.

Kirk, M. (2006). Teaching science for social justice. *Feminist Teacher, 16*(2), 150–151.

Kleon, A. (2012). *Steal like an artist: 10 things nobody told you about being creative*. New York, NY: Workman Pub.

Larner, M. (2007). *Tools for leaders: Indispensable graphic organizers, protocols, and planning guidelines for working and learning together*. New York, NY: Scholastic.

Lee, H. (2002). *To kill a mockingbird* (1st Perennial classics ed.). New York, NY: HarperCollins. (Original work published 1960)

Leedy, L. (2007). *It's probably Penny* (1st ed.). New York, NY: Henry Holt.

Leonard, H. B. (1991). With open ears: Listening and the art of discussion leading. In C. R. Christensen, D. A. Garvin, & A. Sweet (Eds.), *Education for judgment: The artistry of discussion leadership* (p. 150). Boston, MA: Harvard Business School Press.

Lewicki, R. J., & Wiethoff, C. (2000). Trust, trust development, and trust repair. In M. Deutch, P. T. Coleman, & E. C. Marcus (Eds.), *The handbook of conflict resolution: Theory and practice* (pp. 92–119). San Francisco, CA: Jossey-Bass.

Lewis, J., & Aydin, A. (2016). *March: Book three*. Marietta, GA: Top Shelf Productions.

Lobdell, T. (2011, November 18). Getting off the treadmill. *Palo Alto Weekly*. Retrieved from http://www.paloaltoonline.com/weekly/morguepdf/2011/2011_11_18.paw.section2.pdf

Lowry, L. (1993). *The giver*. New York, NY: Houghton Mifflin Harcourt.

Macaulay, D. (2016). *The way things work now: From levers to lasers, windmills to Wi-Fi, a visual guide to the world of machines*. Boston, MA: Houghton Mifflin Harcourt.

Marzano, R., Pickering, D. J., & Pollock, J. E. (2001). *Classroom instruction that works: Research-based strategies for increasing student achievement*. Alexandria, VA: ASCD.

McCandless, D. (2012). *Information is beautiful* (New ed., revised, recalculated and reimagined). London, England: Collins.

McLaughlin, M. W., & Talbert, J. E. (2001). *Professional communities and the work of high school teaching*. Chicago, IL: University of Chicago Press.

McLeod, C. (2015). Trust. In E. N. Zalta (Ed.), *The Stanford encyclopedia of philosophy*. Retrieved from https://plato.stanford.edu/archives/fall2015/entries/trust

McTighe, J., & Wiggins, G. (2013). *Essential questions: Opening doors to student understanding*. Alexandria, VA: ASCD.

Mehta, J. (2018). A pernicious myth: Basics before deeper learning [Blog post]. Retrieved from http://blogs.edweek.org/edweek/learning_deeply/2018/01/a_pernicious_myth_basics_before_deeper_learning.html

Meister, C. (2014). *Cinderella stories around the world: 4 beloved tales*. North Mankato, MN: Picture Window Books.

Myers, W. D. (2004). *Monster*. New York, NY: HarperTempest/Amistad.

Nails, D. (2014, Spring). *Socrates*. Retrieved August 06, 2016, from http://plato.stanford.edu/archives/spr2014/entries/socrates

National Association for Gifted Children. (n.d.). Standard 3: Curriculum Planning and Instruction. Retrieved May 23, 2018, from https://www.nagc.org/resources-publications/resources/national-standards-gifted-and-talented-education/pre-k-grade-12-3

National Coalition for Core Arts Standards. (2014). *National core arts standards*. Dover, DE: State Education Agency Directors of Arts Education. Retrieved from http://www.nationalartsstandards.org/sites/default/files/NCCAS%20PhilosophicalFoundations%20-%20Lifelong%20Goals_0.pdf

National Council for the Social Studies. (2010). National curriculum standards for social studies: A framework for teaching, learning, and assessment. *The ten themes of social studies*. Retrieved from https://www.socialstudies.org/standards/strands#1

National Council of Teachers of Mathematics. (2018). Principles, standards and expectations. Retrieved May 16, 2018, from https://www.nctm.org/Standards-and-Positions/Principles-and-Standards/Principles,-Standards,-and-Expectations

National Governors Association Center for Best Practices and Council of Chief State School Officers. (2010). Common core state standards. Retrieved from http://www.corestandards.org

National Research Council. (2012). *A framework for K–12 science education: Practices, crosscutting concepts, and core ideas*. Washington, DC: The National Academies Press.

Palmer, P. J. (1998). *The courage to teach: Exploring the inner landscape of a teacher's life*. San Francisco, CA: Jossey-Bass.

Pattison, K. (2008). Worker interrupted: The cost of task-switching. *Fast Company* [Blog post]. Retrieved from https://www.fastcompany.com/944128/worker-interrupted-cost-task-switching

Paulsen, G. (2017). *Six kids and a stuffed cat*. New York, NY: Simon & Schuster.

Peeples, S. (2015, May 25). Buying and selling hope, one student at a time. *The Blog, HuffPost*. Retrieved from https://www.huffingtonpost.com/shanna-peeples/buying-and-selling-hope-o_b_7438272.html

Peeples, S. (2017, April 27). Finding grace in small spaces. Retrieved from https://www.shannapeeples.com/finding-grace-in-small-spaces

Perkins, D. N. (2014). *Future wise: Educating our children for a changing world*. San Francisco, CA: Jossey-Bass.

Pew Social Trends. (2015, November 4). *Raising kids and running a household: How working parents share the load*. Retrieved December 3, 2015, from http://www.pewsocialtrends.org/2015/11/04/raising-kids-and-running-a-household-how-working-parents-share-the-load

Phillips, C. (2002). *Socrates cafe: A fresh taste of philosophy*. New York, NY: W. W. Norton.

Plato. (1892). *Laws*. In B. Jowett (Ed. & Trans.), *Internet classics archive*. Retrieved from http://classics.mit.edu/Plato/laws.1.i.html (Original work written 360 BCE)

Raczka, B. (2006). *No one saw: Ordinary things through the eyes of an artist*. Minneapolis, MN: Millbrook Press.

Schaefer, L. M., & Schaefer, A. (2016). *Because of an acorn*. San Francisco, CA: Chronicle Books.

Schein, E. H. (2013). *Humble inquiry: The gentle art of asking instead of telling*. Oakland, CA: Berrett-Koehler.

Schroeder, A. (2016). *Abe Lincoln: His wit and wisdom from A–Z*. New York, NY: Holiday House.

Dr. Seuss. (1984). *The butter battle book*. New York, NY: Random House Books for Young Readers.

Sheppard, J. (1993). *The right number of elephants*. Carson, CA: Lakeshore Learning Materials.

Stanford University. (n.d.). Retrieved May 17, 2018, from http://shc.stanford.edu/what-are-the-humanities

Stanford University News. (2005, June 14). *"You've got to find what you love,"* Jobs says. Retrieved from https://news.stanford.edu/2005/06/14/jobs-061505/

Swan, K., & Griffin, S. (2013). Beating the odds: The college, career, and civic life (c3) framework for social studies state standards. *Social Education*, 77(6), 317–321.

Texas Higher Education Coordinating Board & Texas Education Agency Division of Curriculum. (2009). *Texas college and career readiness standards*. Retrieved from http://www.thecb.state.tx.us/collegereadiness/CRS.pdf

Thomson, R. (2014). *Photos framed: A fresh look at the world's most memorable photographs*. Somerville, MA: Candlewick Press.

Thoreau, H. D. (1983). *Walden and civil disobedience* (The Penguin American Library). New York, NY: Penguin Books. (Original works published 1852 and 1849)

Tippett, K. (Producer). (2014, December 4). *On being* [Audio podcast]. Retrieved from https://onbeing.org/programs/seth-godin-the-art-of-noticing-and-then-creating

Twain, M. (2003). *Adventures of Huckleberry Finn*. New York, NY: Random House. (Original work published 1884)

Vygotsky, L. S. (1986). *Thought and language* (Rev. ed.; A. Kozulin, Ed. & Trans.). Cambridge, MA: MIT Press. (Original work published 1962)

Wagner, T. (2012). *Creating innovators: The making of young people who will change the world*. New York, NY: Scribner.

Webb, N. L. (2002). Depth-of-knowledge levels for four content areas. Retrieved from http://facstaff.wcer.wisc.cdu/normw/All%20content%20areas%20%20DOK%20levels%2032802.pdf

Wheatley, M. J. (2009). *Turning to one another: Simple conversations to restore hope to the future*. San Francisco, CA: Berrett-Koehler.

Willis, J. (2014, September 22). *Cognitively priming students for learning*. Retrieved June 5, 2017, from https://www.edutopia.org/blog/cognitively-priming-students-for-learning-judy-willis

Zak, P. J. (2017, January/February). The neuroscience of trust. *Harvard Business Review*, 84–90. Retrieved from https://hbr.org/2017/01/the-neuroscience-of-trust

Zwiers, J., & Crawford, M. (2010). *Academic conversations: Classroom talk that fosters critical thinking and content understandings*. Portland, ME: Stenhouse.

INDEX

Curated questions:
  abstract reasoning goal and,
    104–105
  classical philosophical questions,
    student questions and, 104,
    105 (figure)
  classroom content, connected
    student learning and, 101–102,
    101 (figure)
  controversial issues, management
    of, 96, 100–101
  cross-content thematic connections
    and, 104, 104 (figure)
  cross-content use of, 92–93, 95
  essential questions and, 100, 101
  flipped learning, student questions
    and, 101–105
  in-class debate, interdisciplinary
    connections and, 96, 97, 100
  in-class debate protocol and, 97–99
  nontraditional students and, 95
  questions, multiple perspectives
    on, 95
  teacher planning questions and,
    96–97
  See also Career and Technical
    Education (CTE) questions;
    Fine Arts questions; Literacy;
    Math questions; Questioning
    classroom culture; Science
    questions; Social Studies/
    Government/Humanities
    questions
Curiosity, 14–15, 29, 95, 109, 110,
  146, 190
Current events, 198–199, 227–228

Damon, W., 5
de Montaigne, M., 204
Debate, 96
  See also Academic discussions;
    In-class debate protocol

Deep learning experiences:
  agency in learning and, 14, 40–41
  co-created learning and, 3, 14
  cross-course connections and, 95
  culture of inquiry and, 25
  curiosity, encouragement of,
    14–15, 95
  meaning/purpose and, 5–6, 7
  nontraditional students and, 95
  philosophical matters and, 2, 6
  questioning, brain function
    and, 15
  scaffolded questions and, 15
  social learning, participation in,
    14, 96
  Socratic method and, 7–8
  student inner life, welcoming of, 6
  student meaning-makers and, 7
  See also Academic discussions;
    Active listening; Culture of
    thinking; Curated questions;
    Design thinking; Engagement
    strategies; Student questions;
    Thinking process
Descartes, R., 117
Design thinking, 27
  class/school design, student
    disengagement and, 27
  content value, communication
    of, 27
  convergent thinking and, 30–31
  cubing design strategy and, 29–30,
    30 (table)
  curiosity and, 29
  definition of, 29
  distracting designs, avoidance of,
    28–29
  divergent thinking and, 29–30
  innovation and, 29
  parent participation,
    encouragement of, 28
  play in learning and, 45–46

Perkins, D. N., 118
Personalized learning. *See* Inquiry-
    based learning; Project-based
    learning
Peru's Challenge, 224
Phillips, C., 227
Philosophical matters, 2, 6, 234–237
Photography sample resources, 242
Pickering, D. J., 68
Plato, 45, 78, 152, 173, 189
Play in learning, 45–46
Pollock, J. E., 69
Polybius, 127
Pomodoro technique, 29
Privileges:
    agency in learning and, 40–41
    choice and, 41–43
    collaboration/independence
        privileges and, 45–46
    hierarchy of needs and, 40
    privacy, right to, 41–42
    respect and, 40–41
    self-regulation/responsibility and,
        40–41
    social reproduction, educational
        inequities and, 92
    student physical needs and, 40
    thought/purpose, privileges of,
        43–44
    See also Inquiry-based learning
Problem-based learning, 5, 45
    play in learning and, 45–46
    team collaboration and, 46
    See also Inquiry-based learning;
        Project-based learning; Real-
        world work
Productive struggle, 118, 133
Professional development:
    Center for Courage and Renewal
        and, 205–206
    common pattern of, 205, 206–208

community, power of, 205
effective approach to, 206–207
empowerment practices and,
    223–224
energy creation, force multiplier
    effect and, 223–224
fear/perceived powerlessness and,
    224
inquiry team observation/
    evaluation protocol and,
    222–223
numbing experience of, 204–205
outcomes/results, obsession with,
    207
productive conversation and, 212
professional identity, realization of,
    209–211, 212
professional learning community
    conversation routine protocol
    and, 220–221
professional silence and, 205
public narrative/leadership
    storytelling, power of, 211
reflection, absence of, 205
teacher autonomy, importance of,
    206–207, 208
teacher design of, 212
"tips/tricks/techniques," shallow
    approach of, 205
workshop opening questions and,
    13
See also Staff meetings; Teacher
    questions
Professional learning communities
    (PLCs), 220–221
Project-based learning, 5, 180, 189
    authentic audiences, provision of,
        190–191
    community, creation of, 197–198
    community outside school,
        engagement with, 200–201

ReadWriteThink, 232
Real-world work, 178
   disadvantaged students, test prep
      and, 180
   inquiry project planning/
      implementation protocol and,
      184–187
   interdisciplinary learning and, 95
   productive struggle and, 118
   service learning and, 180
   soft skills, value of, 180–181
   strengths-based approach and, 180
   student questions and, 181–184
   test results/future success,
      correlation of, 178–180
   See also Curated questions;
      Inquiry-based learning;
      Project-based learning
Reflection, 5, 56–58, 60, 71–72, 169,
   205, 246
Resources:
   art/photography samples sources,
      242
   assessment rubrics, 247–250
   documented expository essay
      requirements, 260
   English Language Arts sample
      weekly schedule, 229
   Fine Arts instruction resources,
      150
   flash fiction resources, 241
   high school reading list by topic,
      251–256
   in-class debate handouts, 243–246
   inquiry project contract, 261
   inquiry project guidelines handout,
      257–259
   leveled questions thinking, poetry/
      flash fiction/literature for,
      240–241
   Math instruction resources, 126

   parent-teacher call template,
      230–231
   philosophical questions, songs as
      texts for, 234–237
   poetry resources, 240
   questions of the heart discussion,
      videos as texts for, 238–239
   Science instruction resources, 116
   Social Studies instruction
      resources, 137–138
   speaking/listening skills practice,
      texts/lesson ideas for, 232–233
   See also Protocols
Respect, 6, 39, 76
Reverso, 168
Rief, L., 71
Right action, 39
Risley, T., 82
Rogers, T., 39
Rothenberg, C., 68
Ryan, J., 153, 154, 155, 156

Sackman-Ebuwa, D., 167, 168, 170
Safety, 76–78, 82–84, 83 (table), 146,
   168, 212
Scaffolded literacy tasks, 87–89,
   88 (figure), 91
Scaffolded questions, 15
SCANS Competencies, 160
SCANS Foundational Skills for
   Entering the Workforce, 160
Schaefer, A., 112
Schaefer, L. M., 112
Schein, E. H., 6, 7
Schopenhauer, A., 100
Schroeder, A., 134
Science questions, 104, 107
   big questions, encouragement of,
      109–110, 112–114
   child intuitions/prior conceptions
      and, 109

writing exercise for, 218–219

See also Professional development; Teacher questions

Strohl, J., 180

Student questions, 13

agency in learning and, 14

authentic question generation protocol and, 21–23

authentic questions and, 14, 21–23

classroom content, connected student learning and, 101–102, 102 (figure)

conditions for questioning and, 21

curiosity, encouragement of, 14–15

essential questions and, 100, 101

flipped learning and, 101–105

questioning, brain function and, 15

real-world work and, 181–184

scaffolded questions and, 15

social learning, participation in, 14

Socratic circle discussion protocol and, 31–35

student concerns, questions about, 18–19, 18–20 (figures)

teacher listening, importance of, 16–17, 18

thinking skills, development of, 15

See also Academic discussions; Curated questions; Deep learning experiences; Project-based learning; Questioning classroom culture; Teacher questions

Tchesnokov, P., 143

Teacher questions, 17

adults as learners, expectation of, 216

authentic question generation protocol and, 212–215

authentic questions and, 17–18, 212–215

"coffee house," parent involvement and, 227

conversation sparks, larger world stage and, 224–226

cubing design strategy and, 29–30, 30 (table)

deep discussions, participation in, 215–216

in-class workshop technique and, 227–228

parent participation and, 226–228

practices questions, inquiry groups around, 216–220

Socrates Cafe technique and, 227

Socratic circle protocol and, 216–217

storytelling, prompts for, 215

student concerns, connection to, 17, 18

vulnerabilities, exposure of, 216, 218

See also Curated questions; Professional development; Staff meetings

Teacher talk, 217–218

Teachersplaining, 6–7, 61

Technical education. *See* Career and technical education (CTE)

Texas Education Agency Division of Curriculum, 68

Texas Higher Education Coordinating Board, 68

Thinking process:

in-class debate, interdisciplinary connections and, 96

learning to think and, 51

meaning/purpose and, 5–6, 7

philosophical matters and, 2, 6

questioning, brain function and, 15

reflective writing, scheduling of, 56–57

skill development and, 15

student meaning-makers and, 7
teachersplaining, "telling" culture
    and, 6–7
See also Culture of thinking;
    Curated questions; Deep
    learning experiences;
    Engagement strategies; Inquiry-
    based learning; Literacy
Thomson, R., 134
Thoreau, H. D., 198, 199
Tiny tasks for small groups protocol,
    46–48
Tolstoy, L., 25
Trust, 17, 38, 41, 42, 43, 55, 62, 73
    actions of, 73–74
    co-created safe spaces and, 77–78
    difficult students, validation for,
        74–76
    English language learners
        and, 168
    first-day questionnaire and, 79–80
    first-day questionnaire answers,
        processing of, 81–82
    healthy relationships, building of,
        82–84, 83 (table)
    management behaviors, high trust
        levels and, 83–84
    neuroscience of, 82, 83
    positive regard, power of, 82–83
    safe spaces, ground rules
        for, 77–78
    safety, trusting climate and, 76–78
    smiling, power of, 78–79
    strengths-based approach and,
        79, 82
    teaching presence and, 78
    vulnerabilities, exposure of,
        211, 216
    See also Belonging; Culture of
        thinking; Empathy
Trustworthiness, 74

Truth and Reconciliation
    Commission (TRC), 131
Twain, M., 103
20/20 technique, 29
Tyson, N. D., 107

User experience, 27–29

Vazquez, D., 167, 171
Vilson, J. L., 104, 119,
    121, 216
Vogelsang, K., 190
Vygotsky, L. S., 14, 96

Wagner, T., 95
Walden Challenge, 199
Wallace, D. F., 51
Wheatley, M. J., 62, 64, 207,
    211, 225
Wiethoff, C., 74
Wiggins, G., 100, 101
Wiley, K., 145
Willis, J., 15
Wilson, E. E., 71
Women Inspiring Serving and
    Educating (WISE), 182
Writing group creation/meeting
    protocol, 52–54
Writing groups/circles, 49
    assessment rubric for,
        249–250
    Career/Technical Education
        instruction and, 159
    classroom physical arrangement
        and, 49
    "coffee house" author celebrations
        and, 49
    Fine Arts instruction
        and, 148
    gradual release of writing process
        and, 50, 50 (figure)

A SAGE Publishing Company

CORWIN HAS ONE MISSION: to enhance education through intentional professional learning.

We build long-term relationships with our authors, educators, clients, and associations who partner with us to develop and continuously improve the best evidence-based practices that establish and support lifelong learning.

Confident Teachers, Inspired Learners

No matter where you are in your professional journey, Corwin aims to ease the many demands teachers face on a daily basis with accessible strategies that benefit ALL learners. Through research-based, high-quality content, we offer practical guidance on a wide range of topics, including curriculum planning, learning frameworks, classroom design and management, and much more. Our suite of books, videos, consulting services, and online resources, developed by renowned educators, are designed for easy implementation and to provide you AND your students with tangible results.

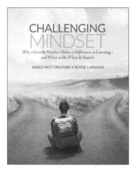

James Nottingham and Bosse Larsson

Create the right conditions for a growth mindset to flourish in your school and your students.

James Nottingham

Embrace challenge and celebrate eureka!

Carla Marschall and Rachel French

Develop a thinking classroom that helps students move from the factual to the conceptual.

Kimberly L. Mitchell

Discover inquiry for yourself with this interactive guide.

Lisa Westman

Build collaborative student–teacher relationships as a precursor to student growth.

John Antonetti and Terri Stice

Analyze, design, and refine engaging tasks of learning.

Silvia Rosenthal Tolisano and Janet A. Hale

Discover a new approach to contemporary documentation and learning.

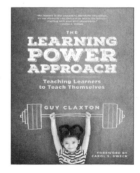

Guy Claxton

Become mind-fit for life with a groundbreaking set of design principles for strengthening students' learning muscles.

corwin.com